INTELLIGENCE
GAMES

Franco Agostini — Nicola Alberto De Carlo
U.S. Editor: Michael Stueben

INTELLIGENCE GAMES

Color plates by Lino Simeoni
Drawings by Chiara Molinaroli and Vittorio Salarolo

A Fireside Book
Published by Simon & Schuster Inc.
New York London Toronto Sydney Tokyo

Photographs
Mondadori Archives, Milan, Italy

Copyright © 1985 by Arnoldo Mondadori Editore S.p.A., Milan
English language translation copyright © 1987 by
Arnoldo Mondadori Editore S.p.A., Milan
All rights reserved including the right of reproduction in whole or in
part in any form

A Fireside Book
Published by Simon & Schuster Inc.
Simon & Schuster Building
Rockefeller Center
1230 Avenue of the Americas
New York, New York 10020

Originally published as GIOCHI DELLA INTELLIGENZA by
Arnoldo Mondadori Editore S.p.A., in Italy

FIRESIDE and colophon are registered trademarks of
Simon & Schuster Inc.
Printed and bound in Italy by Officine Grafiche,
Arnoldo Mondadori Editore, Verona
10 9 8 7 6 5 4

Library of Congress Cataloging in Publication Data

Agostini, Franco.
  Intelligence games.

  Translation of: Giochi della intelligenza.
  ''A Fireside book'' – Verso t.p.
  1. Mathematical recreations.   I. De Carlo, Nicola.
II. Title.
QA95.A3313   1987   793.7'4   86-33908
ISBN 0-671-63201-9 (pbk.)

Contents

Foreword

All of us more or less know what intelligence is: we have probably classed some of our friends as more intelligent than others. We might say that someone has reached a high position because of their intelligence, or we might—perhaps wrongly—think that another has only a humdrum job because he is not very intelligent. Again, we claim that humans are more intelligent than apes, and apes in turn more intelligent than cats, and so on. The man in the street will have a rough and ready concept of what intelligence is, which helps him to assess and orientate himself in the society in which he lives. But on what is this concept based? What is intelligence, really?

It is not easy to anwer this. A book entitled Intelligence Games *will naturally be expected to offer some precise definition. And we shall try to meet such expectations. Yet not even the experts (for example, the psychologists) can give a conclusive definition. The subject is in the end so vast that it seems impossible to wrap up neatly: whenever one discusses intelligence, one is always left with a feeling of incompleteness—that something important has been left out. Intelligence is part of what makes a human being. And it is no easy business sorting out what makes a human being! However, it is possible to describe certain facets and behaviour patterns of humankind, starting for instance with the discoveries and formulations of psychology. In particular, skill with words, a facility with numbers, and the ability to argue clearly are all accepted as characteristics of intelligence.*

Using games, puzzles, and stories, this book deals with verbal, visual, mathematical, and logical forms of intelligence. It must be stressed, though, that while psychology tends to concentrate on those aspects of intelligence that are most easily accessible to objective analysis, it also acknowledges that intelligence is a single faculty, at once a unified whole and an immensely complex entity, embracing the individual's entire psyche, and is determined by genetic, environmental, and cultural factors.

This book is an opportunity for you to reflect about yourself. Some of the exercises are versions of material used in intelligence tests, adapted here in the form of games. Yet there is always the danger of feeling somehow "judged." Often, newspapers and magazines promise an objective "measurement" of intelligence that in fact creates much doubt and disappointment, because the methods adopted are not set in proper proportion. Rather than helping people to know themselves better, they seem designed to instil a certain unease. The tests in this book are simply games. Through them, each individual will be able to express his or her intelligence and personality freely and entertainingly.

Intelligence has been understood differently over the years, and this book also traces the evolution of our primitive faculty for solving problems of survival to abstract notions of intelligence such as were held by the Greeks; then on to Roman calliditas—*a down-to-earth, practical quality; thence to the quick, lively, dynamic ability of the emergent mercantile bourgeoisie in the late Middle Ages to attain a certain goal or resolve unforeseen crises; and finally to the developments of modern psychology, which sets the problem of intelligence in a systematic, organic overall view. If our intelligence is expressed not merely in the traditionally understood ways, but involves our total being, then we are entitled to ask how it manifests itself in relation to other people—to friends especially, or in our choice of a partner, our work, or our desire for a successful career and financial position. We attempt to answer these questions, always inviting the reader to step outside his or her own self by means of games, tests, and exercises. Intelligence is to some degree the ability to see oneself from the outside, with that irony and spirit of freedom through which we are able to feel both mastery of and solidarity with our own selves. And this is not all: every moment of life can be lived with intelligence! Good humour, a sense of the comic, the ability to see problems and difficulties for what they are—real* savoir-vivre, *in fact—all help dispel that sense of boredom,* ennui, *and emptiness that some days can bring. Life becomes a true joy when wine, good food, company, wit, and humour appropriate to the time and place combine with a basically balanced life-style, dictated by good sense. Intelligence under these conditions can be seen as the ability to spend one's days happily, rather than fixed on a distant, abstract happiness projected into the future. The sixteen colour plates show "mental games" from all over the world and from every age. Cards, checkers, chess, dominoes, and other very common games have not been included. Many books already exist on such games (some are included in the bibliography at the end of this book).*

A general survey

Intelligence is . . .

Intelligence is a credit card. Anyone possessing it is thought to be able to face the most tangled problems and solve them. In everyday use, the adjective "intelligent" implies a number of qualities: the ability to identify objectives quickly and to achieve them; sensitivity in dealings with others; skill in assessing people's characters; balanced judgment; and readiness to alter one's own ways.

A child behaves intelligently if it abandons its tantrums, once it is clear they lead nowhere. In business a sign of intelligence is the ability to ignore lesser problems in order to concentrate on the major ones in the fields of accounting, production, or management. Parents who recognize and can help their children to see the most vital elements of the educational process are similarly "intelligent."

Intelligence is thus a virtue with many practical features, so highly prized and so useful that it is something we can admire even in our enemies.

Intelligence is a safety door. Much is forgiven "intelligent" people, both male and female: lack of practicality, inconstancy, laziness, irritability, and inattentiveness. Some people rarely seem able to do a job on time. Yet if they are held to be intelligent, they are judged much more tolerantly. Tribute always seems to be paid to those with intellectual potential, even if it is never properly used and is mostly hypothetical.

A pun, a witty remark, or a clever riposte can turn the most awkward situation to one's advantage. "My friend," said the highly revered professor of anatomy Riccardo Anzalotti to Francesco Lalli, a third-year student, "your work has not been what it should have been. For your efforts in this exam, I shall offer you a seventeen and a cigarette." "Thank you," Lalli replied, fresh from a week's wild living and a successful amorous encounter. "Give me sixteen, will you, and a light?"

Accused by her husband, Sir Andrew, after being surprised kissing the young gardener Pettygreen, Lady Miligham contemptuously denies the evidence: "How can you possibly say you love me, Andrew, if you prefer to believe your own eyes rather than my words?"

Intelligence is a proof of breeding. It is associated with important things such as good taste, success, agreeable feelings, and hopes, wealth, and power.

Margaret, flattered by Faust's compliments, laments over the untold numbers of women more intelligent than herself on whom he has exercised his powers of seduction. Here intelligence goes with culture, ancestry, and personal magnetism.

Intelligent people enjoy brilliant careers, earn fortunes, and have an intense emotional life. "Sir Francis Drake is an intelligent man," Queen Elizabeth observed, "and we owe a great deal to intelligence." And with that she boarded the admiral's ship and spent the entire night in conversation with him.

Like an official title or honour, a reputation for intelligence can compensate for many defects. Quirks, oddities, and negative personality traits that would be considered serious in an "ordinary" person are looked on more kindly. Wit can even make meanness seem entertaining: "Ah, virtue is priceless. Alas! Were it not, we could sell or mortgage it!"

Intelligence is knowing how to live well. In the office, at school, in the factory, the theater, or hotel, on a cruise, walking about a city center, out in the country, alone, in company, with a date or with somebody one loathes, with children or with an old friend—in any of those countless everyday situations that make up our lives, intelligence represents the ability to achieve the greatest possible satisfaction, the best results, the most experience, and the truest pleasure. Intelligence is knowing how to eat well without putting on weight or suffering from indigestion. It is, however, also knowing when to ignore the rules of "healthy" eating and enjoy the pleasures of the table to the full (and take the consequences) without suffering from guilt at doing so.

Thus intelligent behaviour goes hand in hand with awareness. It entails an ability to approach problems, people, facts, and events in a constructive way: anticipating possible developments, balancing positive and negative factors, and making decisions accordingly. Such considerations will determine whether one copes with any given predicament with a touch of humour, say, or with a decisive attack.

Intelligence is a game. Surely a characteristic of intelligent people is also that they are able to see themselves, events, other people, and the world about them in all its beauty and all its awfulness, with humour. This is wise. Reality is not wholly within our powers: old age and the whims of fortune still loom over us. While remaining totally committed to all we hold most dear (family, profession, science, art, ideas, the ethical life), it is useful, too, to maintain a certain detachment—to be able to smile, to take things with a pinch of salt. Setbacks and frustrations can then be turned to good account. At the same time, any moment of the day can become a source of unexpected pleasure, affording something comic, curious, grotesque, stylish, or new and original. A card game is more interesting when one knows its origins, its ancient esoteric symbolism, its history as it evolved into a pastime, and the importance it has for those who regularly spend their evenings playing it, over a liter or two of wine. With due detachment, a "nonevent"—a love affair that never got off the ground, for example—can give cause for laughter rather than misery. There will be others. The English novelist J. R. R. Tolkien tells a touching but entertaining story of a young man greatly in love with a rather haughty young lady. The man went to a ladies' outfitters, accompanied by his sister, to buy his beloved a pair of fine gloves. It being a typical English winter, the sister took the opportunity of buying herself a pair of woolly drawers. Sadly, of course, the shopgirl made the inevitable mistake of sending the drawers, instead of the gloves, to the lady in Belgrave Square. The error might have been rectified had not the young man left a letter to accompany them.

Dear Velma,
This little gift is to let you know I have not forgotten your birthday. I did not choose them because I thought you needed them or were unaccustomed to wearing them, nor because we go out together in the evenings. Had it not been for my sister, I should have bought long ones, but she tells me you wear them short, with just one button. They are a delicate colour, I know, but the shopgirl showed me a pair she had worn for three weeks, and there was not the slightest stain on them. How I would love to put them on you for the first time myself.

Doubtless many another man's hand will have touched them before I am able to see you again, but I hope you will think of me every time you put them on. I had the shopgirl try them, and on her they looked marvellous. I do not know your exact size, but I feel I am in a position to make a better guess than anyone else. When you wear them for the first time, put a bit of talc in them, which will make them slide on more smoothly; and when you remove them, blow into them before putting them away; obviously they will be a little damp inside. Hoping that you will accept them in the same spirit in which they are offered, and that you will wear them to the ball on Friday evening, I sign myself.
Your very affectionate
John

P.S. Keep count of the number of times I kiss them over the next year.

Two facets of intelligence

It will be clear by now that "intelligent" behaviour as commonly defined takes many different forms. And the connotations of such "intelligence" are equally many and varied: success, charm, originality, independence of judgment and action, and so on.

An unusual, to say the least, picture of Einstein that perhaps belies the normal image of the scientific genius who revolutionized traditional physics. Yet at the right time and place, joking high spirits, and extrovert good humour are very much part of human intelligence.

tion in which they appear give us a chance to investigate our own "self" as well as that of others. No area of human life, individual or social, is outside the field of the study of intelligence.

This book

Together with the reader, we should like to consider the different forms that "intelligent" behaviour takes. A tale by Boccaccio, the ability to remember series of numbers, the social use of some particular talent, the solutions to specific problems, all provide ways of exploring "how the mind works." We shall adopt two levels of approach. First, various data will be given (stimuli, problems, "unusual" cases) and different ways of understanding them suggested. The first chapter will thus be a sort of introduction.

In the second chapter we shall give a brief survey of present scientific knowledge about intelligence —about its development within the individual, the ways it is expressed, its connection with creativity and with personality traits.

The succeeding chapters will follow up these themes and, most important, provide "stimulus opportunities" for the reader to exercise his or her own faculties.

The key feature is the games—a pointer in everyday life for developing and maintaining good spirits in difficult circumstances. In a way it is a sort of training for one's ability to "see the funny side," both in others' lives and our own.

Conventional wisdom and intelligence

From the Greeks we inherited an essentially abstract notion of intelligence, which expressed itself mostly in cultural forms. It was thus above all intellectual, centered on words, distinct from practical matters and other aspects of human behaviour. The institution of schools is based on—and in a sense also continues—this idea. Intelligence is commonly considered in terms of performance in study and school exams, although in fact the equation of intelligence with academic ability is less popular now than it was not so long ago, when fewer people went to school. Schoolwork certainly still remains an objective factor in assessing intelligence, but it is not all. Indeed, it has been seen that the institutionalization of school (its structures, the categorization of subjects, the relationships between teachers and pupils) often actually blunts children's liveliness and curiosity for learning. Gradually, a less strictly academic concept of intelligence has thus evolved. Different kinds of ability are recognized as constitut-

But alongside this notion of what, broadly speaking, is meant by intelligence, is a more precise understanding. A more academic approach tries to define the specific features that distinguish intelligence from other psychological traits and to create categories into which those features can be ordered (skill in problem solving, ability with language, mastery of figures, speed and efficiency of response to physical stimuli, and so forth). And then there is the further question as to whether intelligence is an innate quality or more a matter of something acquired through teaching.

Each of these two aspects of intelligence—the "practical," everyday side, and the theoretical, analytical side that is the particular preserve of psychologists and researchers—are worth studying. The diversity of human behaviour and condi-

ing intelligence, other than brilliance at solving mathematical problems or translating Latin tags.

We would like here to concentrate on aspects of intelligence that are perhaps not ordinarily thought of as having a bearing on "intelligence." It was modern psychology that broke the traditional mould of ideas about intelligence, seeing it as basically a capacity for wholeness—just as the individual is one whole being. And while different aspects are identified (verbal intelligence, performance, and concrete, synthetic, and analytic intelligence), it is only because human beings need to analyze, make distinctions, and classify.

As a faculty for wholeness of being, intelligence involves all of human life. Thus it can be found where one would least expect—in joking, in the way someone faces up to difficulties, in irony, inventiveness, artistic taste, feelings, or just the humdrum business of getting on with others.

Horny hands and intelligence

The ancient Romans took their idea of intelligence from the Greeks as something basically intellectual and cultural. They had not always thought thus, however. Study of the Latin language reveals that it was at one time viewed as something more practical and concrete. "Intelligence" is a Latin word, so it is worth finding out what the Romans meant by it.

Etymologically, "intelligence" means "to read into" (*intus legere*) and refers to the ability to comprehend; in a more limited use, it meant sensitivity and good sense. It was in the classical period (first century B.C.), however, that *intellegentia* became widely employed by educated people, when Hellenism had penetrated deeply into Roman society. And the more aware and sensitive intellectuals such as Cicero sought to adapt Latin to the new cultural demands. The word *"intellegentia"* thus came to denote essentially intellectual characteristics. Yet the Romans are noted historically for their practical bent of mind and their administrative, organizational, and juridical genius. When they used words like "ingenious," "dexterous," or "sagacious" (in their Latin forms, of course), they were referring mainly to practical talents of such a kind. An intelligent or wise person was also called *callidus* (one who possessed *calliditas*). This understanding of intelligence is most clearly evident in the plays of Plautus, who lived in Rome in the third and second centuries B.C. We know that his comedies were aimed at popular audiences. It may be supposed, therefore, that *calliditas* was used mostly by the common people and those who were least Hellenized. The word is commonly translated as "skill,"

Scenes from an old edition of Boccaccio's *Decameron*, illustrating the tale of Andreuccio of Perugia, in which native wit, good fortune, and the element of the unexpected give a lively and realistic picture of real life.

"aptitude," or "ability," but a meaning closer to the original would be "knowledge of that which arises from experience, from practice," and the qualities stemming therefrom. Often rendered as "expert" or "skillful," *callidus* is clearly related to practical intelligence by its own etymology: for *callidus*, *calliditas*, and the associated verb *calleo*, all derive from *callum*, meaning a callus—the areas of thick, hard skin that develop on the soles of the feet after much walking, or on the hands of manual labourers.

Now we can get an idea of the true meaning of *calliditas*: intelligence is wisdom acquired by experience, the ability to understand things because they are the materials of experience. Roman intelligence was thus first and foremost a practical quality—wisdom drawn from experience.

A history of intelligence?

For a long time the notion of intelligence as intellectual or cultural activity, to do with study and contemplation, reigned supreme over the more practical meaning of the term.

In the eleventh century, with the revitalization of economic and urban life, a new concept of intelligence emerged—thoroughly down to earth, concerned with concrete, contingent problems. The intelligent person was now the person who was able to achieve aims (be they economic, amorous, or political) without illusion and with fixed determination, using every tool available in the real world. We find such a view of intelligence in the tales of Boccaccio (1313–1375). For him it is a faculty raising the individual above the common run of human beings, driving him to pursue his ends, letting nothing divert his energies. It might almost be said that intelligence is one of the main characters in his writing—a dynamic, ever-active force. Abstract contemplation ceases to be a sign of intelligence, in favour of that faculty of self-control that is able to profit from the passions of others in order to obtain a set goal. (See "The Tale of Alathiel," pages 45–50.)

It was this concept of intelligence that undergirded the activities of the new merchant class that dominated the European economic and cultural revival of the Middle Ages. Boccaccio reflected the world and the outlook of this mercantile class. For them a man could only be fulfilled through his intelligence, which was seen as an ability to get the best out of any situation however complex or difficult. The same utilitarian urge extended also to relations between men and women: Boccaccio was fascinated by the way lovers managed to overcome obstacles placed in their way by parents who had forgotten the delights they themselves had once enjoyed, or by jealous spouses outmaneuvered by sharper intelligence. This supremacy of the intelligence is manifested in an individual's quickness of response to unforeseen hurdles or in the ability to turn the tables in an embarrassing situation and gain the upper hand. Such intelligence was thus not a prerogative of any one social class but could occur in anyone, plebeian, merchant class, or nobility. Clearly, this accorded well with the ethos of the nascent bourgeoisie, for whom individual merit counted more than birthright.

The dwarf

Here is quite a well-known trick question, to which people normally give the first answer that happens to come to mind. Being creative also involves being able to direct our imagination to seeking the most probable answers and not allowing spontaneous fancy to have its head. The story goes as follows.

On the twentieth floor of a skyscraper there lived a dwarf. Methodical in his habits, and dedicated to his work, he would rise early, get himself ready, make breakfast, take the lift down, and go off for the day. Every evening at the same hour he would return and relax. All so far seems perfectly normal. However, one feature of the dwarf's day was odd: on his way back in the lift in the evenings, he would stop at the tenth floor and walk the remaining ten. A fair hike!

Why did he not take the lift all the way to the twentieth floor? Was there some reason?

This question evokes, interestingly enough, a vast range of answers, all quite original in their own way,

all in some sense creative. The most common are:
– the dwarf wants some exercise, so he uses the ten flights of stairs every day for this purpose;
– he is a rather overweight dwarf who has been advised by his doctor to take some exercise;
– he has a friend, who may be ill, living between the tenth and twentieth floors.

Less frequent replies (though equally, in a sense, original and quite entertaining) are:
– the dwarf comes home drunk every night, late, and climbs the last ten flights on tiptoe for fear his wife should hear him and be waiting for him with a rolling pin;
– the lift once got stuck between the tenth and twentieth floors, giving him such a fright that now he prefers to climb the last ten flights of stairs;
– between the tenth and twentieth floors the lift shakes slightly and makes a noise, which is rather worrying, and the dwarf climbs this section on foot to avoid the unpleasant sensation.

All these answers are clearly related to the subjective experience of those who give them, in some manner or another. The simplest solution, and also the likeliest, is that the dwarf is unable to reach any button higher than the tenth. Thus, while he is able to press the bottom button and descend all the way in the lift, on the upward journey he cannot go higher than the tenth floor and is thus obliged to do the last ten on foot.

Let's exercise our intelligence

At an intuitive level, we all know what intelligence is. The problems start when we try to define it. Some view it as "the ability to adapt to new circumstances" or "the ability to learn from experience"; others more often define it as "the ability to find solutions to the problems raised in everyday life." All, however, agree that it is an ability, a potential, that is manifested in many and varied ways. There are in fact all kinds of modes of behaviour that we would unhesitatingly call "intelligent."

On the basis of such a concept, experts have devised intelligence tests characterized by their sheer variety. In line with the historical developments we have traced, it is worth stressing that these tests are confined to the conditions of a certain culture. The figurative, numerical, and verbal material of which most are composed all relate to contemporary Western culture. Their value is thus relative. Together they test a number of faculties that all, to varying degrees, make up "intelligence." Those presented on the following pages are verbal, numerical, spatio-visual, and evolved from certain psychological experiments.

①

From the five words listed below, choose the two that share basic common features:

a) **TOKEN**
b) **MONEY**
c) **TILL**
d) **COIN**
e) **FINANCE**

②

Insert the missing number.

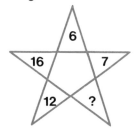

③

If ... goes with ... then ...

goes with ... d ... e ... f

④

Identify the two words with essential characteristics in common:

a) **FABLE**
b) **WOOD**
c) **TREE**
d) **CHAIR**
e) **WRITING DESK**

⑤

Supply the missing number.

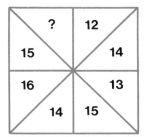

⑥

If ... goes with ... b

then ... c ... goes with

d ... e ... f

⑦

If FOX goes with DEN, then BIRD goes with

a) **TREE**
b) **FLYING**
c) **NEST**

(8)

Complete the series.

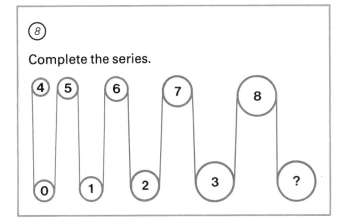

(9)

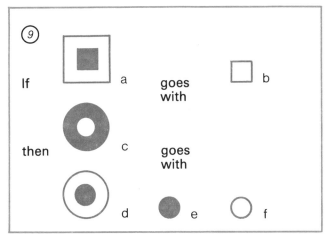

If [a] goes with [b]

then [c] goes with

d   e   f

(10)

If WHEEL goes with CART, then HOOF goes with

a) **GALLOP**
b) **RACE**
c) **HORSE**

(11)

How does the series continue?

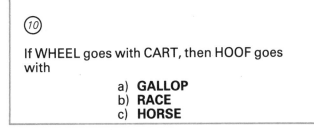

(12)

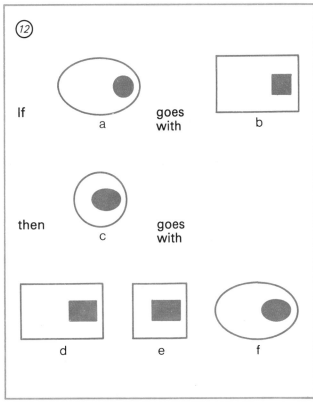

If [a] goes with [b]

then [c] goes with

d   e   f

(13)

In the five words below, the letters are jumbled up. Four of them are anagrams of countries. Which is the odd one out?

a) **ACFERN**
b) **ARMYNEG**
c) **AAIRECM**
d) **ANINLFD**
e) **AANATLA**

(14)

These words can be rearranged to form a sentence. If the sentence is true tick T, if false tick F

TO DOLPHINS THE BELONG FAMILY MAMMALS OF

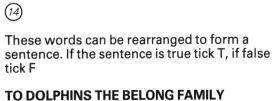

T   F

(continued on page 20)

SENET

Judging from the evidence that has come down to us, the ancient Egyptians invented and played numerous board games as pure mental diversions. The most widespread of these games would appear to have been *senet*, the rules of which have been worked out by the archaeologists C. Jéquier (Swiss) and E. B. Pusch (German). It was a game played by all, from the common people, to the rich nobility and even the pharaoh. The photograph below is of a fresco in the tomb of Nepheronpet (nineteenth dynasty), showing the deceased and his wife playing *senet*. The game is in fact a contest of speed, played by two, on a board consisting of three parallel lines divided into ten compartments each (see diagram above—the

1	2	3	4	5	6	7	8	9	10
20	19	18	17	16	15	14	13	12	11
21	22	23	24	25	26	27	28	29	30

order of the numbers indicates the direction to be followed), with 5 counters of different colours (normally 5 black and 5 white) to each player. To start with, these counters are placed alternately in the first row, as shown on the opposite page.
* To move, the Egyptians would appear to have had four special dice, with only two faces (such as one black and one white), thus allowing only two possibilities each throw. The scoring for each throw could

therefore be as follows:
– 1 white and 3 black   1 point
– 2 white and 2 black   2 points
– 3 white and 1 black   3 points
– 4 white   4 points
– 4 black   6 points
* To start, the players throw the dice in turn until one of them throws a 1. That player then takes black and moves the first counter from square 10 to square 11. Then he throws the dice again. If he throws either a 1-, a 4-, or a 6-point throw, he can move any of his counters

according to his score and throw the dice again; if his throw earns him 2 or 3 points, however, he can move whichever counter he wishes two or three places but then has to pass the dice to his opponent. At his first throw, the other player must move the counter on square 9. After that he can move any piece he may wish to. He, too, throws the dice until he scores a 2 or 3, at which it once again becomes the other player's turn. (Their turns always change with a 2 or 3.)
* The counters can be moved either forwards or backwards. However, certain rules have to be respected. If your counter moves to a square already occupied by your opponent, the latter has to move to where you have just come from: there can never be more than one counter on any one square. If there are counters of the same colour on two consecutive squares, they cannot be attacked, and the opponent must make a different move. Where there are three consecutive counters of the same colour, not only can they not be attacked, they cannot even be passed. The opponent must make other moves, until the throw of the dice forces the stronger one to move on. Counters of the same colour are of course permitted to cross such a "castle."
* Every throw of the dice entails a move, but if the move is backwards, the counter cannot land on a square already occupied by the opposition—for that would merely advance the relevant counter to your own disadvantage. If a player cannot move, he has to forgo his turn.
* As appears on the opposite page, the square corresponding to number 27 is marked X. Any counter that lands here must return to number 1, or to the first unoccupied square after 1, and begin again. Squares 26, 28, 29, and 30, however, are "free zones," and no counter can be forced backwards from them.
* When all the counters of one colour are in the last row (from 21 to 30), they can come out, one at a time, as each lands exactly on the final square. If, however, during this operation one counter lands on 27 and has to go back to the beginning, the other counters of that colour must all wait until it has again reached the end row before being able to leave the board. The winner is the first player to clear the board of all his pieces. The board, counters, and dice for *senet* are not available commercially, but any reader who wants to will easily be able to improvise well enough.

THE ROYAL GAME OF UR

In the Sumerian section of the British Museum is a finely inlaid game board from the royal tombs at Ur (the ancient city mentioned in the Bible as Ur of the Chaldeans). This board (illustrated below) was used for a game played some four and a half thousand years ago in the palace of the Sumerian kings. Models of the board are available in some gift shops, together with the rules of the game—or at least such rules as have been supposed by scholars to be the probable original game.

The board on display in the museum is valuable not only as an historical curiosity, but also for its exquisite inlay work of stone, mother-of-pearl, and lapis lazuli (a deep blue mineral used as a gem or pigment). Along with other objects of similarly skilled craftsmanship, the board testifies to the sophistication of Sumerian culture and the luxury and lively refinement of court life. It was discovered together with other game boards by an archaeological expedition led by Sir Leonard Woolley, which was mounted by the British Museum and the University of Pennsylvania in the 1920s and 1930s to work on sites in southern Iraq. Similar boards have been found in Egypt and Cyprus. This suggests that the various wealthy courts of those ancient civilizations shared a game (or variants of one basic game) in common. Whatever the links between these different pastimes, and whatever the

rules that can be inferred for them at this distance in time, we shall here set forth those for the royal game of Ur, which Woolley described as "the most striking example found" during his excavations.

As the illustration below and the reconstruction (opposite page) show, the board is made up of 20 squares, arranged in three sections: at the bottom, having 12 squares (4 rows of 3), at the top, having 6 (2 rows of 3); and 2 squares connecting them. Five are specially marked with a rosettelike star with eight points; 5 have little circles; 5 have designs that resemble eyes; and the remaining 5 are variously patterned. As we shall see, however, only those squares with stars have any particular significance.

To play the game you need 14 counters (7 white and 7 black) and six special dice (three for each player) shaped like triangular pyramids, of which two apexes are coloured. The point of the game is for each of the two contestants to get his pieces around one of the two tracks (shown arrowed in the diagram at the right). The counters are moved according to the throw of the dice, the possible scoring for each throw being as follows:

– three coloured apexes: 5 points (⅛ probability);
– three plain apexes: 4 points (⅛ probability);
– two coloured and one plain: 1 point (⅜ probability);
– one coloured and two plain: 0 points (⅜ probability).

A throw of the dice decides who

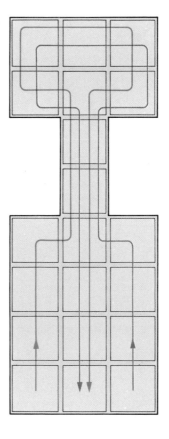

starts. Then the first piece can only be put on the board after a score of 1 or 5; for example, it has to enter on the first or fifth starred square. Subsequently, the other pieces can be brought into the game on square 1 whenever a counter of the same colour lands on a starred square. Once started, no piece can move backwards. Once a piece has moved 14 squares (so has crossed back over the 2-square "bridge") it is turned upside down. Several pieces can be piled on top of each other. When a piece is on the bridge or in the top section, it can attack its opponents, whether single or piled up, by landing on the same square. When this happens, the opponent's pieces are removed from the board and have to start again. The starred squares and the final square are "free zones," where tokens of either colour are immune from attack.

Upside-down pieces can only be attacked by other upside-down pieces. The same principle applies to pieces the right way up. To end the course, each piece has to land exactly on the final square (where any number can accumulate), and then a 4 has to be scored—at which point all the tokens on the end square finish together. The player who gets all his pieces around the course first is the winner.

As one might imagine, although the game is largely determined by the throw of the dice, the fun consists in choosing how to move once each player has more than one piece on the board. The royal game of Ur is to some extent a game of strategy, in which reason and intuition can help win the day.

15

How does the series continue?

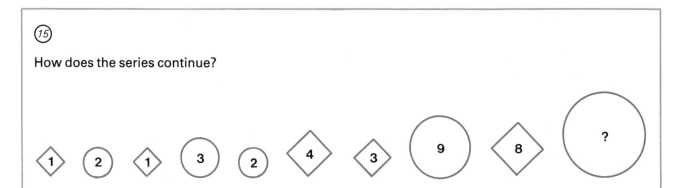

16

How does the series continue?

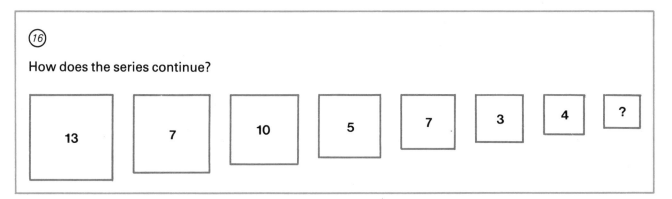

17

If   a   goes with   b   then   c   goes with   d   e   f

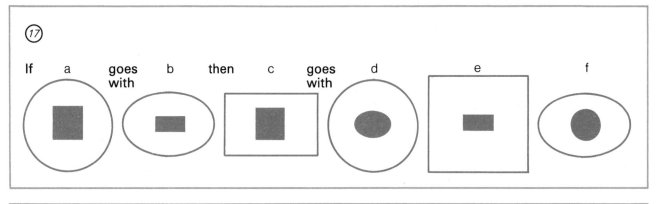

18

If   a   goes with   b   then   c   goes with   d   e   f

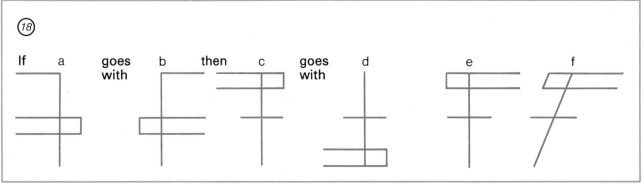

Here are five words with jumbled-up letters. Four of them are anagrams of birds. Which is the odd one out?

a) **CCNIHEK**
b) **CAANYR**
c) **CCOUOK**
d) **CEIALNP**
e) **CISFTAH**

These words can be rearranged to read as a sentence. If the sentence is true, tick T; if false, tick F.

FLOATS ALL NOT WOOD

T

F

How does the series continue?

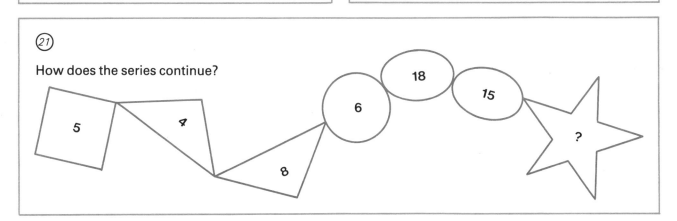

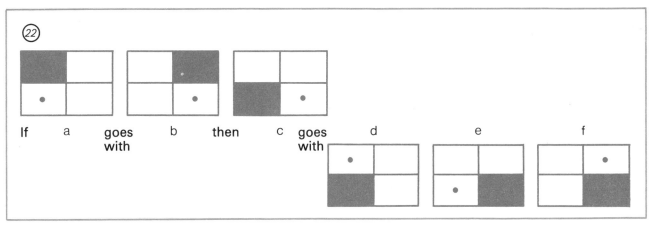

If a goes with b then c goes with d e f

Two of these words are similar in meaning. Which ones?

a) **VIVACIOUS**
b) **SUPERFICIAL**
c) **INCAPABLE**
d) **SPIRITED**

How does the series continue?

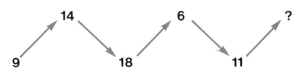

25

Figure a can be constructed with four of the six fragments designated b, c, d, e, f, g. Which are the unnecessary fragments?

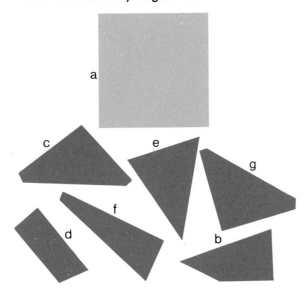

26

Figure a can be constructed with three of the five fragments designated b, c, d, e, f. Which are the two unnecessary fragments?

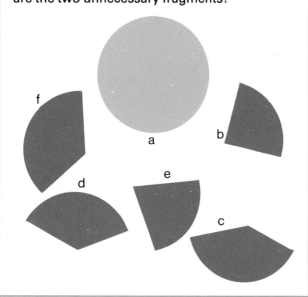

27

Fill in the gaps so as to make each line into two complete words.

a) **MIST(..)ROR**
b) **LEM(..)LY**
c) **LO(..)XED**

28

Which of sections a, b, and c are contained in line d?

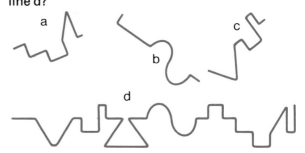

29

Figure a can be constructed with three of the five fragments designated b, c, d, e, f. Which are the two unnecessary fragments?

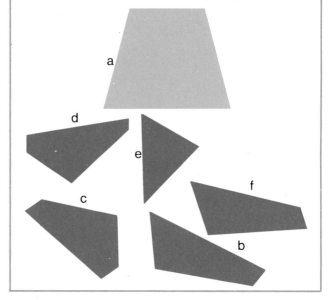

(30)

Complete these three series of numbers.

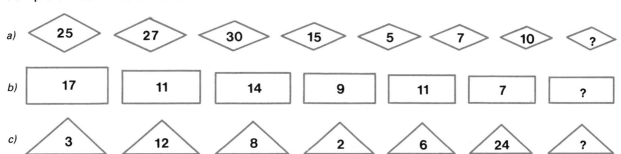

a) 25 27 30 15 5 7 10 ?

b) 17 11 14 9 11 7 ?

c) 3 12 8 2 6 24 ?

Answers

(Of course, there are other solutions besides the ones given by the author—for example, "token" and "money" both have five letters. A coin is called money, and money can be referred to as coin or coins.)

1) a, d

2) 9: 6 (+1), 7 (+2), 9 (+3), 12 (+4), 16

3) e (2:00, 5:00, 8:00, 11:00)

4) d, e

5) 13 or 17 depending on whether the number begins or ends the series: 13 (−1), 12 (+2), 14 (−1), 13 (+2), 15 (−1), 14 (+2), 16 (−1), 15 (+2), 17

6) d

7) c (a fox has a den; a bird a nest)

8) 4: 4 (−4), 0 (+5), 5 (−4), 1 (+5), 6 (−4), 2 (+5), 7 (−4), 3 (+5), 8 (−4), 4

9) e

10) c (a wheel has the same function as a hoof for a horse)

11) 44: 2 (+2), 4 (×2), 8 (+2), 10 (×2), 20 (+2), 22 (×2), 44

12) e

13) Except for e, which conceals the word ATLANTA, which is not a country.
a) FRANCE, b) GERMANY, c) AMERICA, d) FINLAND

14) The sentence reads: DOLPHINS BELONG TO THE FAMILY OF MAMMALS, and is true

15) The series continues with 16: 1 (×2), 2(−1), 1 (×3), 3 (−1), 2 (×2), 4 (−1), 3 (×3), 9 (−1), 8 (×2), 16

16) The series continues with 1: 13 (−6), 7 (+3), 10 (−5), 5 (+2), 7 (−4), 3 (+1), 4 (−3), 1

17) e or f

18) e (Figs. *a* and *b* are visually symmetrical, and the only figure similarly symmetrical to c among d, e and f is e)

19) e (CATFISH is the odd man out. The others are a) CHICKEN, b) CANARY, c) CUCKOO, d) PELICAN

20) The sentence reads "NOT ALL WOOD FLOATS." This is true: the specific weight of some types of wood is greater than that of water, and will therefore make them sink.

21) 60: 5 (−1), 4 (×2), 8 (−2), 6 (×3), 18 (−3), 15 (×4), 60

22) e is visually symmetrical with c

23) a, d

24) 15: 9 (+5), 14 (+4), 18 (÷3), 6 (+5), 11 (+4), 15

25) The unnecessary fragments are b and c

26) The unnecessary fragments are e and f

27) a) MIST(ER)ROR
b) LEM(ON)LY
c) LO(VE)XED

28) a, c

29) The unnecessary fragments are b and d

30) a) 5: 25 (+2), 27 (+3), 30 (÷2), 15 (÷3), 5 (+2), 7 (+3), 10 (÷2), 5
b) 8: 17 (−6), 11 (+3), 14 (−5), 9 (+2), 11 (−4), 7 (+1), 8
c) 20: 3 (×4), 12 (−4), 8 (÷4), 2 (+4), 6 (×4), 24 (−4), 20

Language and intelligence

Can a faculty such as intelligence be independent of verbal language? It is true that not all "language" is verbal: we communicate also through gesture and with figures and other symbols. These are often spoken of as codes, artificial languages, or animal communication. It is nevertheless hard to imagine another language capable of encompassing such a huge variety of objects and expressing such a vast range of experiences and feelings as our everyday verbal language.

Hence it is natural to suppose that what we call "intelligence" finds particularly good expression in ordinary language. One need only observe how, in babies learning to speak (which can start at the age of one), their relationship with others (parents and strangers) is extended, and they begin to be able to master many of the mysteries of their immediate environment. Yet it must be remembered that while for animals the development of crude communication is a natural thing and does not evolve, in humans it is the fruit of learning and does evolve, both in the lives of individuals and in history, changing in form and content. This learning process is in turn determined by the family, the environment, the cultural atmosphere, and the stimuli present in these. Thus it is true that thought finds a natural vehicle in language; yet it is also true that this very language has resulted from a slow, continuous process of cultural evolution. It is necessary to bear this in mind when one looks at intelligence as manifested in language. We also know that the richness, variety, and distinguishing characteristics of language, and the accessibility of abstract concepts, vary among social groups. Someone brought up in a narrow cultural environment, speaking mostly a local language or dialect, will find it hard to shine in verbal tests relating to the language as it is spoken nationwide and to a culture very remote from his own experience. The risk in tests of verbal ability is that rather than showing merely lack of expertise with words, they can suggest low intelligence, since they are moulded according to certain cultural contexts. It is, however, difficult to devise verbal tests of universal applicability in a society in which great linguistic and cultural variety still exists.

Finally, it must also be remembered that verbal intelligence is normally deemed to consist of being able to speak clearly and expressively, with ready comprehension of information read or heard, and with the facility for conversation.

However, we shall return to such detailed considerations of the phenomenon of intelligence in the second chapter. For now we can confine ourselves to introductory observations.

Playing with words

Here is a series of tests in which the reader can exercise his or her ability with words. They go from easy to difficult, from simple to complex: the first concrete, the later ones more abstract.

These little tests should be entered upon in the spirit of a game. There is no scoring system, and any results are entirely for the player's own interest and benefit.

Two of these words refer to objects with basic characteristics in common.
Which are they?

a) **BELFRY**
b) **SPIRE**
c) **TERRACE**
d) **EMBRASURES**
e) **BATTLEMENTS**
f) **KEEP**
g) **BELL TOWER**

Two of these words refer to objects with basic characteristics in common.
Which are they?

a) **WINE**
b) **CASK**
c) **BOTTLE**
d) **VINTAGE**
e) **BARREL**

Two of these words refer to objects with basic characteristics in common.
Which are they?

a) **PYLON**
b) **BRIDGE**
c) **SCAFFOLD**
d) **PARAPET**
e) **VIADUCT**

4

Two in this series refer to objects with basic characteristics in common.
Which are they?

a) HAY
b) SICKLE
c) GRAIN
d) EAR
e) BILLHOOK
f) RAKE

5

Two of these words refer to objects with basic characteristics in common.
Which are they?

a) MUSIC
b) GUITAR
c) FLUTE
d) PIANO
e) PIPE

6

Here are five words with their letters jumbled up. Four are names of planets.
Which is the odd one out?

a) ETHAR
b) TEENPUN
c) ASIRUN
d) ASTRUN
e) IPURJET

7

Fill in the empty spaces to create two full words:

a) NO(..)AL   b) CA(..)AR

8

Two of these words are similar in meaning.
Which are they?

a) SAD
b) SERIOUS
c) MALEVOLENT
d) GRAVE
e) SPIRITED

9

Two of these words are similar in meaning.
Which are they?

a) REFUSAL
b) LISTLESSNESS
e) INTROVERSION
d) APATHY
e) REPROOF

10

Two of these words are similar in meaning.
Which are they?

a) CONVENIENCE
b) CONVENTION
c) CONVECTION
d) CONCESSION
e) CONVOCATION

Answers

1) a, g

2) b, e

3) b, e

4) b, e

5) c, e

6) c (is *not* URANUS)

7) a) NO(SE)AL
   b) CA(GE)AR

8) b, d

9) b, d

10) b, e

Natural "tools" for games

The history of human civilization reveals the presence of games of one kind and another among all peoples of every society. Games seem to satisfy a basic need in human nature.

They have always stimulated the imagination, and mankind has been able to make use of the most unlikely objects for play. Even when there was nothing to provide entertainment, human beings managed to play games with their own most vital means of communication—words!

One needs only listen to a child beginning to articulate sounds: it is as though new horizons were opening up to it. It derives visible pleasure from being able to control the sequence of its own sounds ("ta-ta," "pa-pa," "ma-ma," "ga-ga"), until finally it can utter words with meanings (relating to parents, useful objects, other people in the home, and so forth). Its verbal ability then improves steadily, along with understanding. Then the first sentences are spoken, bringing with them satisfaction and pleasure. As the child develops further, this same basic pleasure will act as a powerful stimulus, encouraging it to use verbal language to extend and master its own world of relationships.

First games with words

The acquisition and mastery of verbal language by children is manifested by increased confidence and self-awareness, and is a feature of the general growing-up process. Another clear sign of this is their delight in constructing odd sequences of words, as soon as they begin to have a vocabulary and to know how to construct sentences. They seem to have a facility for making games with words, both for adults' entertainment and their own. Words and the different meanings they acquire in conjunction with other words are a constant source of surprise and discovery for young children, bringing them closer to a world of adult control. They use words as if they had an independent existence and were all parts of a huge puzzle—bits to be played around with in ever new ways, to create ever new results. Thus it is quite normal to hear children playing with rhyming words:

mouse	→	house
ground	→	drowned
jelly-cake	→	belly-ache
trees	→	breeze

dollar	→	scholar
nose	→	toes

Words that are associated with each other in this way often sound strange and comical because of the unusual or non-sensical meaning they assume. Many nursery rhymes are based on this principle and can often provide parents and teachers with an amusing and lighthearted way of teaching children how to count, or recite the alphabet, as the following two examples illustrate:

A was an Archer
who shot at a frog

B was a Butcher
who kept a bull-dog

C was a Captain
all covered with lace

D was a Drummer
who played with much grace

E was an Esquire
with pride on his brow

F was a Farmer
who followed the plough

G was a Gamester
who had but ill luck

H was a Hunter
and hunted a buck

I was an Italian
who had a white mouse

J was a Joiner
and built up a house

K was a King
so mighty and grand

L was a Lady
who had a white hand

M was a Miser
who hoarded up gold

N was a Nobleman
gallant and bold

O was an Organ boy
who played about town

P was a Parson
who wore a black gown

Q was a Queen
who was fond of her people

R   was a Robin
    who perched on a steeple

S   was a Sailor
    who spent all he got

T   was a Tinker
    who mended a pot

U   was an Usher
    who loved little boys

V   was a Veteran
    who sold pretty toys

W   was a Watchman
    who guarded the door

X   was eXpensive
    and so became poor

Y   was a Youth
    who did not love school

Z   was a Zany
    who looked a great fool

ANON

One, two, buckle my shoe,
Three, four, knock at the door,
Five, six, pick up sticks,
Seven, eight, lay them straight,
Nine, ten, a big fat hen,
Eleven, twelve, dig and delve,
Thirteen, fourteen, maids a-courting,
Fifteen, sixteen, maids in the kitchen,
Seventeen, eighteen, maids in waiting,
Nineteen, twenty, my plate's empty.

ANON

The game of question and answer

This is played with friends, in a circle. The first player asks his right-hand neighbour a question; he answers, then puts a question to the neighbour on his right—and so on, until all have replied to their left-hand neighbours and put questions to those on their right. Everyone has heard all that has been said. Then each player has to repeat the question he was asked and the answer he received to his own question. In other words, he does not repeat his own question, but does repeat what his neighbours on either side of him said—the question asked on his right and the answer given on his left!

A variant of the game of question and answer is often played by mixed groups of teenagers, who sit alternately boy-girl-boy-girl. On a sufficiently long

piece of paper, they then one after another write sentences on a predetermined theme (in block capitals, to conceal identity as far as possible).

It is interesting, for instance, to suggest they write a compliment or a love message to one of the girls there (chosen at random). The first person writes something, then passes the sheet to his neighbour after carefully folding over the top of the paper to hide what he has written. The next player writes a sentence, again folds over the top of the sheet (that thus gradually becomes a thicker and thicker wedge), and passes it on. Finally the sheet of paper is unrolled, and everything read out in one go, as though written as a single piece. The results are always good fun.

Definitions

Defining a word, either concrete or abstract, means describing what it means by using other words and related meanings. The game of definitions consists of guessing a word from its definition. A number of people can play. Either at random or turn by turn, the players one at a time take a dictionary and (without showing which page they are reading from) read out a definition. Before the start of the game, it should be decided how the answers are to be given—whether by individual players in turn or in a free-for-all. The winner is the player who guesses most words. The fun of this game is that it is not always the simplest or most common words that are easiest to guess. Here are a few examples.

possible: that which comes within the bounds of abstract or concrete supposition; that which comes within the bounds of an objective or subjective faculty

gramophone: an instrument for reproducing sounds by means of the vibration of a needle following the spiral groove of a revolving disk

emulation: praiseworthy effort to imitate, equal, or surpass others

corbel: architectural element jutting out from the face of a wall serving to support a structure above

cerulean: the blue of the sky, used for example to describe a small patch of water

misoneist: one who through fear, hatred, or intolerance is opposed to novelty or change

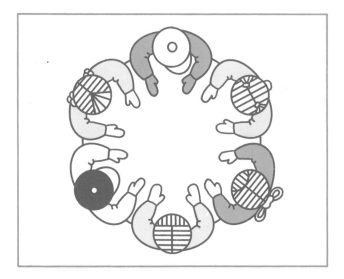

humour: the vision of the ridiculous in things, not necessarily hostile or purely entertaining, but reflecting an acute wit and frequently a kindly human sympathy

beautiful: capable of arousing physical or spiritual attraction; worthy of admiration and contemplation

This game can be played the other way round: each player in turn chooses a word to be defined. The winner is the one who gives the most precise definition. Words that are too difficult, too abstract or too idiomatic are naturally excluded. Nor is it necessary to give a definition strictly according to the one in the dictionary. An approximation will do. After all, dictionaries do not always exactly agree even among themselves!

The players can agree on a judge who will be the final arbitrator, to maintain good sense and fairness.

Word chains

The society we live in, with its frenetic pace of life and timetabled mode of working, seems to leave few idle moments in the day. However, there are occasionally times when we find ourselves with nothing to do: waiting to leave somewhere, waiting for a delayed train, or a long car journey all can seem to be wasting more time than they in fact are taking up. Often on such occasions we cannot think how to "kill" time. Games are an ideal way not only of making the most of these tedious hours, but above all of relaxing the tension during a period of waiting

or overcoming the boredom of a long journey.

One game, which even children can join in with, is to go from one word to another by changing only one letter at a time. For example . . .

LOVE → LOSE → LOST → LUST

Every word must mean something, and all conjugations of verbs and declensions of nouns are permitted.

Two boys waiting for a plane at an airport adopted the following sequences: one had to go from ROME to BONN, the other from YUMA to RENO. Both managed their respective word chains, the first one went as follows:

ROME, TOME, TONE, BONE, BONN,

and the second:

YUMA, PUMA, PUMP, RUMP, RUMS, RUNS, RUNT, RENT, RENO.

It can be agreed before the start of the game that the winner will be the player who reaches the second word within a certain time limit. And then if that results in a tie, the winner can be the one who went through the fewest word permutations.

In the example of the boys at the airport, the first one was thus the winner.

This game can also be played as a sort of patience, alone. Here are some word chains to try out:

   I) GAME—BALL
  II) MORE—CARD
 III) FEEL—GOOD
 IV) THICK—BRIDE
  V) REAR—BACK

Palindromes

Another game to play with words is to think which words are palindromes, or symmetrical in their spelling. "Palindrome" itself is a word of Greek origin, meaning "running back again." It therefore

---

Answers
  I) GAME—GALE—GALL—BALL
 II) MORE—MARE—CARE—CARD
 III) FEEL—FELL—TELL—TOLL—TOLD—GOLD—GOOD
 IV) THICK—TRICK—TRICE—TRINE—BRINE—BRIDE
  V) REAR—BEAR—BEAK—BECK—BACK

refers to words that are the same when read forwards or backwards.

In our language we write and read from left to right, at the end of each line returning to the left again to start the next. However, some languages (such as Arabic and Hebrew) adopt the opposite system and read from right to left.

Words read in a single direction, either left to right or right to left, are mostly asymmetrical. To take a simple example, "apple" in our language has a precise meaning when read from left to right, yet if read from right to left is a meaningless muddle of letters. The word "elppa" conjures no object in our mind and is merely a haphazard group of letters without reference to any objective reality. The game of palindromes consists of hunting through the language for words that have the same meaning regardless of which way they are read. The word "radar," for instance, means the same whether it is read from left to right or from right to left.

Other examples are "level" and "rotor."

Try to think which is the longest palindrome in the English language. (Here is a long one: "Malayalam" —the language spoken in Kerala, southern India. But perhaps even better ones exist.)

Numbers and intelligence

When we talk about language we tend to think of that which we pick up naturally, and which is the main means of communication between humans. But there is another language, not commonly thought of as such, though in constant use in daily life. That is the language of mathematics.

Often, unfortunate mental habits picked up at school, where different mental disciplines are kept very separate, mean that we view mathematics as a world of its own, abstract and quite apart from normal everyday language. Thus we ignore the essentially linguistic nature of mathematics, which uses signs and symbols (numbers) to convey thought. Though basically a language, the main purpose of mathematics is not communication between individuals, but systematization of human powers of knowledge and ability to present it as a unified, objective experience. Hence it is above all the language of the sciences. Intelligence must therefore necessarily include the capacity for using numbers, for establishing the relationships between them and handling them effectively.

Intelligence is by no means purely mathematical, but equally it is commonly accepted that mathematical ability is an expression thereof. It is for good reason that intelligence tests contain a significant proportion of numerical exercises.

Games with numbers

Let us now test our ability with numbers, using the following exercises. Each is a numerical series in which the idea is to discover the general law governing it. The first ones are simple, the later ones more difficult. Having discovered a law of the series, it is then possible to guess the next number.

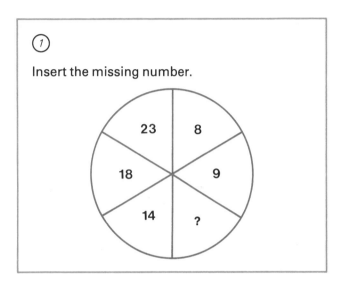

① Insert the missing number.

23   8
18   9
14   ?

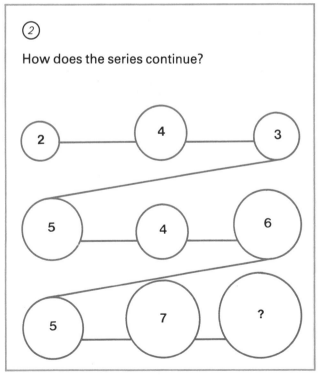

② How does the series continue?

2 — 4 — 3
5 — 4 — 6
5 — 7 — ?

③

How does the series continue?

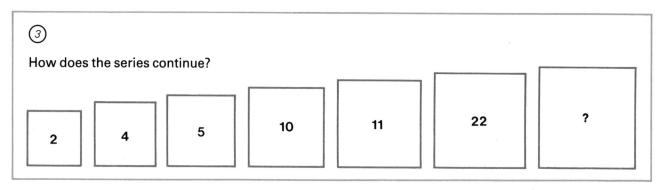

④

How does the series continue?

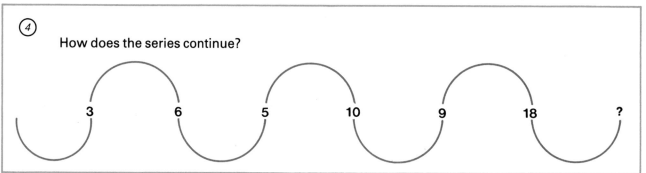

⑤

How does the series continue?

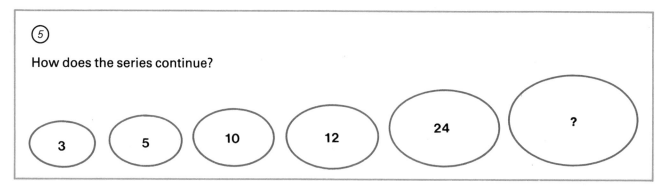

⑥

How does the series continue?

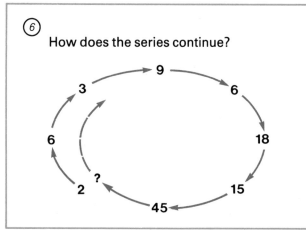

⑦

How does the series continue?

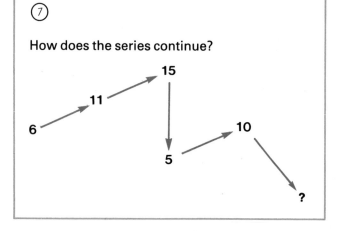

⑧

How does the series continue?

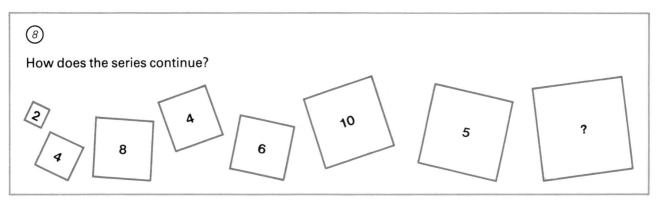

⑨

How does the series continue?

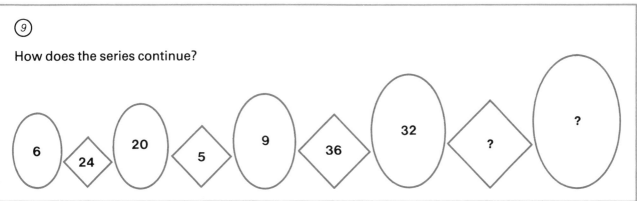

⑩

How does the series continue?

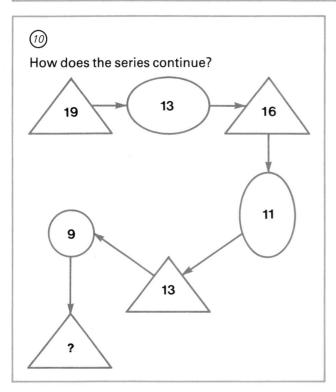

Answers and explanations

1) 11: 8 (**+1**), 9 (**+2**), 11 (**+3**), 14 (**+4**), 18 (**+5**), 23

2) 6: 2 (**+2**), 4 (**−1**), 3 (**+2**), 5 (**−1**), 4 (**+2**), 6 (**−1**), 5 (**+2**), 7 (**−1**), 6

3) 23: 2 (**×2**), 4 (**+1**), 5 (**×2**), 10 (**+1**), 11 (**×2**), 22 (**+1**), 23

4) 17: 3 (**×2**), 6 (**−1**), 5 (**×2**), 10 (**−1**), 9 (**×2**), 18 (**−1**), 17

5) 26: 3 (**+2**), 5 (**×2**), 10 (**+2**), 12 (**×2**), 24 (**+2**), 26

6) 42: 2 (**×3**), 6 (**−3**), 3 (**×3**), 9 (**−3**), 6 (**×3**), 18 (**−3**), 15 (**×3**), 45 (**−3**), 42

7) 14: 6 (**+5**), 11 (**+4**), 15 (**÷3**), 5 (**+5**), 10 (**+4**), 14

8) 7: 2 (**+2**), 4 (**+4**), 8 (**÷2**), 4 (**+2**), 6 (**+4**), 10 (**÷2**), 5 (**+2**), 7

9) 8 and 12: 6 (**×4**), 24 (**−4**), 20 (**÷4**), 5 (**+4**), 9 (**×4**), 36 (**−4**), 32 (**÷4**), 8 (**+4**), 12

10) 10: 19 (**−6**), 13 (**+3**), 16 (**−5**), 11 (**+2**), 13 (**−4**), 9 (**+1**), 10

Visual intelligence

The attitudes of an individual or a community are expressed above all through verbal language. This supremacy of language in turn affects the development of the individual's other faculties (especially the logical and cognitive faculties). A rich, well-articulated language influences the whole culture of a social group, feeding it with terms and concepts. There are, however, other faculties and modes of human activity that are also indisputably "intelligent." The architect's ability to order space in a house, is without doubt a clear form of intelligence. Perhaps, too, a painter, in the treatment of shapes and colours within the limitations of his materials, displays a similar kind of "intelligence." Intellectual ability is exhibited in many activities in which similar or dissimilar geometrical figures have to be discerned.

Games with shapes

Let us now exercise our visual powers in the following tests. The object is to recognize similarities in dissimilar figures and vice versa, to discern the individual shapes that all together make up a single geometric form. Some of these exercises are presented as a progression: the development of the visual features of one unit into those of the next—a mental step that can be taken without the aid of verbal language. Intelligence is a unifying faculty.

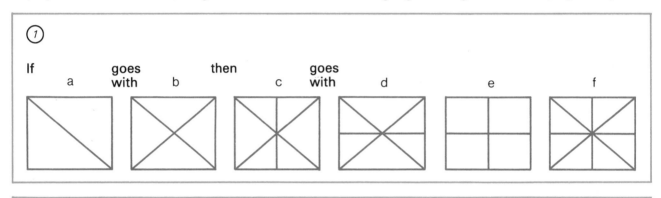

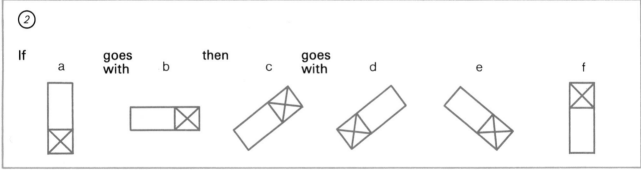

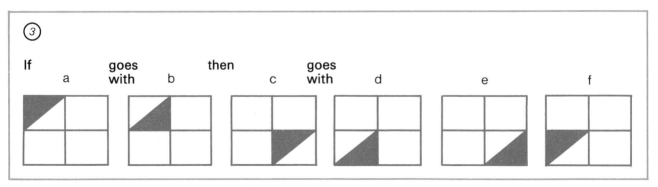

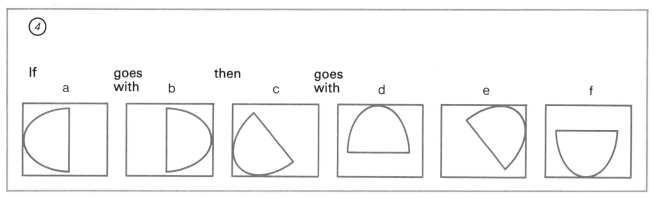

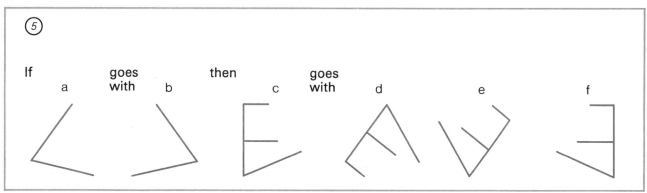

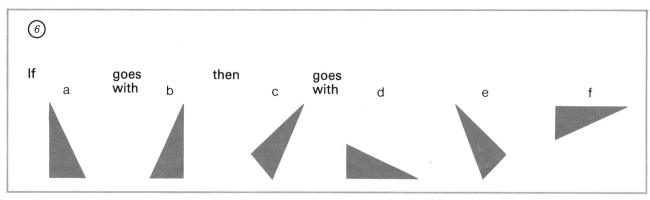

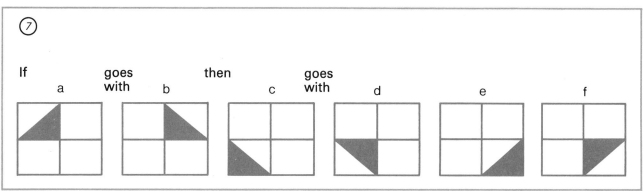

(continued on page 38)

ALQUERQUE

In the thirteenth century, when Spain was largely ruled by the Moors, Alfonso X of Swabia, known as the "the Learned," was king of Castile and León for thirty-two years (1252–1284). He earned his nickname through his transformation of the court of Seville into an international cultural center. A poet himself, he wrote numerous secular and religious songs. One undertaking he encouraged was the translation of Greek and Arabic philosophy into Spanish. He also endeavoured to compile a collection of all the knowledge of his age, and the scholars working on this project produced a remarkable body of legal works (*Las siete partidas*), historical works (*Grande e general Estoria; Crònica general*), and artistic, literary, and scientific documents (the Alphonsine astronomical charts, for instance). Among these there was a book of games, the so-called *Libro de juegos*. This is a large illustrated collection of every game known and played at that time, some of which are mentioned as being "played with the mind." One of the most interesting is called *alquerque de doce* ("for twelve pieces"), the name being a Spanish approximation to the Arabic *el-qirkat*. In fact, although this game may have been introduced into Spain by the Moors, it had

fig. a

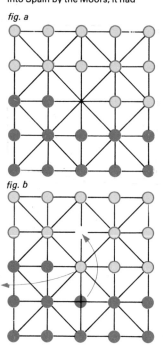

fig. b

for a long time been familiar to the ancient Egyptians and the peoples of the Near East and is essentially an early variant of checkers. It is still widely played today—not only in the houses and *bodegas* of Spain, but also in certain areas of Asia, Africa, and Central America. Like checkers, it is a board game for two players. The board is divided up with 5 horizontal lines, 5 verticals, and 6 diagonals, creating 25 points of intersection (see opposite page, below). There are 24 pieces: 12 per player, of two colours (usually 12 black and 12 white), and at the start of the game they are positioned as indicated in *figure a*. The players move one at a time, turn by turn. Unlike checkers, the pieces can be moved in any direction along the lines of the board, and the player who has the advantage at the beginning is not the starter (who is constrained by having only the one empty space) but the second. Really, though, the outcome depends on each player's ability to gauge the possible moves—using both reason and intuition—and to choose the best, predicting his opponent's moves. Any piece can be moved (one at a time) from where it is to any empty neighbouring place. However, when a piece—let us say, white—moves to a position next to a black piece, leaving an empty space behind it, the black can jump the white and "gobble it up"—for example, take it and eliminate it from the game (see *figure b*). If the position of the pieces allows, it is possible to take more than one of an opponent's pieces at a single go, even when changes of direction are involved. At the same time, if it is possible to take a piece, it is not permitted *not* to take it. If a player fails to notice that he can take a piece, and makes another move, his opponent can remove the piece that should have taken a "prisoner" from the board. Once a player has moved and taken his hand away from the piece, the move is irreversible—unless he has previously said, "Testing," to indicate that he is not making a proper move but is just trying the ground to see what he wishes to do. The winner is the one who takes all the other player's pieces or forces him into a position where he cannot move. It is quite common to end in a draw, when the players are evenly matched. Many variants of *alquerque* are to be found throughout the world, the differences depending primarily on differences in board design.

fig. c

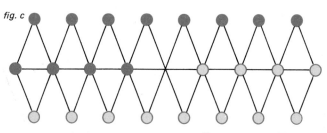

fig. d

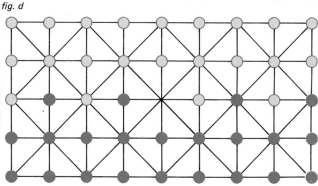

Some are simpler than the Spanish-Moorish version, others more complex. Among the former is the version played by the Zuni Indians in New Mexico, who learnt it from the Conquistadors, naming it *Kolowis Awithlaknannai* ("snake fight"). This version still has 24 pieces, but the board consists of 8 lozenges intersected by a line. At the start of the game, the pieces are arranged as in *figure c*. A more complex variant of *alquerque* is played on the island of Madagascar, where the game is known as *fanorona*: the board is as illustrated in *figure d*, and each player starts with 22 pieces (thus 44 pieces in all).

Another complex variant is to be found in Sri Lanka, where it is known as *peralikatuma*. The board for this is the one shown on the opposite page (above). Each player has 23 pieces, arranged as in *figure e*. At the outset there are three empty spaces in the middle. This version takes somewhat longer to play, but all the different variants share the same rules. Like the better-known games of checkers and chess, *alquerque* and its variants belong in the category of "games of intelligence," for they all demand a combination of intuition, strategy, and reasoning power.

fig. e

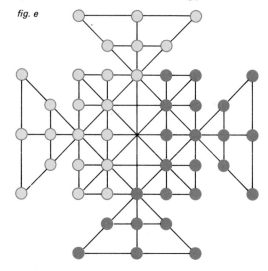

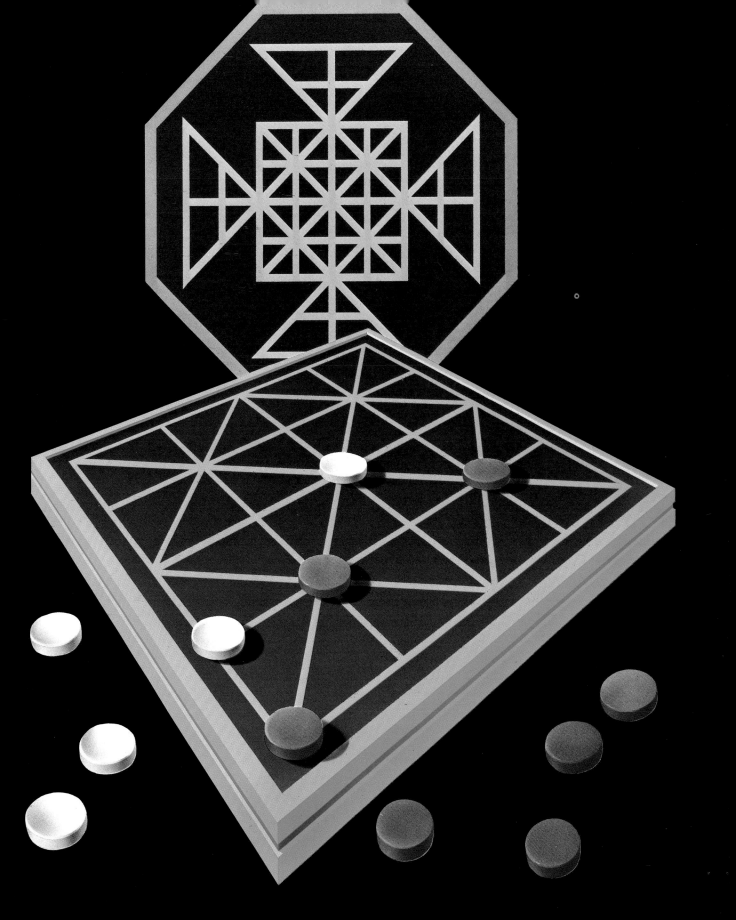

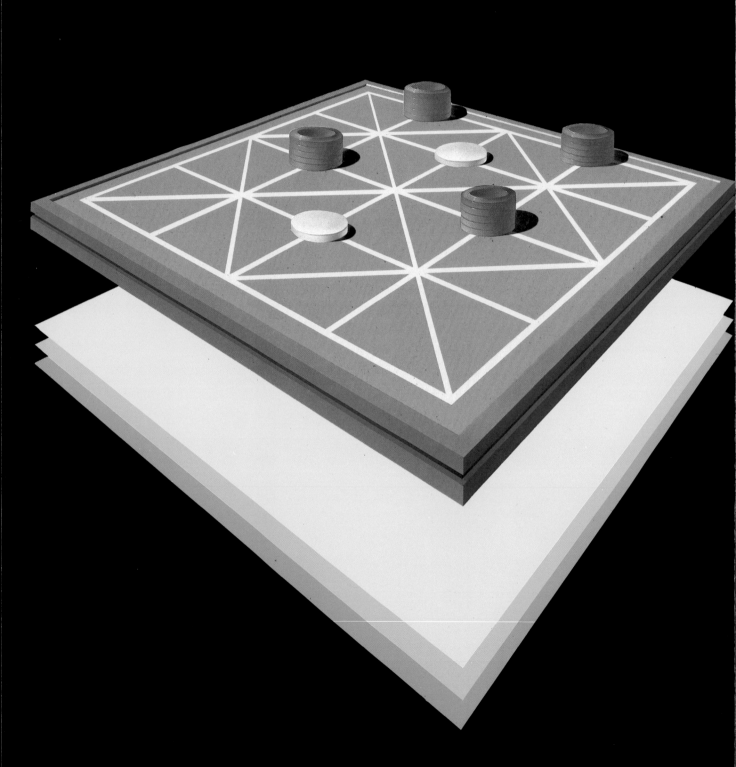

BAGH-BANDI

Bagh-bandi—the game of tigers and goats—is an entertaining Indian game for two players, played throughout the vast expanse of Asia under different names and with rules of varying degrees of strictness. The example given here is one of the more easily graspable forms, with a simple board and rules. *Bagh-bandi* is the Bengali name (Bengal being famous for its tigers), and the board (see *figure a*) is in fact the simplest of all. As can be seen, it is square, with 5 horizontal lines and 6 diagonals, intersecting to form 32 equal triangles, exactly as for *alquerque* (see pp. 34–35). Anyone can make this board with squared paper, (the handiest size being approximately 8 × 8 in. (20 × 20 cm). To start, one player takes 2 pieces of the same shape and colour, while the other (generally the more experienced player) has 20 pieces, which are all the same but different from those of the other player. It is possible to use coloured buttons or painted coins—one colour for the tigers and another for the goats, which should also be smaller and stackable). There are thus 2 tigers and 20 goats. The tigers start off from intersections *a3* and *c3*, while the goats, in piles of 5, start on *b2*, *b4*, *d2*, and *d4* (see *figure a*: tigers pink, goats red).
The aim of the game is of course to win: the tigers win if they manage to eat all the goats (or if the goat player capitulates when it is impossible for him to win); the goats win if they manage to hedge the tigers in so that they are unable to move.
Each player moves in turn, as follows.
First, the goats move. They can only travel one at a time, to a next-door intersection connected to where they are by a straight line, corresponding to the side of a triangle, both on the area of the board and around the perimeter. The top goat of the pile moves first, with the others following in successive moves. Actual piles of goats cannot be moved. It takes some skill to maneuver the goats well—which is why, as was indicated above, the more experienced player should take them. The best way to defeat the tigers is to dismantle the piles and move the goats around as much as possible.
As well as being able to make the same moves as the goats, the tigers can jump the latter, both individually and when in piles, as long as there is a free

fig. a

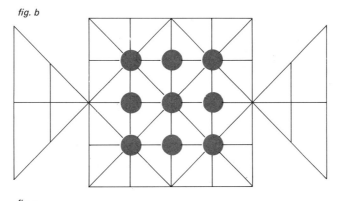

intersection to the other side. (The intersections thus correspond to the squares on a checkerboard.) Every time a tiger jumps a goat, it "eats" it, and the "dead" goat is removed from the board. When it jumps a whole pile of goats, however, it

fig. b

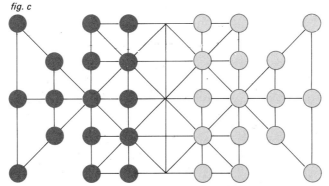

fig. c

eats only the top one. If the goats have been so foolish as to permit it, a tiger can devour several at once, in a series of leaps (including the top goat of any pile). Of course, the tiger cannot jump back and forth, over the same pile of goats eating them all in a single turn!
The following rules must be observed, however:
1) goats cannot eat tigers;
2) when a tiger is able to eat a goat, it must do so whenever the goat player insists. If, however, there are two "eatable" goats in different directions, the tiger can choose which one to eat;
3) when a tiger becomes hedged in and cannot move, it is removed from the board.
Expert players will play several (say, four) games in a row, swapping sides each time. If the result is 2–2, they then play on until one of them wins two games in a row.

Rimau-rimau
Farther east, in Malaysia, a different tiger-hunting game is played. Known as *rimau-rimau*, it is played on a board similar to the Sinhalese *peralikatuma* board (see pp. 34–35), but in a simplified form. (See *figure b*.) Another game for two players, it consists of 1 tiger (white) and 24 hunters (black). To start, 9 hunters are positioned on the board as shown in *figure b*. The tiger then moves, devouring 3 of them (whichever 3 it likes) and ending up on any of the 3 freed positions. At each successive move, black introduces another piece onto the board, placing it on any empty intersection, until all the hunters have entered the game. They can then move, one step at a time, in any direction but are not able to jump the tiger. Meanwhile, the tiger also moves one space at a time, though it then has the advantage of being able to jump and devour hunters, as long as there are an odd number of hunters on the board.
The hunters win if they manage to trap the tiger so that it is unable to move. The tiger wins if it is able to eat at least 14 hunters.

Mogol Putt'han
Using the same board as for *rimau-rimau*, but with 2 armies of 16 pieces each, the game of *Mogol Putt'han* is played in India. To start, the pieces are positioned as shown in *figure c*. The moves are the same as in *alquerque*. Whoever captures all the enemy soldiers, or manages to prevent their moving farther, is the winner.

Figure a is composed of three of the five fragments indicated b, c, d, e, f.
Which are the unnecessary fragments?

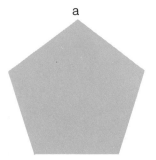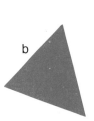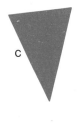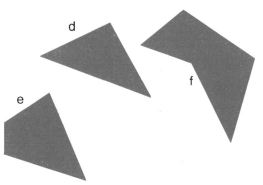

Figure a is composed of three of the five fragments indicated b, c, d, e, f.
Which are the unnecessary fragments?

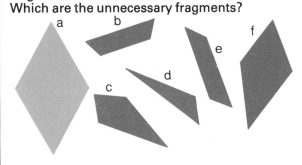

⑩

Figure a is composed of four of the six fragments indicated b, c, d, e, f, g.
Which are the unnecessary fragments?

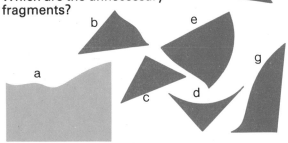

Answers and explanations

1) f

2) e

3) e

4) e (If the half-moon a in its position is visually symmetrical with b, then c is similarly symmetrical with e.)

5) f (Here, too, a and b are related by visual symmetry; hence c must go with f.)

6) e (for the same reason as above)

7) e (b is clearly visually symmetrical with a, thus c goes with e.)

Tests 4–7 work on visual perception of *symmetry*. This is a common phenomenon found almost everywhere, from the arts to the natural sciences, occurring in objects of widely differing nature. In these problems, basic data in a given set of visual stimuli are arranged in a certain pattern (described as "symmetrical") in relation to the other elements of the whole. The distinctive feature of such data is that they are seen as equivalent, in their spatial arrangement, with respect to a term of reference (a point, a plane, a straight line, or some more abstract factor). The concept of symmetry is of particular interest in science.

8) The unnecessary fragments are c and d.

9) The unnecessary fragments are c and e.

10) The unnecessary fragments are g and f.

City mirages

Our car has stopped at a red light. The lights then change and turn green, and we proceed. What we have experienced is a sort of movement from red to green. The same kind of visual impression is even clearer when we watch the strings of lights on a Christmas tree flashing on and off, or fairground lights and neon signs lighting up and switching off. In fact, of course, nothing moves; the individual lights stay where they are, and electricity as such is a physical phenomen, which cannot be seen. And yet that illusion of movement remains, even for those who are unaware that electric current is generated by the movement of electrons. The movements we see are pure illusion.

How is this possible?

We know that such visual tricks occur because images remain on the retina of our eye, thus fusing with the next, so producing an impression of movement. It is not hard to see here the basic principle behind the projection of images in movie films.

Figures in motion

Let us exercise our powers of perceiving motion. These are problems in which we need to "follow" mentally—in our imagination—a moving figure or group of figures. In some the correct answer will be immediately evident but others will require greater attention.

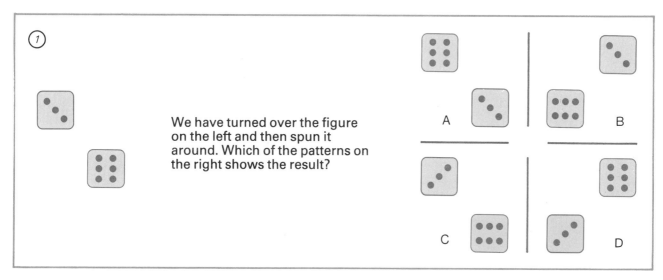

1. We have turned over the figure on the left and then spun it around. Which of the patterns on the right shows the result?

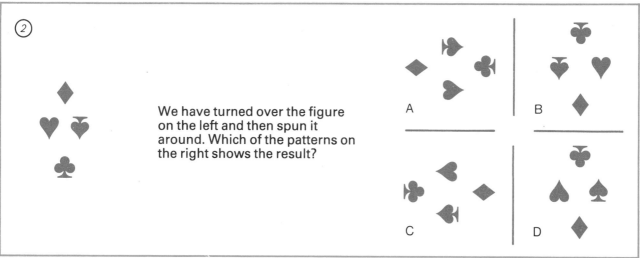

2. We have turned over the figure on the left and then spun it around. Which of the patterns on the right shows the result?

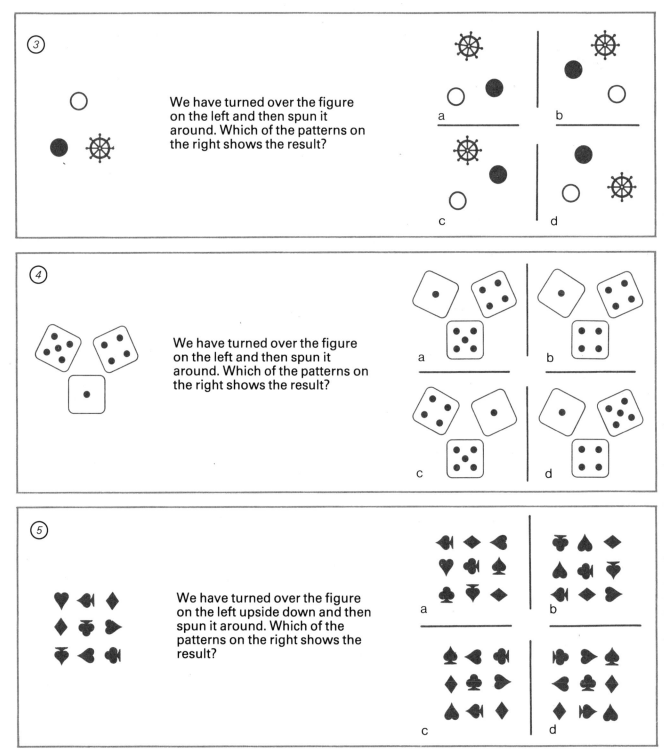

③ We have turned over the figure on the left and then spun it around. Which of the patterns on the right shows the result?

a b c d

④ We have turned over the figure on the left and then spun it around. Which of the patterns on the right shows the result?

a b c d

⑤ We have turned over the figure on the left upside down and then spun it around. Which of the patterns on the right shows the result?

a b c d

Answers:

1) d (To prove this, turn the page over, twist the book 180 degrees, then hold the page up to a strong light and look through it at the original figure. You will see the design shown is answer d.) 2) d 3) b 4) a 5) c

Topological games

Has it ever occurred to you that an ordinary coffee cup with a handle might have a significance beyond its normal function?

A coffee cup is a particular geometrical form, with characteristics that are of great importance for topology, a curious branch of modern geometry. Topology deals with shapes that can be altered (enlarged, shrunk, curved, crushed, twisted, and so on) without their losing certain mathematical and geometrical properties.

In the following exercises, the idea is to identify the "positional" features that remain constant despite the alterations. They test our motor-perceptive faculties, but in a slightly unusual way: concentrating on topology.

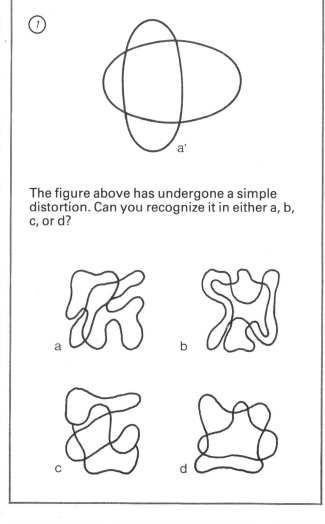

The figure above has undergone a simple distortion. Can you recognize it in either a, b, c, or d?

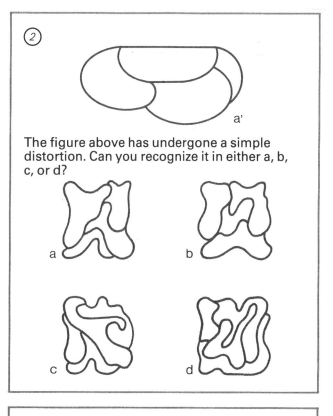

The figure above has undergone a simple distortion. Can you recognize it in either a, b, c, or d?

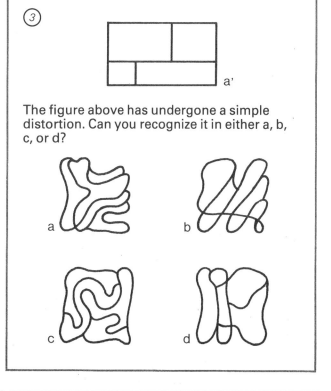

The figure above has undergone a simple distortion. Can you recognize it in either a, b, c, or d?

④

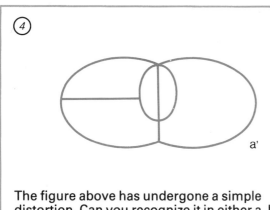

a'

The figure above has undergone a simple distortion. Can you recognize it in either a, b, c, or d?

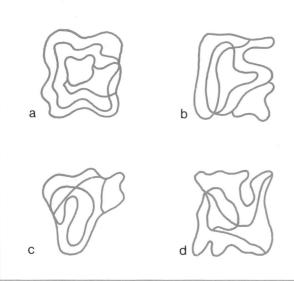

a

b

c

d

⑤

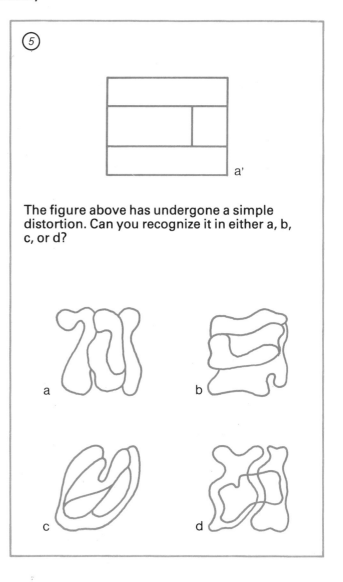

a'

The figure above has undergone a simple distortion. Can you recognize it in either a, b, c, or d?

a

b

c

d

Guide to the answers of the topological tests

1) *Figure a'* consists of an almost regular intersection of two ellipses and thus has unique spatial characteristics that distinguish it from other figures: there is an inner area, defined by four curved lines exactly adjacent to four outer areas. Of figures a, b, c, and d, the only one to share the same positional (topological) features is b, in which a central area is bordered by four peripheral areas. Figure a is not possible because in the top right there is a side that touches two peripheral areas; and it is easy to see that c and d do not perpetuate the same geometrical form.

2) This figure is slightly more complex than the previous one. Let us consider what the unique features of *figure a'* are. Clearly it has two internal points at which three lines intersect.

Of figures a, b, c, and d, which shares this characteristic? Obviously the only one to do so is a.

3) *Figure a'* has four distinct areas and two internal points at which three lines intersect: of a, b, c, and d, the only one to share these topographical features is c.

4) It is always best to start by analyzing the essential features of *figure a'*. Here there is a clear internal point at which four lines intersect. Of a, b, c, and d, the only one to share this feature is d.

5) *Figure a'* has two internal points where two lines intersect. Of the four figures a, b, c, and d, only a retains this feature.

Games with numbers or figures?

The variety of ways in which intelligence is manifested is a symptom of the human mind's need to divide into components whatever is under examination or analysis. Here is an exercise in which the boundary between mathematical reasoning and visual thought is highly tenuous.

In each column, identify the two displaced boxes.

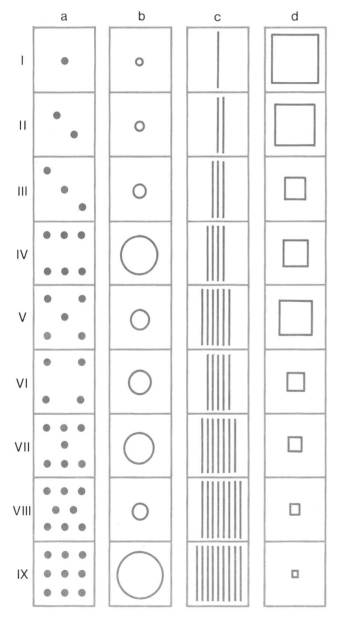

Answers: a) IV and VI b) IV and VIII c) V and VI d) III and V

Memory and intelligence

In preparing for an exam, the exactness, the completeness, or the partiality of certain answers can rest on the degree of visual memory of the books studied. It is probable that successful results will correspond to the degree of clarity of memory of relevant explanations and illustrations. The layout of a page, underlining of certain passages, plans, and so forth, all can aid memory.

Memory plays a vital part in the learning process. And the capacity to retain what has been learned by experience is a powerful contributory factor in our ability to adapt—thus also to our intelligence.

A good memory is a "must" for many activities: for study and intellectual work of any sort, but also, too, for manual work (a mechanic, for instance, has to remember many tiny parts of an engine).

How's your memory?

"Memory shrinks unless exercised," according to Cicero (writing some two thousand years ago). And an important truth is grasped here: memory is a faculty that can be improved.

Psychology offers various methods: associations of stimuli, the use of rhymes in verbal memory, and the use of codes, symbols, and metaphor. The way we learn—our attentiveness, motivation, and application—all affect the working of our memory.

Let us try some concrete exercises for testing our capacity for visual mnemonics. Although memory embraces all the sense experiences, (we have auditory and tactile memory, as well as memories of tastes and smells), the visual is the easiest to try out.

Look carefully at the figures in the orange box below for two minutes, then reproduce them on a separate piece of paper. The order in which they come out does not matter.

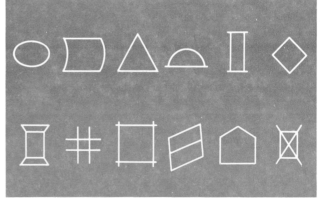

Carefully study the words printed above, for not less than two minutes; then close the book and write down as many of them as you can remember.

The spirit of adaptability

One of the most commonly identified characteristics of intelligence is adaptability—an individual's ability to change according to developments in the physical and social environment.

The events of individual lives are largely unforeseeable. Society, on the other hand, now evolves at a rapid rate. Never before have profound changes in the organization of work and of leisure time—involved whole generations. Industrial methods of production, which were at the source of these changes, proved a considerable test of people's spirit of adaptability. Millions of people left the country for the cities or emigrated to places very different both socially and culturally from where they had originated.

An industrialized society is by nature in a state of constant change. One need only observe current developments: we are at present experiencing a rapid and vast reorganization of production thanks to the computer "revolution"—for example, the introduction of microtechnology into industry. Naturally this creates demands for adaptability.

Let us at this point examine what we mean by "adapt." When our environment (social, economic, physical) changes, then we, too, must change. Knowing how to adapt means being open to the possibility of having to change our habits, our way of life, and even in the long run our whole way of thinking. Thus, intelligence manifests itself in the spirit of adaptability as a willingness to accept for ourselves new values and new standards of behaviour, and to establish new relations with the society around us. It is essentially the ability to change along with the world in which we live.

We may also take an example of the spirit of adaptability from the sphere of individual emotional life: when one falls in love—that is, brings another person into one's life—a new situation is created, in which one has oneself to change. True, in such cases the power of love helps the spirit of adaptability, and often two people who are in love adapt very quickly to each other, without problems. An individual is a complex entity, however, and when one element of a complex system undergoes change, the whole system has to adjust its balance and find a new mode of being. It may be that a change like love can bring a new strength to the whole system; or it may be only a partial adjustment, in which case imbalance can occur. In such cases, intelligence is revealed in the quest for a new equilibrium, a new way of relating to the other.

The tale of Alathiel

In the summer of 1348 the serene city of Florence was struck by plague. The normal scenes of bustling, colourful life were replaced by scenes of death and grief. From this disaster ten youths resolved to flee to the haven of the countryside, seeing life as a mode of reality in which, through intricate interaction of events of all kinds, intelligence, nature, and fortune held sway. This briefly is the unifying background to the *Decameron*, written by Giovanni Boccaccio (1313–1375), a collection of a hundred *novelle* (short stories) evoking the burgeoning, dynamic world of industry and enterprise created by the mercantile middle classes of the late Middle Ages. Upon this broad, wide-open stage was played out the comedy of human life: a contest between two forces, one external (circumstances and fortune), the other internal (natural instinct, manifested predominantly in the experience of love). These forces are both at play in the tale of Alathiel, the unhappy daughter of the king of Egypt, who, although caught up in events beyond her control, still managed to follow her own nature, intelligently enjoying what pleasures offered themselves to her despite the misfortunes of her existence. In the end, Alathiel's ability constantly to adapt to altered circumstances is rewarded.

It is now a long time since there lived a sultan of Babylon, called Beminedab, who was fortunate in all his affairs. Amongst other children, both male and female, he had a daughter named Alathiel, who, in the opinion of all that saw her, was the fairest lady in the whole world. And because the King of Algarve had afforded him great assistance in a defeat occasioned to a most numerous army of Arabians that had assailed him, and had demanded her afterwards in marriage, he consented as a most special favour: and providing a ship, well equipped for the purpose, with all necessary provisions, and sending an honourable train both of lords and ladies to bear her company, he commended her to the protection of Heaven, and took his leave. The sailors, as soon as a fit opportunity offered, hoisted their sails, and leaving the port of Alexandria, sailed prosperously many days; when, having passed the island of Sardinia, and now seeming to be near the end of their voyage, on a sudden, contrary winds arose, which were so boisterous, and bore so hard upon the ship, that they often gave themselves over for lost. Nevertheless, for two days together, they tried all the means they could devise, amidst an infinite number of tempests, to weather it out; but all to no purpose. And not being able to comprehend by marinal judgment where they were, or to see to any distance on account of the clouds and dark night, being now not far from Majorca, they felt the ship split; and perceiving no hopes of escaping, every one caring for himself only, they threw a little boat into the sea, reposing more confidence of safety that way than by abiding any longer in the broken ship. The men therefore that were in the ship went into it, one after another; although those who were first down made strong resistance with their drawn weapons against other followers; and thinking to avoid death by this means, they ran directly into it; for the boat, not being able to bear them all, sunk straight to the bottom, and the people therein all perished. The ship being driven furiously by the winds, though it was burst and half full of water, was at last stranded near the Island of Majorca, no other person remaining on board but the lady and her women, all lying as it were lifeless, through the terror occasioned by the tempest. It struck with such violence, that it was fixed upon the sand about a stone's throw from the shore; where it continued all that night, the winds not being able to move it. When day-light appeared, and the storm was something abated, the lady, almost dead, lifted up her head, and began to call her servants; but all to no purpose, for such as she called for were far enough from her: wherefore, receiving no answer, and seeing no one, she was greatly astonished; and raising herself up as well as she could, she beheld the ladies that were of her company, and some other of her women, lying all about her; and trying first to rouse one, and then another of them, she scarcely found any that had the least understanding left; so much had sickness and fear together affected them, which added greatly to her consternation. Nevertheless, necessity constraining her, seeing that she was alone, she knew not where, she shook those that were living till she made them get up, and perceiving that they were utterly ignorant of what was become of all the men, and seeing the ship driven upon the sands, and full of water, she began with them to lament most grievously. It was noon-day before they could descry any person from on shore, or elsewhere, to afford them the least assistance. At length, about that time, a gentleman, whose name was Pericon da Visalgo, passing that way, with many of his servants, on horseback, upon seeing the ship, imagined what had happened, and immediately sent one of them on board, to see what was remaining in her. The servant got into the ship with some difficulty, and found the lady with the little company that was left her, who had all hidden themselves, through fear, under the deck of the ship. As soon as they saw him, they begged for mercy; but not understanding each other, they endeavoured, by signs, to inform him of their misfortune. The servant carried the best account he could to his master of what he had seen; who ordered the ladies, and every thing that was in the ship of any value, to be brought on shore, conducting them to one of his castles, where he endeavoured to comfort them under their misfortunes by this generous entertainment. By the richness of her dress, he supposed her to be some person of great consequence, which appeared more plainly by the great respect that was paid to her by all the women: and although she was pale and in disorder, through the great fatigue she had sustained yet was he much taken with her beauty; and he resolved, if she had no husband, to make her his wife; or, if he could not have her as such, still not to lose her entirely. Pericon was a man of stern looks, and rough in his person; and having treated the lady well for some time, by which means she had recovered her beauty, he was grieved that they could not understand each other, and that he was unable to learn who she was; yet, being passionately in love, he used all the engaging arts he could devise to bring her to a compliance, but all to no purpose; she refused all familiarities with him, which inflamed him the more. This the lady perceived, and finding, after some stay there, by the customs of the place, that she was among Christians, and where, if she came to be known, it would be of no great service to her; supposing also, that, at last, Pericon would gain his will, if not by fair means, yet by force; she resolved, with a true greatness of spirit, to tread all misfortune under foot, commanding her women, of whom she had but three now alive, never to disclose her quality, unless there should be hopes of regaining their liberty; recommending it farther to them to maintain their chastity, and declaring her fixed resolution never to comply with any one besides her husband; for which they all commended her, promising to preserve their honour, as she had commanded them. Every day did his passion increase so much the more as the thing desired was more near, and yet more difficult to be obtained: wherefore, perceiving that entreaty was to no purpose, he resolved to try what art and contrivance could do, reserving force to the last. And having once observed that wine was pleasing to her, not having been accustomed to it, as being forbidden by her country's law, he determined to surprise her by means of this minister of Venus. And seeming now to have given over his amorous pursuit, which she had used her best endeavours to withstand, he provided one night an elegant entertainment, at which she was present, when he gave it in charge to the servant that waited upon her, to serve her with several wines mingled together, which he accordingly did; whilst she, suspecting no such

treachery, and pleased with the rich flavour of the wine, drank more than suited with her modesty, and forgetting all her past troubles, became gay and merry; so that, seeing some women dance after the custom of Majorca, she also began to dance after the manner of the Alexandrians; which when Pericon observed, he supposed himself in a fair way of success, and plying her still with more wine, continued this revelling the greatest part of the night. At length, when the guests departed, he went with the lady into her chamber, who having at that time more wine than modesty, undressed herself before him, as if he had been one of her women, and got into bed. He instantly followed, and accomplished his purpose. They afterwards cohabited together without any reserve, till at length, fortune, unwilling that she who was to have been the wife of a king, should become the mistress of a nobleman, prepared for her a more barbarous and cruel alliance.

Pericon had a brother, twenty-five years of age, of a most complete person, called Marato; who having seen her, and flattering himself, from her behaviour towards him, that he was not displeasing to her: supposing also that nothing obstructed his happiness, except the guard which his brother had over her; he consequently contrived a most cruel design, which was not long without its wicked effect. There was by chance a ship in the haven at that time, laden with merchandize bound for Chiarenza in Romania, of which two young Genoese were the masters, who only waited for the first fair wind to go out: with them Marato made a contract, to receive him with the lady the following night. When night came, having ordered how the thing should be managed, he went openly to the house, nobody having the least mistrust of him, taking with him some trusty friends, whom he had secured for that service, and concealed them near the house: in the middle of the night, therefore, he opened the door to them, and they slew Pericon as he was asleep in bed with the lady; seizing upon her, whom they found awake and in tears, and threatening to kill her if she made the least noise. They took also everything of value that belonged to Pericon, with which Marato and the lady went instantly on board, whilst his companions returned about

their business. The wind proving fair, they soon set sail, whilst the lady reflecting on both her misfortunes, seemed to lay them much to heart for a time; till being over persuaded by Marato, she began to have the same affection for him that she had entertained for his brother; when fortune, as if not content with what she had already suffered, prepared another change of life for her. Her person and behaviour were such, as to enamour the two masters of the ship, who neglected all other business to serve and please her; taking care all the while that Marato should have no cause to suspect it. And being apprised of each other's love, they had a consultation together about it, when it was agreed to have her in common between them, as if love, like merchandize, admitted of partnership; and observing that she was narrowly watched by Marato, and their design thereby frustrated, they took the opportunity one day, as the ship was under full sail, and he standing upon the stern looking towards the ship, to go behind and throw him over-board; whilst the ship had sailed on a full mile before it was known that he had fallen in: as soon as the lady heard of it, and saw no likely means of recovering him again, she fell into fresh troubles, when the two lovers came quickly to comfort her, using many kind and tender expressions, which she did not understand; though indeed she did not then so much lament Marato as her own private misfortunes. After some little time, imagining that she was sufficiently comforted, they fell into a dispute together which should have the first enjoyment of her; and from words they drew their swords, and came to blows, the ship's crew not being able to part them, when one soon fell down dead, the other being desperately wounded; which occasioned fresh uneasiness to the lady, who now saw herself left alone, without any one to advise and help her: she was fearful also of the resentment of the two masters' relations and friends: but the entreaties of the wounded survivor, and their speedy arrival at Chiarenza, saved her from the danger of death. She went on shore with him there, and they continued together at an inn; whilst the fame of her beauty was spread all over the city, till it reached the ears of the Prince of Morea, who was then by chance at Chiarenza. He was impatient to get a sight of her; and after he had seen her, was so charmed, that he could think of nothing else: and being told in what manner she came hither, he began to contrive means how to obtain her; which when the man's relations understood, they immediately sent her to him, to her great joy, no less than the prince's, now thinking herself freed from all danger. The prince perceiving her rare accomplishments, joined to a matchless person, though he could have no information concerning her, yet concluded that she must be nobly descended; and such was his fondness for her, that he treated her not as a mistress but a wife. She now recollecting what she had already suffered, and being pretty well satisfied with her present situation, began to be easy and cheerful, whilst her charms increased to that degree, that she was the chief subject of discourse throughout Romania. Hereupon the Duke of Athens, a young and gay person, a relation also to the prince, had a mind to see her; and came one day thither under pretence of a visit to him, as usual, with a noble retinue, when he was handsomely entertained. Talking together, after some time, concerning the lady's great beauty; the duke asked whether she was such as fame had reported; to which the prince replied, "she far exceeds it; but let your own eyes convince you, and not my bare assertion." The duke soliciting the prince very earnestly to gratify his curiosity, they went into her apartment together, when she received them with great good manners and cheerfulness, being apprised of their coming; and though they could not have the pleasure of conversing together, as she understood little or nothing of their language, yet they looked upon her, the duke more especially, as a prodigy of nature, scarcely believing her to be a mortal creature; and, without perceiving how much of the amorous poison he had taken in by intently gazing upon her, and meaning only to gratify himself with the sight of her, he soon became over head and ears in love. After they had parted from her, and he had time to reflect, he began to think the prince the happiest person in the universe, in being possessed of such a beauty; and, after much musing upon it, having more regard to his lust than to his honour, he resolved at all adventures to deprive him of that bliss, and to secure it

for himself: and having a heart to put what he had resolved into execution, setting all reason and justice aside, his mind was wholly taken up in devising a fit stratagem for his purpose. One day, therefore, according to a most wicked agreement, which he had made with a valet de chambre belonging to the prince, whose name was Ciuriaci, he gave secret orders to have his horses and things got ready for a sudden departure; and the following night, taking a friend with him, and being both completely armed, they were introduced by that servant into the prince's chamber, whom they found in his shirt, looking out of a window towards the sea, to take the cool air, the weather being very hot, whilst the lady was fast asleep. Having then instructed his friend what he would have done; he went softly up to the window, and stabbed him with a dagger through the small of his back, and threw him out. Now the palace was seated upon the sea-shore, and very lofty; and the window at which the prince stood looking from, was directly over some houses, which the force of the waves had beaten down, and which were but little frequented; on which account, as the duke had before contrived it, there was no great likelihood of its being discovered. The duke's companion when he saw that it was over, took a cord which he carried

with him for that purpose, and seeming as if he was going to caress Ciuriaci, threw it about his neck, and drew it so tight, that he prevented his crying out, whilst the duke came to his assistance, and they soon dispatched, and threw him down after the prince. This being done, and plainly perceiving that they were not heard or seen by the lady, or any one else, the duke took a light in his hand, and went on softly to bed, where she lay in a sound sleep, and he stood beholding her for some time with the utmost admiration; and if she appeared so charming before in her clothes, what was she not without them? Not at all dismayed with his late-committed sin, his hands yet reeking with blood, he crept into bed to her, she taking him all the while for the prince.

After he had been with her for some time, he ordered his people to seize her in such a manner, that she could make no outcry; and going through the same back door at which he had been introduced, he set her on horseback, and carried her away towards Athens. But, as he was married, he did not choose to bring her thither, but left her at one of his country seats, a little way out of town, where he secretly kept her, to her great grief; allowing her, in a most genteel manner, everything that was necessary. The prince's servants waited till nine o'clock that morning, expecting his rising; but hearing nothing of him, and thrusting open the chamber doors, which were only closed, and finding nobody within, they concluded that he and the lady were gone privately to some other place to divert themselves for a few days, and therefore thought no more about the matter. The next day it happened, by great chance, that a fool going amongst those ruinous houses where the dead bodies were lying, took hold of the cord that was about Ciuriaci's neck, and dragged him along after him: which surprised many people to whom he was known; who, by fair words and much persuasion, prevailed upon the fellow to shew them where he had found him; and there, to the great grief of the whole city, they saw the prince's body also, which they caused to be interred with all due pomp and reverence. Inquiring afterwards who should commit so horrid a deed, and perceiving that the Duke of Athens was not to be found, but was gone privately away, they judged (as it really was) that he had done it, and taken the lady with him. Immediately they elected the prince's brother to be their sovereign, inciting him to revenge so horrid a fact, and promising to assist him to the utmost of their power. He being afterwards fully assured of the truth of what they had but before surmised, collected together all his relations, friends, and vassals, and mustering a powerful army, directed his course against the duke: who had no sooner heard of these preparations, but he also levied a great army, and many princes came to his relief. Amongst the rest, Constantius, son to the Emperor of Constantinople, and Emanuel the nephew, attended by a goodly body of troops, who were kindly received by the duke, and the duchess more especially, being their sister-in-law. Things tending every day more and more to a war, the duchess had them both one day into her chamber, when, with abundance of tears, she recounted to them the whole history and occasion of the war, and the ill-usage she had received from the duke on account of this woman, whom she imagined he kept privately; and complaining very earnestly to them, she conjured them, for his honour, and her own ease and comfort, to give her their best assistance. The two young lords knew all this matter before, and therefore, without asking many questions, they comforted her as well as they could, and informing themselves where the lady was kept, they took their leave. Hearing much talk of her beauty, they became very desirous of seeing her, and entreated the duke to shew her to them; who, never remembering what had happened to the prince, promised to do so; and ordering a magnificent entertainment to be prepared in a pleasant garden belonging to the palace where the lady was kept, the next day he took them, and some more friends, to dine with her. Constantius, being seated at the table, began, full of admiration, to gaze upon her, declaring to himself that he had never seen anything like her, and that the duke, or any other person, was excusable, who, to possess so rare a beauty, should commit any act of baseness or treason: and looking still more and more upon her, and evermore commending her, it happened just to him as it had done to the duke; for, going away

quite enamoured of her, he had given over all thoughts of the war, contriving only how to steal her away from the duke, at the same time that he concealed his love from every one. Whilst he was in this agitation, the time came when they were to march against the prince, who was now advancing near the duke's territories: upon which the duke, with Constantius and the rest, according to the resolution that was taken, marched out of Athens to secure the frontiers, and to prevent the prince's passing any further. Continuing there for some days, and Constantius having still the lady at heart, and concluding, now the duke was absent, that he might more easily compass his intent, he, that there might be a pretence for his return, feigned himself extremely sick: and, with the duke's consent, leaving the command of his troops to Emanuel, he returned to Athens to his sister's, where, after some days, having encouraged her to talk of her husband's baseness in keeping a mistress, he at last said, that if she would give her consent, he would rid her of that trouble, by removing the lady out of the way. The duchess, supposing that this was spoken out of pure regard to her, and not to the lady, replied, that she should be very glad if it could be done in such a manner as the duke should never know that she was in any way accessory; which Constantius fully promised, and she accordingly agreed that he should do it as he thought most advisable. He provided, therefore, with all secrecy, a light vessel, and sent it one evening near to the garden where the lady was kept, having first informed some of his people that were in it, what he would have them do; and taking others with him to the house, he was kindly received by the servants in waiting there, and by the lady also herself, who took a walk with him at his request, attended by the servants belonging to them both, into the garden; when, drawing her aside towards a door which opened to the sea, as if he had business to communicate from the duke, on a signal given, the bark was brought close to the shore, and she seized upon and carried into it, whilst he, turning back to the people that were with her, said—"Let no one stir or speak a word at the peril of their lives; for my design is not to rob the duke of his lady, but to take away the reproach of my sister." To

this none being hardy enough to return an answer, Constantius, boarding the vessel, bid the men ply their oars, and make the best of their way, which they accordingly did, so that they reached Egina by the next morning. There they landed, and reposed himself awhile with her, who had great reason to curse her beauty. From thence they went to Chios, where, for fear of his father, and to prevent her being taken away from him, he chose to abide as a place of security: and though she seemed uneasy for a time, yet she soon recovered, as she had done before, and became better reconciled to the state of life wherein bad fortune had thrown her.

In the mean time Osbech, king of the Turks, who was constantly at war with the emperor, came by chance to Smyrna, and hearing how Constantius lived a lascivious life at Chios, with a mistress that he had stolen, and no provision made for his safety, he went privately one night with some armed vessels, and made a descent, surprising many people in their beds before they knew of his coming upon them, and killing all that stood upon their defence; and after he had burnt and destroyed the whole country, he put the prisoners and booty which he had taken on board, and returned to Smyrna. Upon taking a view of the prisoners, Osbech, who was a young man, saw this lady, and knowing that she was Constantius's mistress, because she was found asleep in his bed, he was much pleased at it, and took her for his own wife, and they lived together very happily for several months. Before this thing happened, the emperor had been making a treaty with Bassano, king of Cappadocia, who was to fall on Osbech on one side, whilst he attacked him on the other; but they could not come to a full agreement, because Bassano made a demand of some things which he was unwilling to grant; yet now, hearing of what had befallen his son, and being in the utmost concern, he immediately closed with the King of Cappadocia, requesting him to march with all expedition against Osbech, whilst he was preparing to invade him on his part. When Osbech heard of this, he assembled his army before he should be surrounded by two such mighty princes, and marched on to meet the king of Cappadocia, leaving his lady behind, with a faithful servant of his, at Smyrna: they soon came to a battle, wherein his army was entirely routed, and himself slain. Bassano remaining victorious, he proceeded on to Smyrna, the people making their submission to him all the way as he went. But now Osbech's servant, whose name was Antiochus, who had the lady in charge, although he was in years, yet seeing her so beautiful, and forgetting the regard which was due to his lord, soon became in love with her himself; and, as he understood her language, it was a great comfort to her, because she had been forced to live for some years like a deaf and dumb person, for want of understanding other people, or being understood by them. This gave him great advantages, and whilst his master was warring abroad, he spared no pains to gain her consent, in which he succeeded: and when they understood that Osbech was slain, and that Bassano carried all before him, without waiting for his coming upon them, they fled away privately, taking with them what belonged to Osbech of any value, and came to Rhodes. They had not been there long before he was taken extremely ill; and having a merchant of Cyprus along with him, who was his great friend, and finding himself at the point of death, he resolved to bequeath to him the care of his lady and wealth also; and calling them both to him, he spoke as follows: —"I find myself declining apace, which grieves me much, because I had never more pleasure in living than at present; yet one thing is a great comfort to me, viz., that I shall die in the arms of those two persons whom I love and value beyond all the rest of the world; namely, in yours, my dearest friend, and in that lady's, whom I have loved, ever since I have known her, more than my own life. I am uneasy, indeed, when I consider that I leave her here a stranger, and destitute both of help and advice, and should be infinitely more so if you were not with us, who, I know, will take the same care of her, on my account, as you would of myself; therefore I entreat you, in case I should die, to take my affairs and her together, under your protection, and to act, with regard to both, as you think will be most for the comfort of my departed soul.—And you, my dearest love, let me beg of you never to forget me, that I may boast, in the next world,

that I have been beloved by the fairest lady that ever nature formed; assure me of these two things, and I shall die satisfied." The merchant and lady were both much concerned, and promised to fulfil his desires, if he should chance to die; and soon afterwards he departed this life, when they took care to have him decently interred; which being done, and the merchant having dispatched all his affairs, and wanting to return home in a Catalan ship that was there, questioned the lady, to know what she intended to do, because it became necessary for him to go back to Cyprus: she made answer, that she was willing to go with him, hoping that, for the love he bore towards his friend, he would regard her as his own sister. He replied, that he was ready to oblige her in everything; and, that he might the better defend her from all injuries whatever, till they came to Cyprus, she should rather call herself his wife. Being on board the ship, they had a cabin and one little bed allotted them, agreeable to the account they had given of themselves, by which means that thing was brought about, which neither of them intended when they came from Rhodes; for they forgot all the fine promises they had made to Antiochus, and before they reached Baffa, where the Cyprian merchant dwelt, they began to consider themselves as man and wife. Now a certain gentleman happened to arrive at Baffa about that time, on his own private affairs, whose name was Antigonus, one advanced in years, and of more understanding than wealth: for by meddling much in the affairs of the King of Cyprus, he had found fortune very unkind to him. Passing one day by the house where she lodged, the merchant being gone about his business to Armenia, and seeing her by chance at the window, he took more than ordinary notice of her, on account of her beauty; till at length he began to recollect he had seen her somewhere before, but could by no means remember where. She, also, who had long been the sport of fortune, the time now drawing near when her sorrows were to have an end, as soon as she saw Antigonus, remembered that she had seen him in no mean station in her father's service at Alexandria. And having now great hopes of regaining her former dignity by his advice and assistance, she took the

opportunity of the merchant's absence to send for him. Being come to her, she modestly asked him whether he was not Antigonus of Famagosta, as she really believed. He answered, that he was, and added—"Madam, I am convinced that I know you, but I cannot call to mind where it is that I have seen you; therefore, if it be no offence, let me entreat you to tell me who you are." The lady, perceiving him to be the same person, wept very much, and throwing her arms about his neck, asked him, at last, as one confounded with surprise, if he had never seen her at Alexandria? When he immediately knew her to be Alathiel, the sultan's daughter, whom they supposed to have been drowned; and being about to pay homage to her, she would not suffer him to do it, but made him sit down. He, then, in a most humble manner, asked her where she had been, and from whence she now came; because for some years it was believed, through all Egypt, that she was drowned. She replied, "I had much rather it had so happened than to have led such a life as I have done; and I believe my father, if he knew it, would wish the same." With these words the tears ran down her cheeks in great abundance: and he replied, "Madam, do not afflict yourself before it is necessary to do so; tell me only what has happened to you; perhaps it may be of such a nature, that, by the help of God, we may find a remedy." —"Antigonus!" replied the fair lady, "I think when I see you that I behold my father: moved therefore with the like duty and tenderness that I owe to him, I shall reveal to you what I might have kept secret: there are few persons that I should desire to meet with sooner than yourself to advise me; if, therefore, when you have heard my whole story, you think there is any probability of restoring me to my former dignity, I must beg your assistance: if you think there is none, then I conjure you to tell no person living that you have either seen or heard anything about me." After which, shedding abundance of tears during the whole relation, she gave a full account of what had befallen her, from the time of her shipwreck to that very hour. Antigonus shewed himself truly concerned at what he had heard, and (thinking some little time about it) he said to her—"Madam, since it has never been known, in all your misfortunes, who you were, I will restore you to your father, to whom you shall be more dear than ever, and afterwards you shall be married to the King of Algarve." She inquiring how that could be brought about, he let her know in what manner he intended to do it. Therefore, that no delay might intervene to prevent it, he returned directly to Famagosta, and waiting upon the king, he thus addressed him:—"My liege, you may, if you please, do great honour to yourself, and service to me, who am impoverished on your account, and without any expense." The king desiring to know by what means, Antigonus thus answered: —"A young lady is just come to Baffa, daughter to the sultan, who was generally thought to have been drowned, and who, to preserve her honour, hath undergone great calamities, and is now reduced, and desirous of returning to her father: if, therefore, you will be so good as to send her home under my conduct, it will redound greatly to your honour, and prove much to my advantage, nor can the sultan ever forget the favour." The king, moved by a truly royal spirit, replied, that he was well pleased with the proposal, and immediately sent in great state for her to Famagosta, where she was received with all honour and respect, both by him and the queen; and being questioned by them concerning her misfortunes, she made such answers as she had been before taught by Antigonus.

In a few days afterwards, at her own request, she was sent with a great retinue both of lords and ladies, and conducted all the way by Antigonus, to the sultan's court; where, with what joy they were all received, it is needless here to mention. When they had rested awhile after their journey, the sultan became desirous to know how it happened that she was now living, and where she had been all this time, without his being ever able to hear a word about her. When she, who had all Antigonus's lectures perfectly by heart, gave her father the following narration: "Sir, about twenty days after my departure from you, our ship was split in the night by a violent tempest, and driven on the western coasts; nor did I ever learn what befel the men that were in it: I only remember this, that when day-light appeared, and I seemed recovered, as it

were, from death to life, certain peasants of the country spying the ship's wreck, came to plunder it; whilst I was carried first on shore, with two of my women, who were immediately borne away by some young fellows, and taken different ways, so that I could never learn what became of either of them. I also was seized by two of them, making the best defence I could; and as they were dragging me towards the wood by the hair of my head, four persons on horseback came riding by, when they immediately left me and fled. But the gentlemen on horseback, who appeared to possess some authority, came to me, and we spoke to each other, without knowing what either of us said. At last, after conferring together, they set me upon one of their horses, and carried me to a monastery of religious women, according to their laws, where I was received with great honour and respect. And after I had been there for some time, and learnt a little of their language, they began to inquire of me who I was, and from whence I came; whilst I (fearful of telling the truth, lest they should have turned me out as an enemy to their religion) made them believe that I was daughter to a gentleman of Cyprus, who sending me to be married to one of Crete, we happened to be driven thither by ill weather, and shipwrecked. Conforming to their customs in many things, for fear of the worst, I was asked, at length, by the chief among them, whom they call Lady Abbess, whether I desired to return to Cyprus; and I answered, that I desired nothing more. But she, tender of my honour, would never trust me with any persons that were going to Cyprus, till about two months ago, certain French gentlemen with their ladies came this way, one of whom was related to the abbess; who, understanding that they were going to visit the holy sepulchre at Jerusalem, where he, whom they believe to be God, was buried, after he had been put to death by the Jews, recommended me to them, and desired that they would deliver me to my father at Cyprus. What respect and civilities I received both from the gentlemen and their ladies, would be needless to mention. Accordingly we went on ship-board, and came in a few days to Baffa, where, when I saw myself arrived, a stranger to every person, nor knowing what to say to these

gentlemen, who were to present me to my father; behold (by the great providence of God), whom should I meet with upon the shore, but Antigonus, the very moment we were landed. I called to him in our language (that none of them might understand us) and desired him to own me as his daughter. He easily understood my meaning, and shewing great tokens of joy, entertained them as well as his narrow circumstances would allow, and brought me to the King of Cyprus, who received and sent me hither, with such marks of respect as I am no way able to relate; if there be any thing omitted in this relation, Antigonus, who has often heard the whole from me, will report it." Antigonus then turning to the sultan, said, "My lord, according both to her own account, and the information of the gentlemen and their wives, she has said nothing but truth. One part only she has omitted, as not suiting with her great modesty to report, namely, what the gentlemen and their ladies told me, of the most virtuous life that she had led amongst those religious women, and their great concern at parting; which, if I were fully to recount to you, would take up both this day and night too. Let it suffice then that I have said enough (according to what I could both hear and see) to convince you that you have the fairest, as well as the most virtuous daughter of any prince in the world." The sultan was overjoyed with this relation; begging over and over, that God would pour down his blessings on all who had shewed favour to his daughter; and particularly the King of Cyprus, who had sent her home so respectfully: and having bestowed great gifts upon Antigonus, he gave him leave to return to Cyprus; sending letters, as also a special ambassador to the king, to thank him on her account. And now, desiring that what he had formerly proposed should take effect; namely, that she should be married to the King of Algarve; he wrote to give him a full relation of the whole matter; adding, that he should send for her, if he desired the match to proceed. The king was much pleased with the news, and sent in great state, and received her as his queen: whilst she, who had passed through the hands of eight men, now came to him as a pure virgin, and lived happily with him the rest of their lives.

Enigmas, riddles, games of logic

"Contrariwise," continued Tweedledee, "if it was so, it might be; and if it were so, it would be: but as it isn't, it ain't. That's logic."

Lewis Carroll

The tools of the trade

Whatever job one is undertaking, it is necessary to be properly equipped. A carpenter has to have his plane, chisels, gimlets, and so forth constantly at hand, in the same way as a language student needs to have up-to-date dictionaries and texts.

But, it may be objected, such "paraphernalia" is really only of use to those who know how it ought to be used. It is all a matter of "know-how."

In fact we all have personal traits that enable us to do well in some activities and not so well, or downright badly, in others. And it is these characteristics that need to be concentrated on: expertise is acquired and refined all the better according to one's intellectual powers, one's flexibility, and one's imagination. Of prime importance are intelligence and creativity since these form the basis of our more or less habitual, everyday activities, the ways in which we cope with problems, and our work performance in the factory, at school, or wherever it may be.

Defining intelligence

Specialists tend to equate intellective levels with the ability to resolve specific problems. They thus adopt an "operational" mode to identify a certain characteristic—intelligence—through its manifestations.

The tests commonly used by psychologists are on the one hand stimuli and on the other a gauge of ability in those who do well at them. By these means an objective conclusion can be reached, however reductive it may be by comparison with the broader significance of "intelligent" as the word is normally used.

In scientific investigations there is a need for precise definitions. "Intelligent" behaviour reflects an interplay of many different personality traits, such as the ability to control worry, to see problems in context or in their individual details, and skill at certain operations. Things must be ordered. Then come operational definitions.

Mostly the tests are conceived and developed to test ability in the following areas:

- comprehension and use of words and phrases;
- arithmetical calculations;
- perception of relationships, similarities, and differences between given geometrical forms;
- powers of memorization;
- perception of general rules governing certain phenomena.

Hence the "dimension" of intelligence can be split into various categories: verbal comprehension, verbal fluency, numerical ability, spatial ability, memory, perceptual ability, and power of reasoning.

A curious thing: I.Q.

It is difficult to ignore the desire to know oneself better. The serpent that tempted our first parents knew this as well as anyone. I.Q., used for the first time in the Stanford-Binet test at the beginning of this century, provides much information in condensed form. It is arrived at through a variety of exercises and represents an overall score.

The name is associated with the French psychologist Alfred Binet (1857–1911), inventor of the scale for measuring children's intelligence, in collaboration with Théodore Simon. The Binet-Simon scale became widely used in the decades following the first intelligence test (based on a series of exercises linked to the everyday experience appropriate to different ages) evolved by Binet in 1905, in response to government requirements. Of the many revisions of the scale, the so-called Stanford revision (the work of Lewis Terman of Stanford University) is the best known: hence the "Stanford-Binet" method.

The phrase "intelligence quotient" derives from the original way of assessing the final score: establishing the mental age of a child, on the basis of its performance in the tests it is able to do, in relation to its actual age, expressed in years and months. Its performance in these tests is based on the average for any given age. Thus I.Q. was developed as a means of measuring general intellectual ability in relation to the average achievement of others of the same age. It may therefore appear that a given child is either ahead of or behind his or her peers, in terms of mental age.

Today I.Q. is also used for adults, and the concept of mental age has been dropped. The "crude" results of a test are transformed by statistical calculations onto a scale on which 90–110 represents "normal." Above or below these results indicates above or below average intelligence.

A competitive spirit is aroused through all this: a means of gauging the intellectual development of children in relation to the norm, it came gradually to acquire emotive significance and value way beyond mere scores. High performance could be taken to reveal an exceptional individual with unusual qualities. And who would not wish to be that?

What truly, though, is our level of intelligence?

What are the most important "tools of the trade," the skills we need to do well at work, in study, and in our relationships with others?

Let us satisfy our curiosity. The following tests will allow you to assess your general I.Q. Note, however, that the results we supply will only help to gauge higher levels of performance (from 115 to 145—the latter representing a truly outstanding score). It is just a game—so good luck!

Let's gauge our intelligence

Instructions
Thirty minutes are allowed for the entire test. Once you have covered all the questions, it is worth going back once again (if there is still time) and thinking over the questions you were unable to answer.

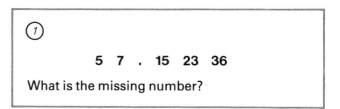

①

5 7 . 15 23 36

What is the missing number?

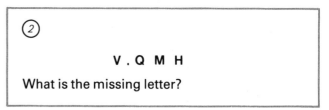

②

V . Q M H

What is the missing letter?

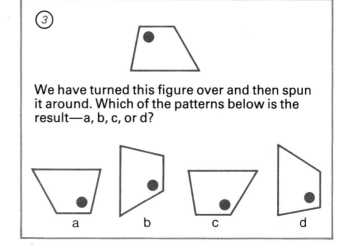

③

We have turned this figure over and then spun it around. Which of the patterns below is the result—a, b, c, or d?

a b c d

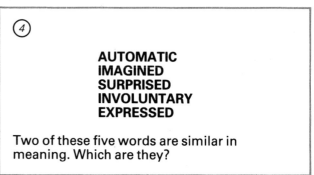

④

AUTOMATIC
IMAGINED
SURPRISED
INVOLUNTARY
EXPRESSED

Two of these five words are similar in meaning. Which are they?

⑤

a'

The figure above has undergone a simple distortion. Can you recognize it in either a, b, c, or d?

a

b

c

d

⑥

G P is to   E R
as   J M is to   . . .

⑦

a

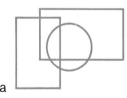
b

Which of these figures is the odd man out?

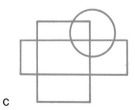
c

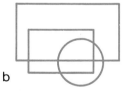
d

⑧

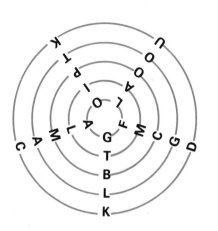

Eliminate one spoke, to leave a complete word on each circle.

⑨

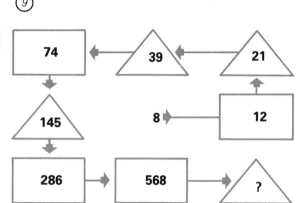

What number should the triangle on the bottom row contain?

⑩

GREEDY
FERVENT
SAVIOUR
AVARICIOUS
ZEALOUS

Which two of these five words are similar in meaning?

⑪

We have turned this figure over and then spun it around. Which of the patterns below is the result—a, b, c, or d?

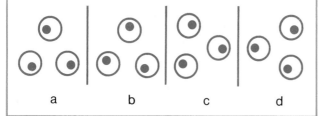

a   b   c   d

⑫

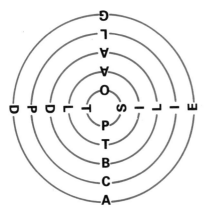

Change the arrangement of the spokes to create a complete word on each circle.

⑬

 . **10   11   21   31   41   1401   16   512**

What number should this series begin with?

⑭

ECH TRW L.O

What is the missing letter?

⑮

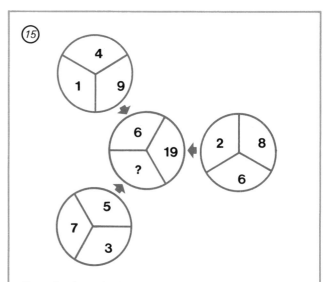

Supply the missing number.

⑯

SURFACE	**— AC**
PLAYING	**— PY**
SINGING	**— GI**
FOLDING	**— DF**
LISTEN	**— EI**

Which line differs from the other four?

⑰

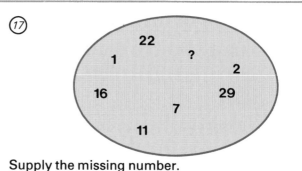

Supply the missing number.

(18)

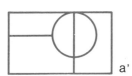

a'

The figure above has undergone a simple distortion. Can you recognize it in either a, b, c, or d?

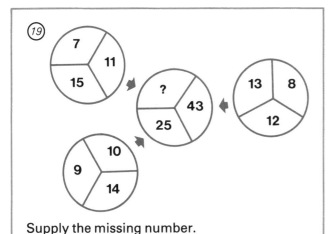

a

b

c

d

(21)

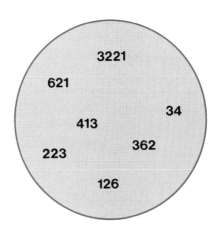

3221

621

34

413

223

362

126

Which of the numbers in this figure is the odd man out?

(19)

Supply the missing number.

(22)

**SPISMISIPSI
LEIN
LAGOV
RHACI
ZONAMA**

The letters of these five words have been jumbled up. Concealed in four of them are names of rivers. Which is the odd one out?

(23)

Which letters does the series continue with?

58   ft   12   te   27   tn   81   . . .

(20)

**BRAGGING
FRAGILITY
BOREDOM
DELICACY
PURITY**

Which two of these five words are similar in meaning?

(24)

	E	**M**	is to	**H**
and	**C**	**I**	is to	**F**
as	**D**	**G**	is to	. . .

(25)

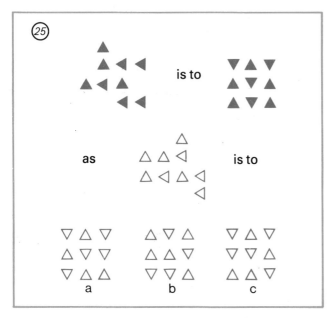

is to

as

is to

a   b   c

(26)

SEOR
OKHCELM
APROLP
TURCARN
SELITTH
DENBIWED

Which word contains the name of a tree?

(27)

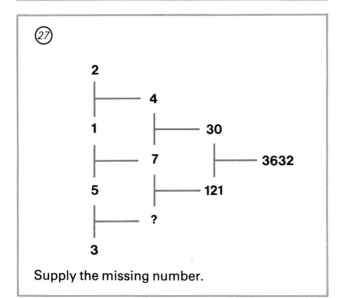

2

4

1 — 30

7 — 3632

5

121

?

3

Supply the missing number.

(28)

I GUARANTEE THAT IT IS UNTENABLE TO DENY THE OPPOSITE OF THE VERACITY OF MY AFFIRMATIONS

Does this mean "I am lying" or "I am telling the truth?"

(29)

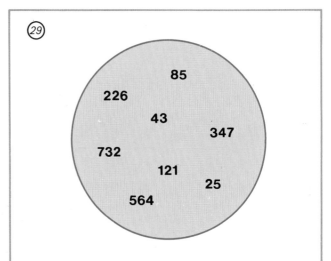

The numbers in this figure go in pairs. With what should 732 be paired?

(30)

MEGRUNIA
PLONPOTT
NERGHEESUO
ROARDHCA
DAPSE

Which of these words conceals the name of a flower?

(31)

LIBIDO	—	DOUBLE
ROME	—	EMIR
GREAT	—	EGRET
EXIT	—	TAXI

Which line is the odd one out?

(32)

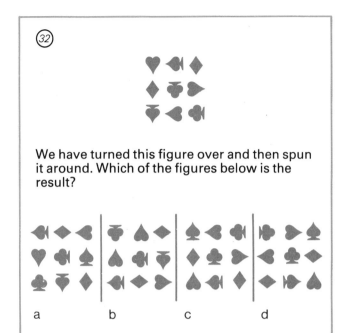

We have turned this figure over and then spun it around. Which of the figures below is the result?

a   b   c   d

(33)

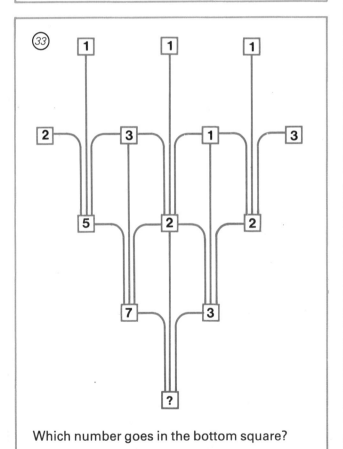

Which number goes in the bottom square?

(34)

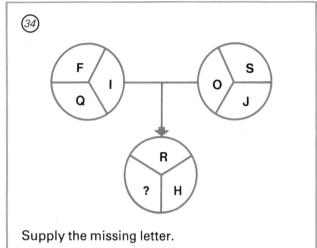

Supply the missing letter.

(35)

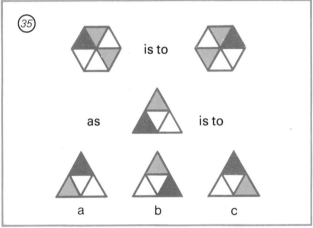

is to

as   is to

a   b   c

(36)

**ALL CATS ARE FURRY
SOME CATS ARE NOT WITHOUT A SENSE OF HUMOUR
ALL FURRY CREATURES ARE SARCASTIC**

Which of the four sentences below contradicts these statements?

a) Certain sarcastic creatures are without any humour.
b) No furry animal is without a sense of humour.
c) Even if sarcastic, no furry animal has a sense of humour.
d) Without humour, no sarcastic creature is furry.

(37)

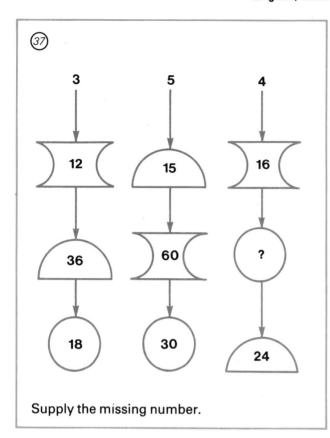

Supply the missing number.

(38)

GREEN DOGS ARE LIVE ANIMALS
ALL LIVE ANIMALS NEED FOOD

Assuming the above statements are correct, which of the following is true?

a) My dog is green because it needs food.
b) All green dogs need food.
c) Certain green dogs do not need food.
d) Some green dogs are not live animals.

(39)

DAMASCUS	— ET
FERRET	— GU
TENDERNESS	— UT
SMILE	— UG

Which is the odd line out?

(40)

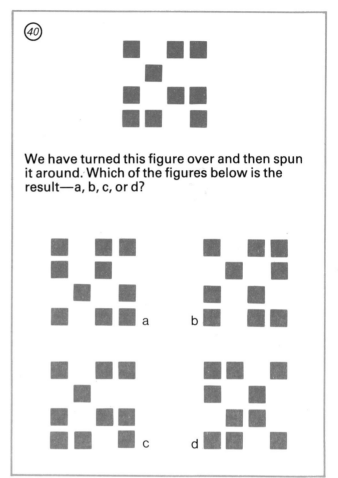

We have turned this figure over and then spun it around. Which of the figures below is the result—a, b, c, or d?

Exact answers

1) 10. The leaps between each number and the next go 2, 3, 5, 8, and 13: each represents the sum of the two previous ones.

2) T. The series is in reverse alphabetical order, with gaps of 1, 2, 3, 4 letters. Thus: VUTSRQPONMLKJIH

3) Figure d.

4) AUTOMATIC and INVOLUNTARY.

5) a, the only one having two internal points where three lines intersect.

6) H O. Two letters before and two letters after.

7) d: d is formed of two circles and a rectangle, while the others consist of two rectangles and a circle.

8) Eliminate OIPTK and leave the circular words FLAG, MALT, COMB, GOAL, DUCK.

9) 1133: each number is double the previous one, less the number of the sides of the polygon in which it stands.

10) FERVENT and ZEALOUS.

11) Figure a. Copy the original figure on a piece of paper, turn the paper over and give it a 180 degree spin. Then place it on each possible answer.

12) Change position of OAALG and SILIE to get: POST, TAIL, BALD, CLIP and AGED.

13) 0: the sum of the digits in each number is successively 1, 2, 3, 4, and so on.

14) J: the first letter of each group is followed by the letters that come two before and three after it in alphabetical order.

15) 20: the three outer circles could have been turned so that 1, 2, and 3 coincide to give 6, and hence:

16) The second: on the other lines the letters on the right represent the two first letters in the alphabet to appear in the word on the left. For instance, in SURFACE, A & C come before S, U, R, F and E in the alphabet.

17) 4: this gives the series 1, 2, 4, 7, 11, 16, 22, 29, wherein the numbers increase by 1, 2, 3, 4, 5, 6, 7 respectively.

18) Figure d: figure a has six regions; figures b and c each have an isolated region that only touches one other region.

19) 34: we turned the three outer circles and added their numbers—25 is the total of the three lowest numbers +1; the inner circle thus adds 1 to each total. Therefore:

20) FRAGILITY and DELICACY

21) 362: the product of the figures in the other numbers is always 12.

22) The fourth: CHAIR (the others were MISSISSIPPI, NILE, VOLGA, and AMAZON).

23) ee: each number is followed by the first and last letter of how it would be written out in full. Thus 58 = fifty-eight, ft.

24) C: the numerical position in the alphabet of the letter on the right corresponds with the difference between the two figures on the left e.g. E = 5, M = 13; 13 − 5 = 8 which corresponds with H.

25) c: by fitting the two left-hand figures one inside the other, the square on the right is obtained; to begin with, however, one is turned over and spun 180 degrees, and the other spun 90 degrees in a clockwise direction.

26) The third: POPLAR.

27) 17: each upended T gives on the right the product of the two left-hand numbers + 2.

28) "I am lying." "TO DENY THE OPPOSITE OF THE VERACITY" = to deny the falsehood = to affirm the truth; "I GUARANTEE THAT IT IS UNTENABLE" = it cannot be maintained.

29) 43: in each pair, one of the numbers is the product of the figures of which the other is composed + 1.

30) The first: GERANIUM.

31) The third: GREAT—EGRET (in the others, the right-hand word shares the same consonants as the left-hand one, but in reverse order).

32) Figure c.

33) 19: in each square with three lines leading to it is the product of the northwest and northeast squares, less that of the north.

34) L: the two upper circles have been spun around and then placed on top of each other. Q placed on S becomes R (the letter between them in the alphabet), F on J becomes H (similarly midway between them alphabetically). The same procedure gives L from I and O.

35) b, being symmetrical on a vertical axis.

36) Sentence c: there are some furry animals—certain cats, at any rate—with a sense of humour.

37) 8: the semicircle multiplies by 3, the circle divides by 2, and the concave figure multiplies by 4.

38) b: all green dogs, since they are living creatures, need food.

39) The last, because in the others, the right-hand letters are those that in the alphabet follow respectively the first and the last letters of the word on the left.

40) Figure b. Copy the figures onto a sheet of paper, turn it over, and spin it 90 degrees anticlockwise, then compare.

Exact answers	Intelligence Quotient
13—16	116—125
17—20	126—130
21—24	131—135
25—28	136—140
29—32	141—145
33—40	145 plus

From the laboratory to everyday experience

Tests place people in artificial situations. They tend to analyze psychological characteristics and evaluate them one by one. This seems rather "unnatural," given that all human actions engage an individual's whole personality, however, this kind of anatomizing of intelligence is necessary if we wish to gain some idea of how the mind "works."

The tests we have just undertaken to discover our I.Q. have been geared towards a variety of personal characteristics, including skill in recognizing similarities, differences and relationships between figures, mastery of words, ability with numbers, and powers of logical thinking.

Such character traits are "tested" continually in everyday life. Under "normal" circumstances (not in exam conditions) we are required, for instance, to recognize road signs, choose the best route to get to a certain spot, express ourselves competently and grasp the possible significance behind certain expressions, and follow a train of thought or the logic of development in both ideas and actions.

Thus it seems clear that the laboratory test situation concurs well with the demands of daily living. It is fair to say, then, that intelligence is exercised in a great variety of ways and by a great many kinds of stimuli both concrete and abstract.

And the results we shall achieve in the games in the following paragraphs will be functions of our intellectual level (though not of that alone, as will emerge later).

Historical digressions

The wisdom of the Jewish King Solomon (c. 973–933 B.C.) was famed throughout the known world. He was indeed a noble and peaceful king, dedicated to justice and to establishing good relations with his neighbour countries. His renown was due not to prowess in battle or any very remarkable achievements, but to his cultivation of wisdom.

In the Bible there is a fine account of the visit, in splendid pomp, of the queen of Sheba, "to test him with hard questions." According to this account, the queen of Sheba had travelled a considerable distance—from far-off Ethiopia—to meet Solomon and test his intelligence. Solomon "answered all her questions; there was nothing hidden from the king which he could not explain to her."

This is perhaps the best illustration of the extent to which, throughout the Near East, intelligence was manifested in riddles and enigmas.

History shows that the earliest human civilizations grew up alongside rivers (the Nile, the Tigris and Euphrates, the Indus), and that they managed to emerge, evolve, and flourish for so long by dint of sheer hard labour. River water was a true life source only once it had been carefully regulated and as long as it was continuously husbanded. Yet even in these early communities, despite the toughness of life, men found time to play games of intelligence. Among the more interesting archaeological finds have been rudimentary chessboards, which must have been used for games similar to our own chess and checkers.

Throughout history riddles and puzzles, too, have developed as a vehicle for intelligence.

In particular, the ancient Greeks enjoyed this rather intellectual kind of pleasure. It is recorded that the comic poet Crates of Athens (fifth century B.C.) livened up his plays with games, curious anecdotes, and riddles that the audience had to answer on the spot. It was an original method of encouraging theatergoers to participate actively, and it must have proved a considerable draw to the Athenians of his day. Sadly his works have been lost, and from the few disconnected fragments that remain it is impossible to make any worthwhile reconstruction.

Riddles as the Greeks understood them were usually short verse compositions, rich in deliberately obscure imagery, ambiguities, and puns, containing an idea that had to be puzzled out and expressed in a straightforward manner. The aura of obscurity and mystery with which they were imbued placed them in the sphere of the sacred. They were part of religious experience. Throughout the Mediterranean world, people would ponder the enigmatic utterances of the oracles and sibyls that they consulted to know the future or to help solve some crisis. Such utterances would then be parodied in the theaters, in a witty, popular mode, in catchy songs with references to ordinary everyday objects and experiences—not infrequently obscene. Hence a riddle could either be of great solemnity, a true enigma, or a jokey kind of comic question-and-answer.

Oedipus and the Sphinx: a tragic precedent!

Enigma in Greek meant "thought or problem expressed in an obscure way," a riddle of the solemn variety.

The existence of enigmas was a reminder of all that was inexplicable about life and suggested a

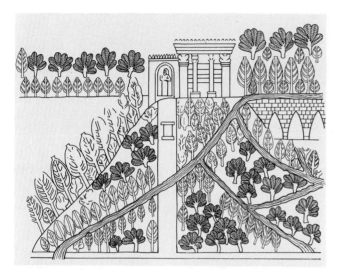

The earliest civilizations evolved alongside rivers (the Nile, the Tigris and the Euphrates, the Indus). Society survived only at the cost of immense labour. Much effort of the human mind was concentrated on regulating and exploiting the natural water supply, on which life depended. We are still impressed today by the devices invented and the huge networks of irrigation channels built, especially in Mesopotamia, to compensate for the irregularity of the water supply (almost tropical in spring and very scant in summer) from the rivers Tigris and Euphrates. The picture above, from a relief in the palace at Nineveh (the ancient capital of Assyria), dating from the seventh century B.C., shows an Assyrian park irrigated by water from an aqueduct supported by arches.

Note the pathway leading uphill to a royal pavilion and altar. Below: a way of raising water uphill by means of the *shaduf*—a kind of bucket suspended from a long pole balanced at the other end by a counterweight. This device (still in use in certain places) was known both in Egypt and in Mesopotamia. One might think that the toughness of life in these early river civilizations would leave little time for leisure games. However, archaeologists have found evidence that in fact, despite the hardships of everyday existence, people still devoted some of their intelligence to entertainment. Thus once again we are made to realize that playing is a natural need, even if mostly expressed at one particular stage of our lives.

degree of coercion and menace, boundaries beyond which only the light of intelligence could venture. To some degree, the play of intelligence can dispose of and put to rout the ghosts and monsters with which human imagination peoples the realm of the uncertain and the unknowable. One story from ancient Greek mythology in particular is worth recalling in this context: the legend of Oedipus. Myths and legends were, in the ancient world, a means of expressing human sensitivity, dilemmas, and ways of perceiving reality.

The legend relates that Laius, king of Thebes, had seriously offended the god Apollo, who, to punish him, condemned him to a "childless death." To an ancient Greek, for whom children and the continuation of the family line were a form of earthly immortality, there could be few harsher punishments. In a moment of folly, Laius fathers a child, Oedipus. But having been told by an oracle that he would die by the hand of this child, he immediately tried to do away with it. He exposed him on Mt. Cythaeron, to be devoured by wild beasts. Discovered by a shepherd, however, Oedipus was taken to the king of Corinth, who, having no children of his own, adopted him.

Years later, Oedipus travelled to Thebes and on the way became involved in a petty argument that then became a fight with a regal-looking dignitary and his escort. Oedipus defeated them all and killed the old dignitary, who in fact was his father, Laius. Meanwhile the inhabitants of Thebes were being terrorized by the Sphinx, a monster with the head of a woman and the winged body of a lion, who had been sent by Dionysus as punishment on the city for not accepting his cult. To all who passed by it, the Sphinx addressed a riddle and mercilessly slaughtered those who were unable to answer it. Oedipus

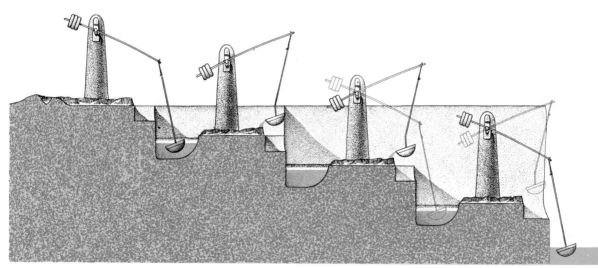

Left: detail of the great Sphinx (74 m long, 20 m high) at Giza in Egypt. As in the Greek myth of Oedipus, it symbolizes all that is dark and obscure in human experience, and which the light of human intelligence alone can transform.

alone managed to give the correct answer, as he entered the city. The following account of their meeting comes from the prologue to *Oedipus Rex*, a tragedy written in the fifth century B.C. by the Athenian playwright Sophocles:

*There is a creature that walks
on two legs, on four legs, and on three legs,
who has only one tenor of voice:
it alone among all creatures that move
on the earth, in the air, and in the water,
changes its shape. But when it walks
on four feet, then
it has least strength in its limbs.*

To which Oedipus replies:

*Listen, whether you wish to or not, O goddess of
   death,
evil-winged goddess, my voice shall pronounce
your end: it is man you mean, who walks
on the earth first of all as an infant
on all fours, away from its mother's womb,
then in old age leans on a stick, as
on a third foot, his neck bowing
under the weight of age!*

The Sphinx then kills itself by hurling itself from a precipice. The grateful Thebans elect Oedipus king

and give him Queen Jocasta as his wife.

Thus the prophecy of the oracle is fulfilled: without knowing it, Oedipus has killed his father and married his mother; and the children of their union are born to equally fated and tragic lives.

It is at this stage that Sophocles' play begins, consisting essentially of Oedipus' step-by-step discovery of the truth about his past and his true identity. The horror of the realization leads him to take terrible vengeance on himself, putting out his own eyes—the eyes that had not recognized his father or mother should no longer be allowed to look on the children of incest. For the rest of his life he would have to make do only with the eyes of his mind, of his intelligence. When Jocasta hears the truth, she, too, kills herself, unable to bear it. Intelligence takes one to the truth, but the truth can be horrifying and repugnant, and may be rejected, as both Oedipus and Jocasta reject it in their different ways. This is the stuff of myth!

Later tradition evolved a shorter version of the Sphinx's riddle: "What walks on four legs in the morning, two legs at noon, and three legs in the evening?"

The answer remains "a human being!"

In more recent times, too, the old Greek legend of Oedipus was given a new lease of life by Sigmund Freud (1856–1939), who used it to describe the complex of unconscious feelings related to early childhood, of desire for one's mother and jealousy of one's father (or vice versa).

Enigma

In the myth of the Sphinx, life itself is at stake. Anyone unable to solve the riddle dies. But then the Sphinx itself, after terrorizing the citizens of Thebes, must disappear. And it is the unconscious parricide, Oedipus, through whom the city is saved.

Through this legend we come to a better idea of what enigma meant for the ancients.

Over the span of life of any individual there were crucial moments, decisive decisions to be taken, steps experienced as trials, which, if overcome, would raise the protagonist's life to a higher level of consciousness and wisdom. Initiation rites in primitive societies, for example, serve rather the same function, marking the passage from childhood into adult life. Enigmas are in some sense the heirs of, and a metaphor for, those ancient rites: forming a
(continues on page 68)

These curious-looking devices are elaborate "toys" from ancient times, which still arouse wonder and delight. Right: the *singing fountain* of Hero of Alexandria; Below, left: *Hero's machine* for opening the doors of a temple. Below, right: the *clock of Ctesibius*. The mechanical principles incorporated in these devices reveal that the Greeks had mastered many of the laws of physical phenomena.

It was these same principles that led to the invention of the steam engine, the commercial use of which was so fundamental to the Industrial Revolution in the eighteenth century. In antiquity, however, machines such as these never had any practical function. They were sheer expressions of *intelligence at play*, designed and made for pure entertainment. Singing fountains, little theaters, and "magic" self-opening doors had no real use. They tended to be commissioned by the wealthy to create a sensation at feasts. To us it is strange and in a way "unnatural" that these bizarre and endlessly fascinating toys did not lead on to machines that could have alleviated the burden of material existence (work in the fields, in mines, on construction sites, at the loom, and so on). Probably it was simply that slave labour was so cheap and plentiful that machines were never considered a necessity. At the same time, a general contempt for these slaves went hand in hand with a contempt for all manual work. This must in turn have meant that people spent less time thinking about basic technology than about more "worthy" subjects (astronomy,

and pure maths).

Let us now look briefly at how these three machines worked. The *singing fountain* (above): the water spouts from the lion's mouth into a covered bowl (1), which, as it fills, expels the air through two tubes (2) leading to whistles concealed in the birds—who thus start to "sing." When the water level reaches the tubes (3) it overflows into another bowl (4). In this bowl there is a float (5) with a cord attached, running around a shaft (6), at the top of which an owl is

perched. At the other end of the cord is a weight (7): so, as the water and the float rise, in (4), the shaft and the owl turn around. Then as (1) and (4) are emptied (perhaps by slaves), the float (5) drops again, and the owl turns back to its original position.

Hero's machine (below, left): when the fire is lit on the altar (1), the air inside expands, building up pressure in the sphere (2), which is part filled with water. The water is thus pushed through a syphon (3) into a container or bucket (4), which, under the weight, drops and turns the door hinges (5) by means of a cord (6) and a counterweight (7). Then, when the fire on the altar goes out, the same process occurs in reverse: the air pressure returns to normal, the water in (4) is sucked back into the sphere (2), and the counterweight (7) rotates the hinges the other way so that the doors shut again.

The *water clock of Ctesibius* (below, right): water drips into a funnel (1) leading to a cylinder (2) containing a float (3) that supports a figure (4). As the water level in the cylinder rises, the float rises with it, causing the figure to rise, too, and indicate the time on the column (5). At the same time the water also rises in the syphon (6) and falls

into a drum (7) divided into compartments. As each compartment fills, the drum turns slightly. A cog on the drum (8) turns three other cogs, one of which is mounted on the shaft supporting the column.

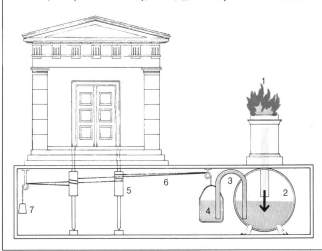

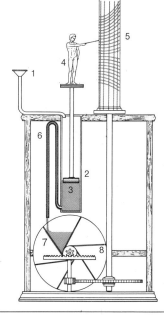

SOLITAIRE

An attractive legend attributes the invention of this game to a French nobleman imprisoned in solitary confinement in the Bastille during the Revolution (at the end of the eighteenth century). He is said to have devised this pastime to divert his thoughts from the sad predicament that he had only too many hours to ponder. However, it is known for certain that in fact solitaire already existed at the beginning of the century. It is mentioned, for instance, by the German philosopher Baron Gottfried Wilhelm von Leibniz in a letter dated January 17, 1716, already under the name "solitaire." Indeed, it would appear to be a very similar game that the Latin poet Ovid (alive in the first century B.C. and the first century A.D.) mentions; and again, it was widely played in ancient China—hence its still frequent alternative name, "Chinese checkers." Whatever its origins, it came very much into vogue in France in the eighteenth century. Undergoing something of a revival today, it still goes mostly by its French name of solitaire. (The "solitaire" played with cards is known in English as "patience.")

Solitaire is played on a small board with 37 holes, and the same number of appropriately sized pegs (see opposite page), or else with 37 rounded depressions and a similar quantity of little balls.

The game starts with the removal of one or more pegs, thus leaving one or more holes free. The remaining pegs are then moved by jumps, over their neighbours, into the free holes. The pegs that are jumped are removed from the board, as happens in checkers. They can move horizontally or vertically, but never diagonally.

The interest of the game varies according to the pattern formed at the start, and the pattern which is ultimately aimed for. The simplest version, though also the most mechanical, is to remove a single peg at the beginning and to end up with just one on the board—perhaps in competition with a friend, to see who can play it out quickest. Let us imagine, however, that the board is numbered as in *figure a*, and that we remove the last peg (37). Peg 35 moves to 37, disposing of 36, then 26 can move to 36, disposing of 32. If we indicate such a move as 26→36 (32 out), it then becomes possible for us to make any of the following moves:

fig. a

30→32 (31 out)	26→12 (19 out)
36→26 (32 out)	28→26 (27 out)
34→32 (33 out)	32→19 (26 out)
20→33 (27 out)	4→ 6 (5 out)
37→27 (33 out)	18→ 5 (11 out)
22→20 (21 out)	5→ 7 (6 out)
20→33 (27 out)	19→ 6 (12 out)
29→27 (28 out)	7→ 5 (6 out)
33→20 (27 out)	1→11 (5 out)
8→21 (14 out)	16→18 (17 out)
12→14 (13 out)	18→ 5 (11 out)
14→28 (21 out)	9→11 (10 out)
2→12 (6 out)	5→18 (11 out)
3→13 (7 out)	18→31 (25 out)
12→14 (13 out)	23→25 (24 out)
15→13 (14 out)	31→18 (25 out)
13→27 (20 out)	

The end result would be one peg in hole number 18: a somewhat dull game!

It can be made more interesting and demanding by deciding that the final peg should end up in the center hole, number 19, rather than 18.

The reader will easily be able to work out how to reach this result, starting with the removal of any peg—say, the central one, number 19.

Here now is a possible sequence of moves to achieve the same result on an "English board" (see *figure b* below), which differs from the other in having 4 fewer holes, thus permitting a slightly simplified game. This type of board is particularly good for children. The end result is a single peg left in the center hole. Renumbering the board as in *figure b*, here are the moves:

fig. b

5→17 (10 out)	4→16 (9 out)
12→10 (11 out)	7→ 9 (8 out)
3→11 (6 out)	10→ 8 (9 out)
18→ 6 (11 out)	21→ 7 (14 out)
1→ 3 (2 out)	7→ 9 (8 out)
3→11 (6 out)	24→10 (17 out)
30→18 (25 out)	10→ 8 (9 out)
27→25 (26 out)	8→22 (15 out)
24→26 (25 out)	22→24 (23 out)
13→27 (20 out)	24→26 (25 out)
27→25 (26 out)	19→17 (18 out)
22→24 (23 out)	16→18 (17 out)
31→23 (28 out)	11→25 (18 out)
16→28 (23 out)	26→24 (25 out)
33→31 (32 out)	29→17 (24 out)
31→23 (28 out)	

There are many *problems with a certain outcome* (with a precise prefixed goal) that can be played on both boards. One version, playable on the French board, is to remove all the pegs except for the 9 central ones (6, 12, 19, 26, 32, 17, 18, 20, 21), which are then left forming a cross on the board, and to reach a single peg at the end in the minimum number of moves. One possible sequence would go as follows:

12→ 2 (6 out)	21→19 (20 out)
26→12 (19 out)	2→12 (6 out)
17→19 (18 out)	12→26 (19 out)
19→ 6 (12 out)	32→19 (26 out)

Another problem with a certain outcome is to start off with the center hole empty and end up with one peg in the center, and all the outer holes filled—like a teacher in the middle of a ring of pupils.

Possible moves for this would be as follows.

21→19 (20 out)	20→33 (27 out)
34→21 (28 out)	33→31 (32 out)
32→34 (31 out)	31→18 (25 out)
30→32 (31 out)	12→14 (13 out)
17→30 (24 out)	17→19 (18 out)
4→17 (10 out)	26→12 (19 out)
6→ 4 (5 out)	11→13 (12 out)
8→ 6 (7 out)	14→12 (13 out)
21→ 8 (14 out)	6→19 (12 out)
18→20 (19 out)	

It is also possible to devise games for which *the outcome is not certain*. Any number of pegs is removed at random (2, 3, 5 . . .), and the aim would be to end up with a single peg left in any one hole. If several boards of the same type are available (either all French or all English), competitions can be arranged, with each player removing the same pegs to begin with, and the winner being the one with fewest pegs remaining after all the possible moves have been made. The games that do have a certain outcome can also be played competitively, of course. It is always worth appointing a referee to check that no shortcuts are being taken! Both boards mentioned here are available in shops, but you can easily make your own by copying the squares in *figure c* onto cardboard and playing with counters.

fig. c

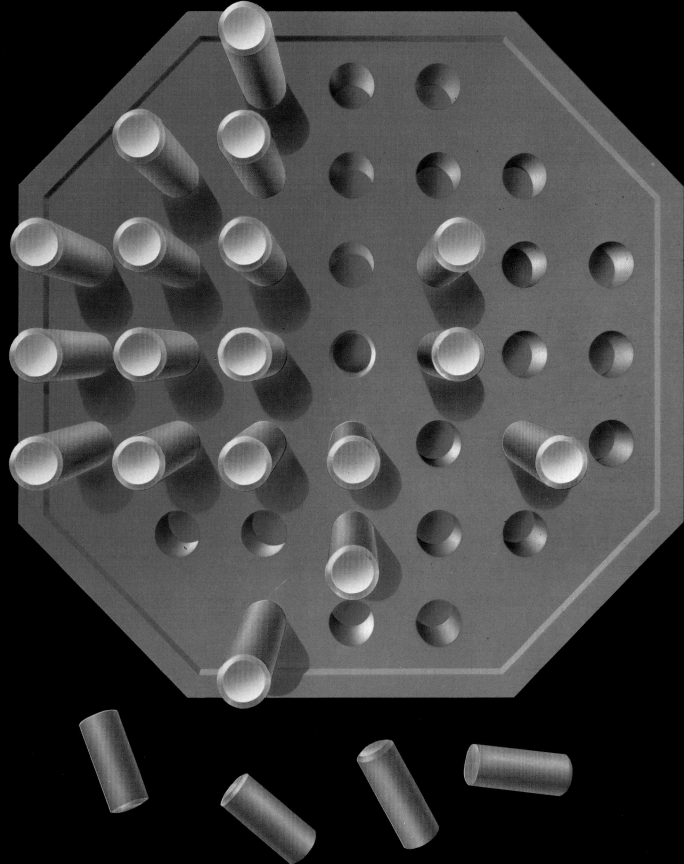

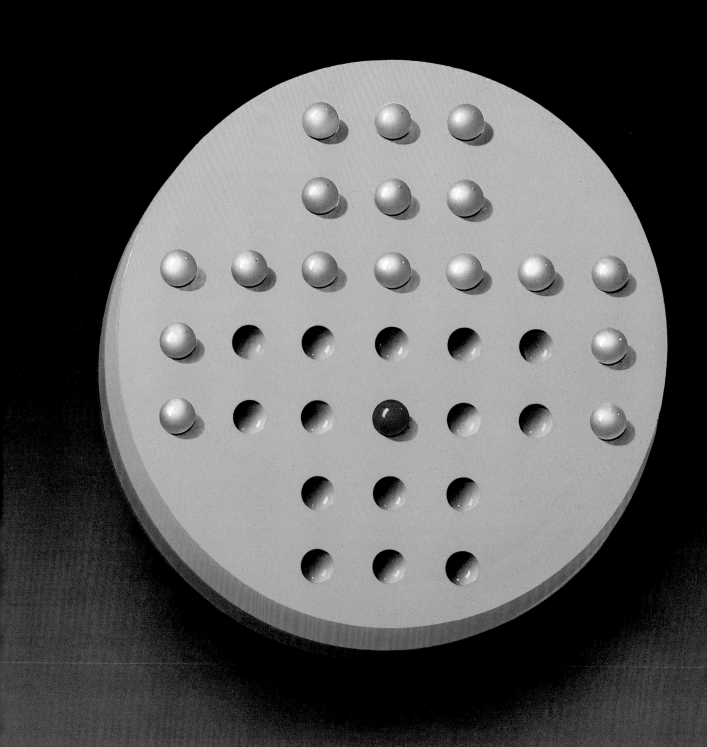

FOX-AND-GEESE

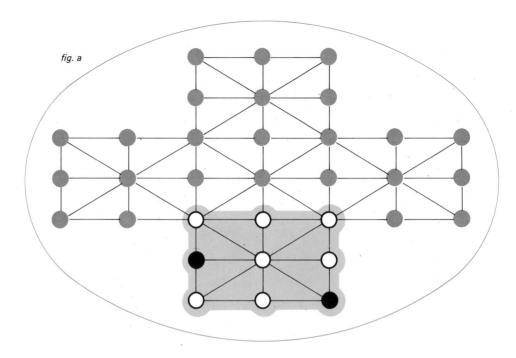

fig. a

Many different games still continue to be played on the solitaire board (see pp. 64–65). Certainly one of the best is fox-and-geese. This game has two features of interest: first, it has been a traditional royal favourite in England (Edward IV—1461–1483—had two complete sets with silver gilt pieces, and the young Queen Victoria used to enjoy playing it with Prince Albert); second, it is a "hunting game" that varies wherever it is played, according to the natural and social environment of the locality. For instance the indigenous Indians of Arizona call it *pon chochoti*, or "coyote and chicken"; to the Japanese it is *yasasukari musashi*, which means "eight ways of hunting out soldiers;" the Spanish know it as *cercar la liebre* ("hunting hares"), and so on. Although some of these games are played on different types of board, they are broadly similar in concept, and all share the basic outlook expressed by Arnold Arnold: "You cannot hunt with the hounds and run with the hare." Unlike solitaire, fox-and-geese is for two players, one of whom has only 1 peg (the fox), while the other has 17 (the geese). To start, they are arranged on the board as shown in the colour plate opposite (p. 67) (which depicts balls in hollows, rather than pegs in holes). The fox is the first to move. Throughout the game it can move *in any direction*, killing as many geese as it can by jumping over them (as in solitaire). The geese can only move one at a time, either forwards (down) or sideways, but not backwards (into the previous position) and not diagonally, to try to hem the fox

in. They win if they succeed in doing this, and the fox wins if it manages to eat at least 12 geese.

Asalto
Here is another game played on the same sort of board, though with lines marked out, linking the holes, and a particular group of 9 holes having special significance (see *figure a*). *Asalto* is Spanish for "assault," and it is the same game as the British *officers and Sepoys* (so called in the last century, after the Indian Mutiny—1857–58—when Indian troops in the Anglo-Indian army, the Sepoys, rebelled against their British officers).
This, too, is a game for two

players, one with 2 pieces (the officers) and the other with 24 (the Sepoys). To start off, the officers are in the fortress completely surrounded by the "mutineers" (see *figure a*). They can move in any direction, while the others must go either forwards (down) or diagonally. Officers capture Sepoys by jumping them. Sepoys can only eliminate officers if they fail to take a possible prisoner.
The Sepoys win if they manage to hem the officers in or to occupy the fort: the officers win if they succeed in capturing enough Sepoys to make it impossible for them to force the officers to surrender.

Other versions
Numerous variants are possible to play on the English solitaire board. Perhaps some of the colour plate illustrations of other games in this book will even help provide ideas for new ones. With a little imagination, for instance, it should be possible to adapt *alquerque* (see p. 34) and *bagh-bandi* (see p. 37) for this board. Easiest of all is to adapt the genuine version of Chinese checkers (see p. 78): all one has to do is arrange the variously coloured pieces as is suggested in *figures b, c,* and *d,* depending on the number of players (two, three, or four), then follow the rules of Chinese checkers.

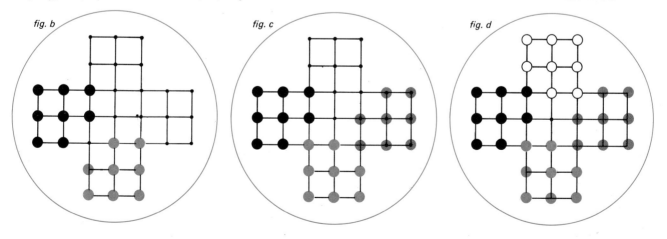

fig. b

fig. c

fig. d

sort of narrowing and intensifying of experience, which many are not able to cope with. All that is involved is a question, an obscure, ambiguous problem; but the person faced with such a question has to answer it. Hence the sense of urgency and panic that enigmas and riddles can create—feelings that are themselves a kind of test from which the individual emerges qualitatively changed. Out of all this esoteric jargon frequently appears a style of language, enigmatic to outsiders, possession of which includes one in a secret circle, holding the key to interpreting and understanding the world, inanimate matter, and animate beings. For the uninitiates, such language has by the nature of things to seem mysterious.

To gain a better grasp of enigma, let us analyze the following riddle: "What has feet but cannot walk?" Put thus, it sounds like a schoolboy trick question—hardly very "enigmatic" in the grand sense. However, all the ingredients of true "enigma" are there: "feet" is not used in the normal sense but refers to something else, in a different context, which the imagination needs to work hard to identify. For instance, the way we speak of the "foot" of a mountain offers, through metaphor, a possible alternative context. Thus "a mountain" could be the answer to the riddle.

This is one form of interpretation. But, as it stands, a riddle is meaningless to anyone who does not understand this way of thinking and referring to things. Another vital aspect of solemn "enigma" in the riddle "What has feet but cannot walk?" is the seriousness of the context—how dramatic or even tragic—in which it is asked.

The philosopher Aristotle (384–322 B.C.) relates that the famous poet Homer (*c.* ninth century B.C.), to whom the *Iliad* and the *Odyssey* are attributed, once asked the god what his native country was and who his parents were. The god's reply was incomplete and enigmatic: he said that his mother's native island was Io, that it was a mortal place, and that he should beware of a riddle put to him by certain youths. Homer realized that if he wished to shed light on his origins, he would have to go to Io, always bearing in mind the god's warning. Once on the island, the poet saw some fishermen approaching the shore and asked them if they had anything to eat. As Aristotle tells it, they had not managed to catch anything, and this was the answer they gave: "What we caught, we left, and what we did not catch, we have with us!"

Aristotle explains that, having caught no fish, the young men had busied themselves picking off their body lice. Thus the lice they had caught, they had left behind, while those they had not managed to remove were still on their bodies. It would appear that Homer, unable to make head or tail of the riddle, died of dejection.

Here, too, then, failure to solve a riddle is associated with the dire problem of penetrating the dark mystery of individual origins—a problem that can actually lead to death. Essentially, a riddle is a kind of contest, a battle with question and answer as weapons, in which life itself is the prize. Not to be able to solve a riddle that "consumes" us with curiosity is tantamount to death—as Homer and the citizens of Thebes found out to their cost. It is noteworthy also, though, that in the tradition of riddles, the opposite may sometimes occur: the ability to conceive an enigma that no one can resolve by one whose mind and awareness of the true nature of things confers life-saving power. A not infrequent example of this is the prisoner condemned to death but offered one last chance by the court: he propounds a riddle, and if the judges are unable to answer it, he is released.

The intelligence behind riddles

For centuries popular culture found in riddles a vehicle of expression appropriate to its own tastes, its own imagination, and its own down-to-earth kind of realism. Many examples survive from the Middle Ages, suggesting a very widespread oral and written tradition. The courts of kings and nobility were particularly favourable to the genre of the riddle. But at the same time, monks and clergy, too, in the solitude of their monasteries, often abandoned serious study in favour of these *nugae* (frivolities), as they called them in their learned Latin. Still, however, it was among the common folk, in popular tradition, that riddles really come into their own. Much dialect literature consists of collections of proverbs and riddles. And it is not hard to understand why. Think back to the days (not so very long ago) before television and radio; in the evenings, especially the long winter evenings, people would gather around the warmth of the hearth to exchange thoughts and stories, seated under the oil lamp hanging from the ceiling. On such occasions tales would be narrated, the news of the day would be discussed, and frequently riddles and guessing games would be bandied about as a good way of sharpening one's wit, as well as providing entertaining, competitive games. For a long time popular intelligence and sensitivity were expressed by these means.

Now let us have a look at the structural and linguistic features of a riddle.

First and foremost, it has a metaphorical meaning, nearly always dealing with external, material reality, and relating to the moral values of the world of the uneducated peasant; second, its purpose was to highlight and give greater effect to the contrast between appearance and reality, between that which has to be guessed and that which at first sight appears; finally, the better the riddle, the harder it would be to solve. Lively images and colourful, imaginative parables tend to sink in much better than abstract, nonfigurative language.

What is that . . .? (Some sample riddles)

Having said all the above, we shall now attempt to satisfy the reader's legitimate curiosity with some examples of riddles that are either very popular or of particular historical interest.

1) What walks all day on its head?

2) What grows bigger the more you take away?

3) What kind of ear cannot hear?

4) He who makes it, makes it to sell,
   He who buys it, does not use it,
   He who uses it, does not know it!

   Still in the same vein:

5) What is it that, having it, cannot be given away?

6) He who does them, forgets.
   He who receives them, remembers.

7) He who does them, remembers them.
   He who receives them, forgets them.

8) I have a comb, but am not a barber,
   I mark the hours, but am not a bell ringer,
   I have spurs, but I do not ride.

"What is it that is twisted and cuts off that which is straight?" King Alboino asked Bertoldo.
   And Bertoldo replied, "A sickle!"

The oldest collection of riddles dates from 1538 and was compiled by Angiolo Cenni of Siena, a humble blacksmith. One of his riddles will convey something of the skill and poetic content of the practice of riddle making:

9) I give at once both heat and cold
   and death to all to whom I give life;
   with my strength I drive away heat and cold.
   See whether my power is infinite;
   if I be not one with you,
   you would have neither death nor life.

From the sixteenth century on, riddles became something of a cult in poetry. New riddles were enjoyed by all social classes, and old ones were refined and polished, made more literary, and generally adapted to suit the salons and courts of the rich and powerful.

Alongside the development of neoclassical poetry in the sixteenth century and later, there grew a whole genre of literature that one might without any pejorative overtones call "enigmatographic:" riddles came to be composed in highly accomplished verse forms (sonnets, ottava rima, terza rima, and so on) worthy of the best literary traditions.

They continued to enjoy ever wider vogue in the seventeenth and eighteenth centuries. With the spread of the first newspapers in the nineteenth century, there came also periodicals devoted to riddles.

It is hardly worth commenting on the present age's love of the enigmatic and of puzzles of all kinds: newspapers and magazines clearly demonstrate that it is now very much a mass pursuit.

How many hares have the hunters bagged?

One well-known riddle, belonging to the dialect literature of Italy, is of special interest in that it could be considered typical of the genre. Originally written in the local dialect of Mantua, it runs roughly as follows:

> Two fathers and two sons went hunting,
> and each killed one hare . . .
> How many hares does that make?

The answer is three, not four. The men who went hunting were grandfather, father, and son: the "two fathers" being the father and grandfather, the "two sons," the father (son of the grandfather) and the son (the grandson of his father's father).

Thus they were three in all, so there were only three hares killed.

In its original form, the riddle is in rhymed verse, while the problem appears to be a simple mathematical question. The solution is not merely to identify an individual character or object, but to give the number of hares caught by the hunters.

Answers to the riddles

1) a nail (in a horseshoe)	4) a coffin	7) favours
2) a hole	5) death	8) a rooster
3) an ear of corn	6) acts of spite	9) breath.

How is it possible?

The trick in the last riddle rests on degrees of family relationships that we do not normally ponder. Any one person may be a father in relation to a son and at the same time a son in relation to his own father.

Following an earthquake, father and son were buried under rubble, severely wounded. When the rescuers reached them, they were immediately seen to be in grave danger and were rushed to the hospital. The father died on the way, and the son was taken at once into the operating theater. The surgeon on seeing him, however, to the great surprise of all said:

"I cannot operate on him, he is my own son!"

How so?

The solution is rather banal: the surgeon was the wounded boy's mother and could not risk the responsibility, if there was the slightest error, of being the cause of her son's death.

What is "entertaining" about this example is not the oddity or the difficulty of the answer, but its very obviousness, once given.

Deceived by the normal male connotations of "surgeon," it is easy to forget that women can also be surgeons, and thus that "the surgeon" in this case might just as well have been the boy's mother, who was not mentioned at the beginning as having been trapped in the falling masonry.

How many are we in our family?

Gone now are the days when small companies of travelling players would advertise their performances with short anticipatory sketches and scenes and question-and-answer routines in the local town or village square. But here is a riddle posed by one such group of actors to the spectators they had managed to attract.

"I have as many brothers as sisters." (The actor is hooded and cloaked so that it is impossible to determine which sex he or she is.) Then onto the stage comes a woman, who in forthright tones declares: "I am the sister that has just been mentioned, and I have twice as many brothers as sisters. So how many are we in our family?"

Anyone who guessed the correct answer would receive a free ticket for the evening show.

A simple process of reasoning will reveal the answer. Let us suppose that the cloaked figure who spoke first is a sister. Then the sister who spoke second should have said the same as the first—for example, should also have said she had "as many brothers as sisters." However, that is not what she said. Hence the first speaker must be a brother.

What conclusions would that lead to?

There must without doubt be one brother more than the number of sisters.

Now let us analyze what the sister who spoke second said: according to her, she has twice as many brothers as sisters—thus half as many sisters as brothers. Half the number of brothers is then two, the number of brothers is four, and there must be (including the last speaker) three sisters, making in all seven brothers and sisters!

How old is Peter?

One day Peter was invited to a meal with an uncle to whom he was close.

"Tell me, Peter," his uncle began, "I've forgotten the date of your birthday."

After a moment's thought, Peter jokingly replied with the following riddle:

"The day before yesterday I was fifteen, and next year I shall be of age (eighteen)."

His uncle was stunned by this answer. He smiled and straight away went and bought a superb present for such a witty reply.

What was the date of Peter's birthday, and how could his reply make sense?

If one thinks about it, Peter (who was sixteen years and one day old) must have been visiting his uncle on the first day of the year: if "the day before yesterday" he was fifteen, that must mean that his birthday fell on the previous day—December 31. This is the only workable date. On December 30 Peter was still fifteen, on the thirty-first he became sixteen, at the end of the year just starting he would become seventeen, and thus "next year" he would be eighteen.

A logical riddle

Solving a riddle often means pursuing a correct line of reasoning through to its conclusion. Sometimes a game or a problem can seem insoluble simply because we lack the patience to exercise our reason. The game that comes next is not a traditional riddle, but it is a problem to which the answer is not immediately apparent. It is necessary to weight the data and then pursue a line of argument.

From a pack of cards three are removed, one black (clubs or spades), and two red (diamonds or hearts). Two players are involved. The three cards are properly shuffled, then dealt as follows: one, facedown, to each player; and the third, also facedown, onto the table. At a sign from the dealer (who is also the referee) each player then looks at his or her card.

The winner is the first one to guess the colour of the other player's card. Thinking ourselves into the position of one of the players, our reasoning should go thus:

1) If I have been dealt the black card, then there is no problem: my adversary must have a red one, and so I cannot lose.

2) If, however, I have been dealt a red card, I should wait (though not too long) to see what my opponent says: if he does not speak immediately, he cannot for certain have the black card, so he must have the other red.

The winner here is the player who first works out the logic of the game and outwits the other. (The game, of course, cannot be played more than once for obvious reasons.)

The eyes of the mind

Sooner or later even convicts have their hour of release! A prison governor, noting the good conduct of three inmates, thought to offer them a chance of parole. Of these three, one had normal

eyesight, one had only one eye, and the third was completely blind. Calling them into his office, the governor posed the following conundrum:

"I have here five caps, three white and two red. I shall put one cap, either red or white, on each of your heads. You cannot see the colour of the cap on your own head, but you can see the caps on the others' heads!"

At this juncture one might think that the trick was unfair to the blind prisoner. However, it was not to prove so.

First of all the governor called the prisoner with normal eyesight and asked him if he was able to say what colour his cap was. He answered no. The one-eyed prisoner was then also asked, and he, too, confessed that he could not give an answer.

Not even thinking to ask the blind prisoner, the governor was then about to send them back to their cells when the blind man stepped forward and asked if he, too, could take part in the game like the others. With a smile, he said:

"I do not need eyes: given what my companions have said, I can see, with my mind's eyes, that my cap is white!"

This was indeed the case, and true to his word the governor granted him his liberty.

How had the blind man's thinking gone?

It must have been more or less along these lines: If I have a red cap, the one-eyed prisoner—seeing that the normal-sighted one was unable to tell the colour of his cap—would have thought that had he, too, had a red cap, then the first prisoner would have been able to know for sure that his was white. And since this had not been the case, he would have concluded that his is white. Now since he had not said white, either, it must mean that I have a white cap!

Weights and scales

What counts in this game is skill at combinations. We have three pairs of balls, similar to those used for putting the shot: two red, two white, and two pink. The two balls of the same colour are indistinguishable except for the fact that one of the pair is three times the weight of the other. Hence there is one set of light balls of identical weight (red, white, and pink) and one set of heavy (red, white, and pink). The game is this: to establish, with the use of scales having two pans, each capable of containing not more than two balls at a time, which is the heavier and which the lighter ball in each pair of the same colour—taking only two weight recordings! How should the balls be combined on the scales?

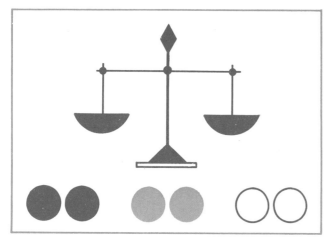

	Wr	WR	Wp	WP
wr	0	0	1	1
wR	0	0	0	1
wp	1	1	0	0
wP	0	1	0	0

There are a number of solutions. We suggest the following: Put two balls of different colours—say, one red and one white—onto one of the measuring pans and a white and a pink on the other. The scales could react in one of two ways:

1) If the scales remain in equilibrium, remove the two balls of different colours (this will then show which of the white balls is the heavier); having once identified the heavier of the two white balls, one can then work out which was the heavier of the two coloured balls with which the white ones were initially weighed; and hence it can be deduced whether the unused balls were the heavy or light ones.

2) If, however, the scales drop to one side or the other, it means that the white ball on that side must be heavier than that on the other (otherwise the scales would stay in equilibrium); yet it is not possible to establish immediately the relative weights of the red and pink balls; the next step, therefore, is to place on one of the weighing pans the red ball already used in the previous step and balance it against the twin of the pink (or vice versa); depending on what happens then, the relative weights of all the balls will be deducible. Let us analyze the various possibilities that may occur, to clarify the procedure.

W (capital) = the heavier white;
w (lowercase) = the lighter white;
R (capital) = the heavier red;
r (lowercase) = the lighter red;
P (capital) = the heavier pink;
p (lowercase) = the lighter pink.

Remembering that one of the pans has proved heavier than the other, and that the white ball on this side must necessarily be the heavier rather than the lighter, the possible combinations are as follows in the chart above.

How, though, are we to read this chart? First of all, 0 = impossible combinations, given the conditions of the test. For instance, the combination Wp–wR is out of the question because it would have held the scales in equilibrium, and in the present case we are assuming that the scales are tipped down on one side. Equally impossible is the combination WR–wR since there are not two heavy red balls. Let us now then consider a slightly more complex example: the combination WP–wr i.e. the bottom pan containing the heavy white and pink balls, and the light white and red in the other; as soon as WP sinks down (during the first step of the procedure), I can identify W and w; I then weigh the unused red ball (in this case R) against P, and since they are of equal weight, the scales will stay in equilibrium. Two assumptions can then be made: if the two balls are p and r, then in the first step, since in the second the unused red ball came into play, it has to be R. Yet that would have given us, in the first step, Wp–wR, which by the very nature of the puzzle could not have been the case: the 0 in the chart opposite Wp–wR indicates this; such a combination would have kept the scales in equilibrium rather than weighted on one side.

Ping-Pong balls

In this game we have to extract balls from a box. The trick behind it, however, is entirely a matter of reasoning, not of calculation.

A team of Ping-Pong players has ordered a supply of six phosphorescent balls (to stimulate and strengthen their visual reflexes): three are red and three white.

The supplying firm sent three small boxes: one

containing two red balls, the second containing two white balls, and the third containing one white and one red. To recognize which was which, the suppliers had labelled each box: *ww* meant two white balls; *rr* two red; *wr* a white and a red. So far so good. Unfortunately, however, the labels had somehow got muddled, and every box was mislabelled.

Here is the game: Removing one ball at a time from any box, what is the minimum number of removals necessary to establish the contents of all three boxes?

It is in fact possible to do it in a single operation. Let us suppose we have removed a white ball from the box labelled *wr*. Since the label is wrong, the other ball cannot be red, so it must be white: thus we have identified the box containing the two white balls.

Let us now examine the box labelled *rr*. We know it cannot contain both red balls, as the labels are wrong. It must therefore contain a white and a red. Hence it is also possible to assume that the last box is that containing the two red balls.

This solution depends on the information that the labels are all wrong.

One last question: If, after the removal of the first ball, we had turned to the box named *ww*, would a single operation still have sufficed? And if we had taken our first ball from the box marked *rr*? (You should each be able to work out the answers.)

In the world of opposites

A sociologist came to hear of a strange society composed of two rigidly opposed groups: one always told lies, the other always told the truth. Feeling he should investigate this he set off for this curious enigmatic land.

The two roads

Our sociologist was making for the main population center of this land when he came upon a fork in the road. Which way should he go? As he stood in a quandary, two people appeared. His first feeling was one of relief. But such feelings had soon to be checked, for he remembered somebody warning him before he left that he would indeed encounter two people—and one would be a liar, the other a truth teller!

There was no telling from mere appearances.

There must be some way out of this predicament, thought the sociologist.

After a moment's hesitation, he asked one of the two strangers a simple question, waited patiently for the answer, then set out confidently in the direction that had been indicated to him.

Here is the riddle: What was the question?

Ponder the situation. Could he not have asked either stranger—no matter which—the following question: "Excuse me, would you please tell me which road your companion would show me, if he were to show me the wrong one?"

Let us analyze the logic of this question. There are two possibilities: the person to whom the question is addressed may be a liar and the other one a truth teller, or it may be the other way around. Let us begin by supposing that the person addressed is a truth teller. Since he always tells the truth, will he not also have transmitted the request faithfully in this case? His lying companion meanwhile will have given the wrong answer—or the *right* direction to the town.

Supposing now that it was the liar who was addressed in the first place: since he cannot but lie and reverse everything, he will change the very content of the question and ask the truth teller: "Which is the right way to the town?" thus resulting again in the correct answer.

In other words, the truth teller, who always tells the truth, will indicate the correct road to the town. Either way, then, the sociologist can be confident in the road he takes.

A variant

We have deliberately introduced the reader to the problems of logic by means of a very popular old story, known sometimes as "The Fable of the Liar

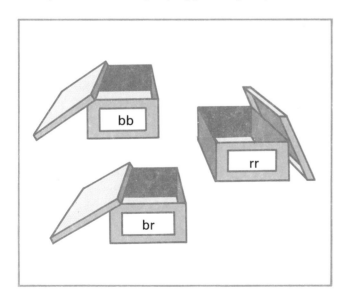

and the Traveller," over which generations of logicians, philosophers, and amateur fans of conundrums and riddles have exercised their minds.

Here we encounter a curiosity of logic that for centuries has proved intellectually stimulating—a paradigm of logical difficulties that are unapparent or apprehended only at an intuitional level.

The different variants of the fable testify to its usefulness.

According to one such variant, the traveller only meets one rather than two strangers. He does not know whether it is a liar or a truth teller he has met; nevertheless, after posing a simple question, he is again able to continue on his way, confident that he is taking the right road.

Once more the problem is: What was the traveller's question?

One solution could go as follows:

"If you belonged to the other group, which road would you direct me onto to reach the town?"

Let us suppose that the stranger is a truth teller: putting himself in the place of a liar, he would then give the wrong road.

Remember, the truth teller *always* tells the truth. Thus, having been asked to answer for a liar, he says honestly what the liar would have said, namely the wrong road. Supposing now that the stranger was a liar: he would put himself in the place of the truth teller, and then say the exact opposite of what the truth teller would have said! Thus in both cases the road indicated would be the wrong one.

Confident of this, the traveller could then happily take the other road.

Shrook!

Sure of being on the right road, the traveller-sociologist now prepared mentally for the quandaries that lay ahead. The problem at the road junction taught him one thing about this society: people at least acted according to rigorous logic. He thus resolved to think along the same lines. This would enable him to understand the inner workings of a rather singular human community!

Suddenly in front of him he spied two people. At once he thought this would be a good chance to test his resolve. He determined to find out which group each belonged to. Courteously approaching them, he addressed the most affable looking of the two: "Are you one of the group that always tells the truth?"

"Shrook!" came the rather confusing reply.

What does "Shrook" mean? he thought to himself. Then, just as he was on the point of addressing the other stranger, he was forestalled.

"He said, 'Yes,'" interpreted the second stranger. "But he's a terrible liar!"

What are the two strangers? Are they both liars? Or both truth tellers? Or is one a truth teller and the other a liar? In which case, which is which? The solution is much simpler than might appear: all rests on patient reasoning.

Let us suppose the first stranger was a liar, who would therefore have answered, "Yes"—just as a truth teller would also have answered, "Yes." In either case, in other words, the initial answer had to be "yes."

Thus in saying that his companion had said, "Yes," the second stranger was telling the truth. His translation of the bizarre answer "Shrook" was reliable. He must be a truth teller.

Satisfied with this conclusion, our intrepid sociologist continues on his way.

Two buffoons

One of the most revealing indicators of the nature of any society is its educational system: the way it projects its own notion of itself toward the future, its aims, its programs of development.

Well aware of this, the sociologist-traveller had, even before setting out, decided to make a special study of local schooling. He had indeed a kind of plan, and top of the agenda was the establishing of links with teachers. It was not hard to find out which were the major educational establishments, and off to one of these he betook himself. Having found the way to the staff room, he was greeted by an unusual scene: elderly people, breathing hoarsely and dressed without taste, some positively in rags, mingled with younger individuals, who were equally odd—absurdly dressed, as if for carnival. It must be to catch the pupils' attention decided the sociologist, doing his best to hide his feelings of disgust.

He was anxious not to waste time by becoming tangled in a web of lies: this would have jeopardized his whole venture. Now a further division among the inhabitants of the world of opposites (besides that of liars and truth tellers) was made, into politicians and ordinary citizens respectively. (For example, "All liars are politicians, and all truth tellers are ordinary citizens.") Wishing for an immediate answer, he approached a young man and a somewhat older man who were reclining on armchairs with a perennially tired air and inquired: "Is one of you an ordinary citizen?"

The younger looking of the two replied, such that the sociologist was able to get a true answer.

What was the young teacher who had replied —truth teller or a liar? And what about his older colleague? Within the terms of the game already given, we have enough information to know for sure. However, it is necessary to argue from certain hypothetical assumptions. First, we know that the teacher's reply was sufficient to tell the sociologist whether he and his colleague were politicians, ordinary citizens, or one of each. Let us therefore imagine the younger teacher's reply as being, ''Yes, one of us is a truth teller.''

Would this have sufficed for the sociologist to discover what the young man really was? Let us reflect: If he was an ordinary citizen, he would of course have answered, ''Yes''—the truth, in that at least one of them was a truth teller; if he was a politician, however, his ''yes'' would have meant that they were both politicians. Hence ''yes'' alone could not have allowed the sociologist to discover what the two men were. Yet the fact is (as we know from the story) that he *did* discover from the answer who was what. And if ''yes'' was not enough for him to have made that discovery, then the answer actually given must have been ''no.''

Now let us consider: Who could have said ''no'' —an ordinary citizen or a politician? Were the young teacher an ordinary citizen, he would not have been able to say ''no'' and yet still be telling the truth. Thus he must necessarily be a politician, telling a lie. His ''no'' would indicate that at least one of them *was* a truth teller, and if it was not the speaker himself, then it had to be the elder teacher. Having established this, then, the sociologist could confidently address his further questions to the truth-telling ordinary citizen—the elder teacher.

The meeting with the prime minister

An interview with the prime minister would considerably aid our sociologist's work; and he eventually contrived to arrange one, after much pushing.

During his preparations for this interview, it occurred to him that he should first find out whether the prime minister was a truth teller or a liar. Only once he knew this would he be able to formulate his following questions. However, there was a further complication; for he had discovered that in this odd country there was yet another division of individuals—those who answered every other question with a lie and every other question with the truth. There were not many of these, but such as there were tended to be found in the upper echelons. Hence the prime minister might very well be one of these . . . ''alternators.''

First of all, therefore, the wily sociologist devised a method of establishing beyond any shadow of doubt what the prime minister was. After a while he wrote two questions on a sheet of paper: what were they? In fact, it was merely the same question asked twice: ''Excuse me, are you an alternator?'' (There are other possibilities here, too.)

If the prime minister replied ''No'' on each occasion, that would make him a truth teller; if each time he replied ''Yes,'' then he would be a liar; and if he replied ''Yes—no,'' or ''No—yes,'' he would reveal himself to be an alternator indeed.

That information would probably suffice for the sociologist. But say he wished to find out whether (should the PM after all be an alternator) he says the truth first and then lies, or vice versa?

Are there a couple of questions that would elicit that information?

The solution would appear obvious: one need only ask him two questions about indisputable facts. One could, for example, ask: ''Do cats have four paws?''

''Yes'' times two would signify a truth teller; ''no'' times two a liar. A ''yes—no'' or ''no—yes'' would indicate both an alternator and the type of alternator. And this could significantly affect the sociologist's inquiries.

At the Assembly of the Wise: all truth tellers or all liars?

How was the country of liars and truth tellers governed?

In the course of his inquiries, our redoubtable sociologist managed to gain access to the supreme house of government, the Assembly of the Wise. This was a chamber of representatives, formed of highly able people, deputed by others to shoulder the burdensome responsibilities of governing. From the very name of this governing body, the sociologist realized that he might be up against problems. Nor were his fears unfounded.

Having gained permission to enter the house of the assembly, he eventually turned up during an important session. All the members were present, arranged around a circular table. At first sight it was impossible to tell the liars from the others.

It has to be remembered, in the interest of truth, that in this strange country, the liars are also politicians, and truth tellers ordinary citizens. These designations were used, for some reason, in political relationships, too.

Now our ingenious sociologist began, as opportunity presented itself, to ask everybody there whom they represented and whether they belonged to either of the ''parties.'' To his surprise, all the members of the assembly claimed to be ordinary citizens and, as such, truth tellers.

Is it possible, thought our hero, that only the truth tellers are represented in this house?

Clearly something was wrong: a bit of cunning would be needed to get to the bottom of this! So he thought up a plan: he asked each member seated at the circular table if his left-hand neighbour was a truth teller or a liar. What was his astonishment when he heard once again an identical reply from everybody, though this time the opposite of what had been asserted the first time. Each member's left-hand neighbour appeared to be a liar!

Not one to be defeated so easily, he returned to his room, sat down, and pored over the data. It was not easy to establish the composition of the Assembly of the Wise and the percentage representation of politicians and ordinary citizens. By now accustomed to thinking logically, however, he had almost reached conclusive results. Yet one detail still remained for him to find out: the number of members present that day at the assembly.

Without that information he would not be able to come to any conclusive decision as to the political makeup of this society.

How many members?

Our indomitable sociologist picked up the phone and got himself put through to the president of the assembly. He asked his question and was told that there had been in all fifty-seven members present. Experience had taught him, though, not to trust the first reply he might receive, all the more since he had not yet been able to gather whether the president was a truth teller or a liar. Picking up the phone again, he called the secretary, who sat beside the president, and asked: "Is it true that there were fifty-seven members in the assembly?"

"No, no," cried the secretary vehemently. "I've already told you, the president is a typical politician, he's the biggest liar of the lot; there were sixty people around the table. I counted them myself."

Whom should he trust? Can a president of an assembly lie so shamelessly?

From the secretary's emphatic, angry tone, the sociologist was inclined to give greater credit to him. But previous experience had made him wary, and he would only trust to the rigorous certainty of logic. Turning to a citizen who he knew for certain was a truth teller, he appealed for help. Without telling him the identity of the liar, the man he asked replied, "Only one of the two is an ordinary citizen."

So who was telling the truth. This information alone was enough for the sociologist to be able to establish the precise number of the members of the assembly: then what was the number of persons seated around the large round table?

Let us try analyzing the situation together.

Asked singly, the members had all declared themselves to be truth tellers; while, according to their right-hand neighbours, every one of them was a liar. These replies already can lead us to two hypotheses. Let us suppose, on the basis of the first reply, that all were truth tellers—in that case they all lied when they said their neighbour was a liar, and therein is a contradiction, since truth tellers here *always* tell the truth; alternatively, let us suppose that all were indeed liars—then they would have replied correctly in saying that they were themselves truth tellers, but there would again have been a contradiction when they declared their left-hand neighbours to be liars.

We thus have to drop any notion that all the members of the assembly were the same, be it liars or truth tellers. We can only conclude that they were a mixed bag of liars *and* truth tellers. Now there is one more bit of information we can perhaps derive from what we have been told: the order in which liars and truth tellers are seated around the table. And perhaps this will then enable us to work out how many members the assembly had and thus to decide which of the two—the president or the secretary—were barefaced liars.

Let us then suppose that (going clockwise, from left to right) we encountered two truth tellers and two liars: the first truth teller, in claiming his left-hand neighbour to be a liar, would not have been telling the truth, so that will not do! The same objection holds if we suppose there were two liars sitting next to each other. Thus, in the Assembly of the Wise, liars and truth tellers must have been seated alternately: no other arrangement would square with what was said by each about themselves and about their neighbours. If, therefore, liars and truth tellers alternated, there must have been an *even* number of members—for otherwise there would at some point around the circle have had to be either two liars or two truth tellers together. And as we have seen, the answers given by the members themselves excludes this possibility.

The diagrams on the opposite page depict a hypothetical large round table with truth tellers (the little circles marked T) and liars (the circles marked L) seated around it: in I there is an even number of members (for convenience sake, only a few, not the full contingent), while II (again less than the full quorum) depicts an odd number.

As can be seen, where there is an odd number of members, two liars end up next to each other, which would mean that one or other would be obliged to say that his left-hand neighbour was a truth teller.

It emerges then that the president was telling an

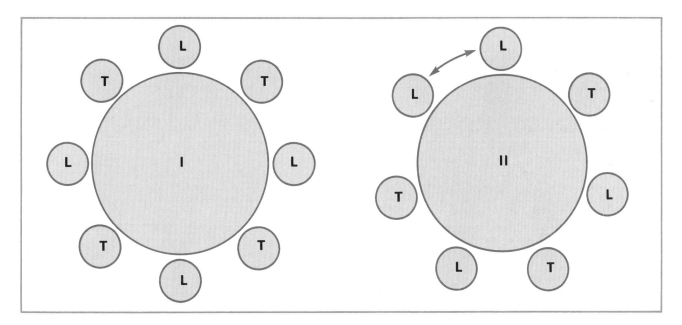

outright lie in claiming there were fifty-seven (an odd number) members. As the secretary was sitting next to him, he must be a truth teller: thus the number of members must truly have been sixty!

The game never ends

To draw out all the possibilities implicit within a game, a riddle, or any kind of problem is not only a matter of methodological habit, it can also prove very useful. Logic in this respect shares the same method of procedure as mathematics. If our aim was simply to find a solution in the simplest and most direct way, our game might be considered over. We can, however, make the solution more complete by following a further line of investigation: by asking what conditions could have made the game insoluble.

Let us suppose that the president of the assembly had claimed there were fifty-eight rather than fifty-seven members. He would still have been lying, but we should not have been able to establish his dishonesty for certain; indeed, we could have assumed him to be honest without thereby creating any logical inconsistencies.

We can be sure he was lying only because fifty-seven is an odd number, while it was logically necessary that the total be even.

We can say, then, that the problem would have been insoluble had both the president and the secretary claimed an even number of members, rather than conflicting even and odd numbers.

A serious game

Within human society it is not possible to make any clear distinction between good and bad people—between liars and truth tellers. Individuals within themselves are never all one thing or the other.

Since our game rested on the assumption that people were thus either entirely honest or entirely dishonest, there is no question but that it was mere imaginative entertainment. It might thus seem that to reduce the complexity and variety of real human society to two clearly demarcated groups is purely fanciful. Nevertheless, there may be more to it.

Strange as it may seem, there are times when taking an unrealistic viewpoint (putting onself in a sense outside reality) actually helps towards reaching a clearer picture of reality—to grasp otherwise elusive aspects of it. Reality (human, social, physical . . .) is too varied and complex for us to grasp wholly in all its aspects. This does not mean, however, that it cannot be grasped. Generally one begins by isolating certain individual aspects, and from this basis one can gradually build up a more complete picture of whatever area one is investigating. To begin with, therefore, only isolated moments and separate elements of reality are considered. Yet this reduction and simplification of things should not be mourned as a loss, but rather seen as a necessary first step. To some extent, this is the way of the rational method in the sciences. Physics, for instance, started as a rational study of external reality, concentrating on only some of the innumerable material phenomena of the natural

(continued on page 82)

CHINESE CHECKERS—ALMA

Chinese checkers is widely played today by both young and old alike. It is a game that requires a certain degree of mental application. Though an American invention, dating from the second half of the last century, it owes its name to the fact that the country in which it is most popular is China, where it is called *xiaoxing tiaoqi*. Some confusion can arise between this game and solitaire (see p. 64), which is also occasionally known as Chinese checkers. Real Chinese checkers is played on a hexagonal star-shaped board, with 121 holes or hollows (depending on whether pegs or balls or marbles are used—see page opposite).

Two, three, four, five, or six players can participate. If there are two or three players, each has 15 pieces; if more, then each has 10, all the same colour, a different colour per player. To start off, the pieces are arranged in the "points" of the star, as shown in *figure a* (in which three players are assumed to be

involved). The object is to move all your pieces into the star point diametrically opposite that in which you started. The first player to manage this is the winner. Pieces can be moved in any direction, one at a time. They can either take one step or jump another piece, but not both in one go. Jumping can continue over any number of pieces, both rivals and pieces of the same colour, finishing at the first empty place bordered by another empty place (see *figure b*). (Note: A popular alternative rule is to jump over only one piece at a time. However, several of these single jumps may be made in one move.) Pieces that have been jumped are not removed from the board, since that is not the point of the game. There are differing versions of rules (such as starting off with 10 rather than 15 pieces, or 6 rather than 10), but there are no basic disagreements.

Chinese checkers is often considered to have derived from a much less well-known game

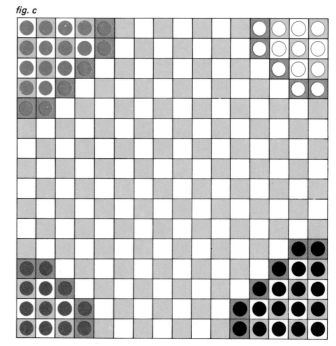

fig. c

called Alma, which was also invented in the second half of the nineteenth century and has similar rules. It takes its name from the river Alma in the Crimea (where the great battle of 1854 was fought), on the start of which the rules were devised. Alma is sometimes written with an *h* at the beginning, after the ancient Greek word *hálma*, meaning "jump"—obviously a more direct reference to the game itself.

The board is square, with 16 places around each side, alternately dark and light (see *figure c*). It can be played with two or four players: if two, each has 19 pieces; if four, 13—all the same colour, though each player having a different colour (for instance, white, black, red, and yellow). To start, each player arranges his pieces in a corner of the board, as shown in *figure c* (if there are 19 pieces, the 19 adjacent corner squares are

used). Each player moves in turn, one piece at a time, not in all directions, but *only* diagonally, such that a piece on a light square will always remain on light squares. As in Chinese checkers, each piece can move either a single square or jump (once or as often as the layout of the other pieces allows) both enemy and friendly pieces; pieces that are jumped are not removed from the board. The winner is the player who first manages to rearrange his pieces in the corner opposite that in which he started.

A rather complicated variant of Alma is the numbered version, in which every piece is numbered in order and arranged on the board as shown in *figure d*. The rules remain the same, but the object is to reconstitute a symmetrical arrangement of one's pieces in the opposite corner of the board, with all the numbers in position.

fig. a

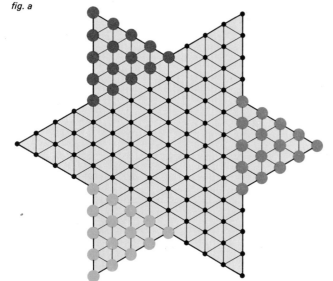

fig. b

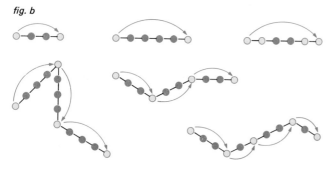

fig. d

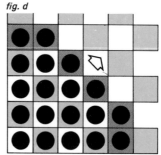
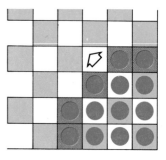

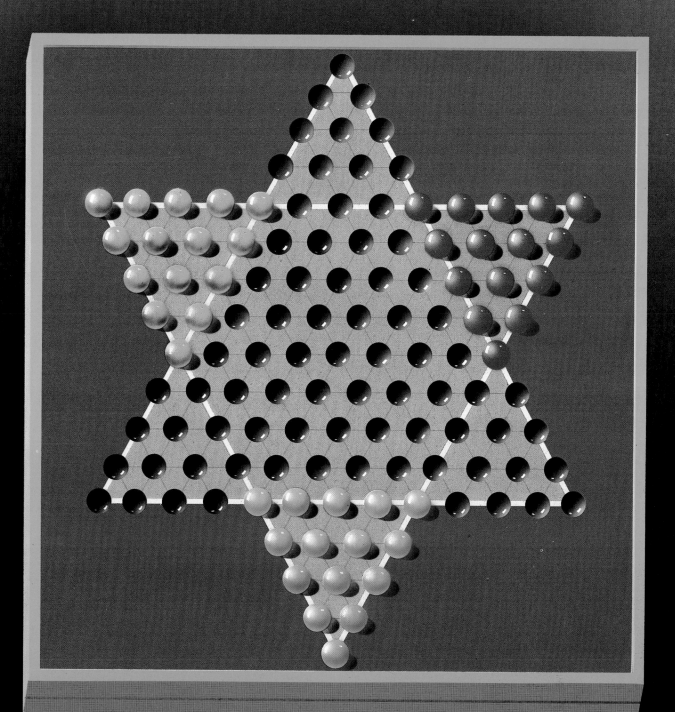

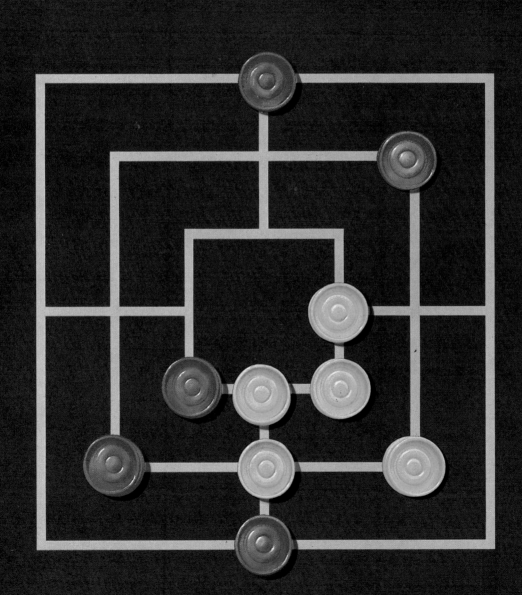

NINE MEN'S MORRIS

This is a simple game, played throughout the world in different forms and under different names. The American and English name nine men's Morris becomes three, six, or twelve men's Morris according to the number of pieces used. The earliest known traces of this game have been found in the temple of Kurna, on the west bank of the Nile at Thebes (fourteenth century B.C.). Remains of boards were also discovered during excavations at the lowest level of Troy, and similar remains have been found in Bronze Age tombs in County Wicklow, Ireland, in the vestiges of a funerary boat at Gokstad, Norway (tenth century B.C.), and in many other places. It is also mentioned in Alfonso X of Swabia's *Libro de juegos* (see p. 34), in the Jewish *Talmud*, and even in Shakespeare's *A Midsummer Night's Dream*.

fig. a

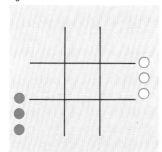

Some of the most interesting variations of this game are as follows:

Tic-tac-toe
This is perhaps the simplest version of nine men's Morris, played by two players on a 9-square board, with 3 pieces each (see *figure a*). The board starts off bare. Each player in turn then places 1 piece on any square, the aim being to create a line of 3 consecutive pieces ("tic-tac-toe"), either horizontal, vertical, or diagonal. The winner is the first player to achieve this. The game is rendered more interesting if 5 pieces are given to each player rather than 3: in this case, having created a line of 3 pieces, the relevant player can take one of his opponent's pieces (though not one that is also part of a complete line). Pieces can be taken either during the process of introducing the "armies" onto the board or

during the maneuvering once they are all in play. In the latter case, pieces are maneuvered simply from one square to the next. The winner is the first player to reduce his opponent's "army" to 2 pieces or to make it impossible for him to form a line.

Three men's Morris
Here the board is slightly more developed than that for tic-tac-toe, but again it is played with 3 pieces (see *figure b*). The rules are the same, but the pieces are positioned on the points of intersection of the various horizontal, vertical, and diagonal lines see *figure b*).

Six men's Morris
On this board the diagonal lines have disappeared, and another central square has been introduced (see *figure c*). Each player has 6 pieces (hence the name of the game). Again, the rules are similar to three men's Morris. Each player tries to form a line along one of the sides of either square.

fig. b

Nine men's Morris
This is the most popular version the world over. Each player has 9 pieces, and the board consists of 3 concentric squares joined by straight lines (see opposite page). The rules are as described earlier, with the following considerations:
1. Once all the pieces are in play, they move one at a time from one point of intersection to any free neighbouring intersection, the object still being to form a row or mill of 3 pieces.
2. Pieces can be aligned along the same axis as many times as desired (though of course to make the game more demanding, it can be ruled that two lines cannot be formed on the same spot, as in a cross or "T" shape).
3. As before, enemy pieces that are part of a line of three cannot be taken.
4. Once a player has only 3 pieces left, he can move them (and jump) one at a time without having to follow the lines as drawn.

fig. c

Twelve men's Morris
Different from the above only in having a more complicated board and in each player's having 12 rather than 9 pieces (see *figure d*).

Morris with numbers
An interesting variant because of its similarity to magic squares (see pp. 169–171). A board is drawn on a sheet of paper and subdivided into 9 circles (see *figure e*) or squares (see *figure f*), and one plays with numbers. One player uses 0 and even numbers (0, 2, 4, 6, 8, 10), the other the odd numbers (1, 3, 5, 7, 9). As the former has one extra "piece," he starts by writing one of his numbers in any of the 9 circles or squares. Then the second player does the same, writing an odd number, and so on, each number being allowed only one appearance. The winner is the player who first succeeds in making a sequence of three numbers, in any direction, totalling 15.
By complicating the board

fig. e

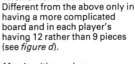

fig. d

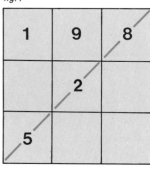

fig. f

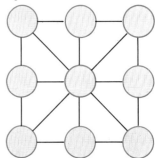

somewhat, and thus increasing the quantity of numbers at each player's disposal, numerous variants of this game can be devised; and new ideas can always be drawn from the description of magic squares later in this book (see pp. 169–171).

world. Other disciplines have evolved along similar lines.

By necessity a starting point is reductive. The final aim, however, is always to achieve as complete a picture as possible of the reality under examination.

In a way we have done the same, postulating a society formed exclusively of liars and truth tellers —simplifying reality, abstracting ourselves from it. But by doing so, we have been able to familiarize ourselves with a method, a viewpoint, that is only apparently remote from everyday reality: namely, that of logic.

The story of the sociologist-traveller in the world of opposites is a serious game because it is fundamentally an exercise of logic—that is, it is based on a discipline that forms the groundwork of scientific reasoning.

A liar from antiquity

One illustration of how, even in antiquity, in the early days of philosophy, thinkers sought a better understanding of natural and human reality by dreaming up hypothetical, unreal stories is the paradox of Epimenides.

Epimenides of Crete was a curious figure. We know little about him, and most of what we do know is legendary in character: for instance, he is said to have lived to the age of 299, with odd bouts of sleep, one lasting fifty-seven years when he was meant to be tending his father's sheep!

A native of Knossos (the site of the celebrated labyrinth of Minos), he is thought to have been called to Athens in the early decades of the sixth century B.C. to purge the city of plague. His philosophy is usually classed as pre-Socratic; that is, simply, that it predates Socrates. It should be remembered that the philosophers who lived before Socrates had little notion of themselves as "philosophers" in the sense in which we now understand the word. They were more like priests, wizards, or sages, or devotees of purificatory rites (as Epimenides of Crete would seem to have been).

The paradox that has immortalized the name of Epimenides in the history of philosophy suggests already a certain mastery of the discipline of abstraction. In its original form, it runs thus: "All Cretans are liars."

Why does this simple statement have such significance? There are many Cretans, but let us accept that they are all liars: now, since Epimenides himself is a Cretan, he, too, must be a liar! Hence his statement is true—which it cannot be, since a liar does not tell the truth. Thus Epimenides is a liar, and his statement is not true. To deny a universal statement such as "All Cretans are liars" is tantamount to saying that there is at least one Cretan who tells the truth.

To conclude, all that can be deduced from Epimenides' paradox is that 1) Epimenides is a liar, and 2) there is at least one Cretan who tells the truth!

The antinomy of the liar

What is known historically as the paradox of Epimenides is not a paradox in the strict sense, even though it has given rise to a whole series of paradoxes, all on the theme of the liar. Usually a paradox is a statement that flies in the face of common sense or the rules of logic. In philosophical jargon, this is more properly known as an antinomy, and although technically there is a distinction between the two terms, for our present purposes they are near enough identical in meaning. So as we trace the process of explication and clarification of Epimenides' paradox in the history of philosophy and logic, we shall speak of the "antinomy of the liar." An antinomy is generally a statement that, either when asserted or when denied, leads to contradiction. The antinomy of the liar is usually presented in the following form: we are to imagine a liar saying, "The statement I am making at this moment is false."

Is the proposition true or false?

The answer is a clear self-contradiction: if it is false, then it is true; and if it is true, then it is false!

It is possible to resolve this antinomy only through a complex analysis of language, which would take all night! Suffice it to say that such statements lack any real base. In other words, the mistake is in the very notion of a statement such as "this proposition is false," since "this proposition" conveys no information and thus has no content.

An invitation to logic

What point is there in imagining a society as absurd, as remote from real life, as "the world of opposites," inhabited only by liars or truth tellers?

Only a cursory, superficial view of the matter will find it confusing. In fact, as we have already seen, it reveals very well a certain method of thought, a way of approaching problems, that is much more down to earth than might appear. The way the sociologist-traveller has to reorientate himself to find out the truth is to some extent similar to the *logic of the scientific method*. Notions of truth and falsehood lie at the heart of the type of knowledge we call "science." More precisely, what partly distinguishes those propositions that we call scientific is their very nature of *being able to be true or false.*

Examples of propositions might be:

3 is a number. (True)
Snow is white. (True)
Birmingham is in Spain. (False)

A moral injunction, a question, or an order are not propositions in the sense understood here. The logic concerned with propositions that are capable of only two values, true or false, is known as two-valued logic. There are now also other types of logic, known as multivalued, to do with propositions that are capable of other values. However, such areas of thought are only relatively recent developments.

The logic with which we have been concerned in the "sociologist" game is basically very traditional (Aristotelian and medieval), in the algebraic and formal mould in which it has been shaped for the last two centuries (and known therefore as "mathematical logic").

Mathematical logic has so far proved to be the most powerful instrument for formulating a rational systematization of the various scientific disciplines. Within the realm of ideas it has furnished concepts and methods appropriate to the basics of mathematics and has shed much light on the rational structure of that discipline. At the same time it has also supplied the other sciences with models for their respective ordering and analysis of the raw material of experience. This has been particularly so in physics, chemistry, biology, medicine, psychology, and law. Finally, it is worth reminding ourselves of the role of logic in computer electronics, cybernetics, and automation in general. One need only look around one to realize how greatly both "pure" and applied logic affect our daily lives, our work, our very culture!

True/false: an old dichotomy

We can in some ways say that civilization began when mankind started to transform his environment according to his own requirements, through agriculture and the domestication of livestock. So long as life was just a matter of hunting and gathering whatever was at hand, nature was a self-enclosed, passive reality. Now, however, mankind's attitude towards it changed; it became a dynamic reality, in which he could intervene and make changes according to his own desires.

This change implies a certain qualitative shift of thinking: it was now understood that some of the workings of nature could be comprehended. More

generally speaking, the transition from a nomadic existence to an agricultural way of life also saw a transition of thought, a first elementary grasp of reality: out of the variety and infinite multiplicity of nature, man had begun to select and distinguish certain constants. It is interesting to see how the earliest "thought categories" went in pairs of opposites—hot/cold, male/female, death/life, bad/good, sacred/profane, and so on. Anthropologists note that a similar way of thinking in opposites is also typical of primitive cultures even today.

It is therefore perhaps no surprise to find the same manner of thinking in terms of opposites in early Western philosophy, among the first Greek thinkers: Heraclitus of Ephesus (c. 550–480 B.C.) saw objective reality as a complex of opposing elements such as—day/night, winter/summer, war/peace. The opposition true/false likewise belongs to this ancient way of thinking, although over the course of history it has acquired rich depths of meaning, finding ever more precise definition, down to the logical systems of thought of our own day. Such "opposition" forms the basis of the logic we applied in our games and stories in this chapter, which for this reason is known as two-valued.

Games of logic

Logic has undergone a long process of evolution, acquiring its own symbols and conventions, so that it has now become a rigorous and precise discipline. It has its own complex jargon and its own rules according to which it functions. Hence it has been able to alter certain aspects of normal language that it sees as obstacles. Normal spoken language is necessarily vague, nuanced, and has more than one way of referring to the same object or concept, because of the infinite variety of situations, individual states of mind and spirit, and objects of perception with which it has to deal. Yet this great quality in everyday language proves a hindrance in logic, which has to define everything precisely and unambiguously. Just as in mathematical calculations symbols and formulae are used, similarly in logic, "calculations" can be done in a more abstract way, without reference to the meaning behind the symbols. Hence the name "mathematical" or "formal" logic. The "formal" character of logical calculation lies in the fact that the same lines of reasoning can be followed to describe certain properties of numbers, a problem in geometry, in physics (dynamics, optics, and so on), or any other science. A book of recreational games is hardly the place to give a detailed picture of this symbol language itself. The questions posed in the next few paragraphs are problems of logic, which require no special style of calculation. However, it will be difficult to understand their logical structure, and so solve them, without a minimum of systematic analysis, without ordering the component statements under categories of F (false) and T (true).

Let us begin with a simple problem, in which the reasoning out of the solution can be diagrammatically illustrated (see figure below).

What colour are their clothes?

Rose, Violet, and their friend, Bianca, which means "white" in Italian, were very close and often used to go out together. On the last Saturday before the holidays, they arranged to have an evening out.

"What a coincidence!" said Rose as they met up, all in high spirits. "Our names are Rose, Violet and Bianca, and look at us! We're wearing just the right-coloured clothes—violet, white, and rose pink."

"So we are!" Bianca replied at once. "But look, none of us is wearing the colour that goes with our name."

"That's true," added Violet, who up till then had remained silent, listening to the others.

Now, Violet was not wearing white. Given this fact, can you say who was wearing which colour?

Simple reasoning will give us the answer. Knowing that Violet is wearing neither violet nor white, she must be wearing pink; Bianca is not in pink, nor

can she be in white, so she must be wearing violet; and Rose therefore can only be wearing white, since Bianca is in violet and Violet in pink.

Let us now try to express this in a chart, using the symbol B for Bianca and w for white, V for Violet and v for the colour violet, and R for Rose and p for the colour pink.

First, draw a chart with three squares on each side, both vertical and horizontal (see figure below).

Knowing that Violet is wearing neither white nor violet, we can mark F (false) in the square corresponding to that option (the intersection of the horizontal columns w and v with the vertical column V.

Since Violet must be dressed in something, we can safely mark T (true) in the pV box. On the basis of this information, we can fill in boxes pB and pR, and there is then little problem about finishing: Bianca being in neither white nor pink, she must be in violet; thus Rose can only be in white.

A mixed bunch

Six people find themselves travelling together on a crowded train. Three are distinguished-looking gentlemen (Mr. Valence, Mr. George, and Mr. Brown), while the other three are ill-dressed, loutish-looking characters with the occupations of thief, mugger, and layabout. By coincidence the three louts share the same names as the three gents. To make our discussion clear, we shall not refer to any of the louts as "Mr.," but rather by their occupations or surnames only.

What is the name of each individual lout?

We can work it out, given the following information:
i)   Mr. Brown lives in Bristol;
ii)   the mugger lives in a large town exactly half way between London and Bristol;
iii) Mr. George has five children;
iv)   of the gents, the one who lives in a town closest to the mugger has three times as many children as he;
v)   the gent with the same name as the mugger lives in London;
vi)   Valence can beat the thief at billiards.

To facilitate our investigation, let us construct a chart with the names of the three gents (V = Valence, G = George, and B = Brown) along the top and the professions of the louts (t = thief, m = mugger, and l = layabout) down the side. (See figure at the top of the page opposite.)

As in the previous game, an F (false) in the appropriate name-profession box will mean that our reasoning concludes that option to be impossible, and T (true) the reverse.

	B	R	V
w	F	T	F
p	F	F	T
v	T	F	F

Of the gents, one lives in London (v) and another in Bristol (i), at the same distance from the mugger. Thus it is the third gent who lives closest to the mugger. This obviously cannot be Mr. Brown, who lives in Bristol, nor Mr. George, who has five children—a number indivisible by three (iv). Thus we are left with Mr. Valence: Mr. Valence lives closest to the mugger. Mr. George, then, lives in London and therefore shares his surname with the mugger.

Now let us start filling in the chart: we can put a T in the Gm box, and this will then allow us to fill in four other boxes: two Fs—in the m (mugger) row corresponding to the names Valence and Brown; and two Fs in the thief and layabout options in the George column.

Let us now continue our process of reasoning. We know that Valence can beat the thief at billiards (vi); thus the thief (who, we know already, cannot be called George) is not called Valence or he would be playing himself at billiards. He must therefore be called Brown, which would leave us with the name Valence for the layabout.

We now only have to fill out our chart with two Ts (one in the Bt box, the other in the Vl box) and the due number of Fs.

Who is the guard?

Richard, Bob, and Nelson are the guard, driver, and steward on a train, though not necessarily in that order. On the train are three passengers with the same names (and again, for the purposes of distinguishing them, and from the employees let us call them "Mr."). Exactly one passenger and one employee each live in the three towns of Bristol, Tonbridge and London. Who is the guard?
i)   Mr. Nelson lives in Tonbridge;
ii) the driver lives in London;
iii) Mr. Bob long ago forgot all the algebra he ever learned at school;
iv) the passenger with the same name as the driver lives in Bristol;
v)   the driver and one of the passengers (a well-known physicist) worship at the same church;
vi) Richard can beat the steward at Ping-Pong.

Here, too, it is vital to make out some sort of visual aid, to see at each stage how much information we have been able to deduce.

Having thoroughly digested the data, let us see what we can make of the problem. Here in fact we shall need two charts: one (see left-hand figure p. 86) with the towns of residence of the three railway passengers along the top and their names down the side; and the other with the job names along the top

and the employee names down the side (see right-hand figure p. 86).

Let us start with the simplest deductions: clue vi tells us that Richard (not Mr. Richard) is not the steward, so we can write F in the box in the right-hand chart corresponding to Richard/steward. Clue i tells us that Mr. Nelson lives in Tonbridge, so we should put a T in the relevant square in the left-hand chart. Having done this, we can then write F in the other squares on the same row and column to indicate that Mr. Nelson cannot live in London or Bristol, since he lives in Tonbridge, and that since that is where he lives, Mr. Bob and Mr. Richard must live elsewhere.

Proceeding further, let us now take a look at clues ii and v together: from these, we gather that one of the passengers, a well-known physicist, lives in London—since he worships at the same church as the driver, who we are told lives in London.

But what is his name?

From clue iii we learn that it cannot be Mr. Bob, who has forgotten all the algebra he ever learned at school; nor can it be Mr. Nelson, who we already know lives in Tonbridge. It must therefore be Mr. Richard, so we can mark T in the Mr. Richard/London box in the left-hand chart, and F in the other squares belonging to that row and column.

Examination of this chart will now tell us a new fact: since it is the only square still empty, we can be sure that Mr. Bob lives in Bristol. Thus the chart can be completed with a T in this box.

The final deductions are not difficult. Clue iv tells

	Tonbridge	London	Bristol
Mr. Richard	F	T	F
Mr. Bob	F	F	T
Mr. Nelson	T	F	F

	guard	driver	steward
Richard	T	F	F
Bob	F	T	F
Nelson	F	F	T

us that the driver's name is Bob (Mr. Bob, we know, lives in Bristol). Thus a T can be placed in the square corresponding to the combination Bob/driver, and F in the other squares of the same row and column, as before. The steward must be Nelson; hence the guard must be called Richard.

Only one sort of logic?

The word "logic" is used in different ways. Here it has always been used in its most common meaning —as a science, a coherent and rigorous discipline. Even someone with the vaguest notion of what logic is probably thinks of it in terms of reasoning and associates it with coherent thinking; in this sense, "logic" is more or less interchangeable with "reasonable" or "rational."

Logic is concerned with the rules of correct reasoning: when these rules are those of inference, one talks of "deductive" logic. The mental teasers in the last few paragraphs were based on an intuitive use of such logic—a method of reasoning towards a *conclusion* by way of *premises*: the premises in our case being the stories themselves and the clues, and the conclusion simply the solution finally arrived at as a result of a process of inevitable, necessary step-by-step thought. Thus it may be said that the conclusion was a *logical consequence* of those premises.

Let us follow the examples of reasoning below:

Premises   *I) The only type of beans contained in this bag are black Mexican beans;*
II) The beans in my hand are from that bag.

Conclusion   *III) Thus these beans are black Mexican beans.*

It is easy to see the necessary link between premises i and ii and the conclusion, iii.

There are cases, however, when the conclusion is not wholly correct, even though the premises are quite correct. There can be degrees of correctness: of *probability*.

Take the following example:

Premises   *I) Stephen is a young eighteen-year-old athlete;*
II) Stephen has pulled a muscle.

Conclusion   *III) Thus Stephen will not run the 200 in twenty seconds tomorrow.*

Between premises and conclusion here there is not the necessity that was apparent in the previous example: it is probable, but not 100 percent certain, that Stephen will not run the 200 in twenty seconds tomorrow.

A tough case for Inspector Bill

A spectacular theft from the vaults of a major bank had occurred: almost every security box had been cleaned out, and the villains had skedaddled with a tidy fortune. When Inspector Bill began his investigations, the situation was not easy. The thieves had obviously been skilled professionals, and the only traces they had left were those that could not be removed. These tracks led to a street running alongside the bank: truck marks were still visible on the tarmac. Obviously, then, the thieves had used a getaway truck. From this slender clue, a long and patient investigation eventually led to the arrest of three young men: "Fingers" Freddy, the lock picker; "Hairy" Barry (so-called because of his distinctive mustache); and "Handy" Tony, a quiet lad, the smoothest handbag snatcher in town.

The inspector knew that one or all of them were the guilty ones. He had only to sift through his findings and order them correctly to be able to identify at least one villain. Eventually he was able to set out the following facts:

i) Nobody was involved in the theft other than Freddy, Barry, and Tony.
ii) Tony never operates without Freddy (sometimes also with Barry, but never alone).
iii) Barry cannot drive a truck.

Which of the three could be definitely accused? Inspector Bill proceeded along these lines: Let us suppose that Barry is innocent; in that case, Freddy or/and Tony must be guilty; on the other hand, if Barry is guilty, then he must have had either Freddy or Freddy and Tony together as accomplices; hence again, we are pointed toward Freddy or Freddy and Tony together. Thus, whether Barry is innocent or guilty, Freddy at least must be guilty.

Let us now concentrate on Tony and Freddy: If Tony is innocent, then Freddy must be guilty (given that clue i tells us that only Freddy, Barry, and Tony are involved); and if Tony is guilty, Freddy must still necessarily be so, too, given clue ii.

The inspector thus charges Freddy, since whoever else might have been involved, he must certainly have been guilty.

Here is an example of deductive reasoning in which the conclusion is a logical consequence of the premises).

A problem of logical deduction

We are so accustomed to reasoning in words that we forget there may be other ways in which thought can proceed. We can be rational without using verbal language. As an illustration of this, here is a little game that can be considered a visual test in logical deduction. We first look carefully at a series of figures (*a, b, c*) that develop according to a "logic" that is purely visual:

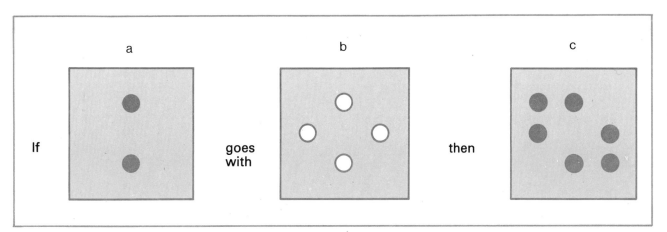

The same sequence is continued logically in one of the figures in the series below, which together constitute all the possible developments.

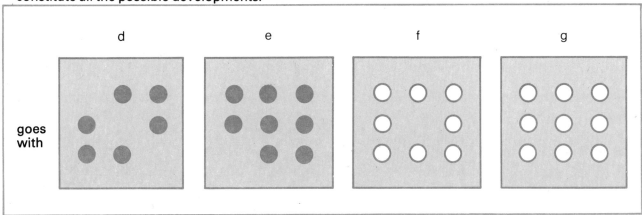

The problem is to identify which of *figures d, e, f,* and *g* follows best in the same sequence. It should not be hard to see that it must be *f*. But let us explore the deductions that lead us to that conclusion. First, it is clear that the circles should not be all red, since in the series *a, b, c* they alternate red-white-red. Thus *d* and *e* are out. As well as the alternation of red and white, we then see that *figure b* has two circles more than *a*, and *c* two more than *b*: thus *g*, which has three circles more than *c*, must also be out. Only *f* remains. Another element is then also to be noted: the circles within the figures are increased symmetrically, two by two; thus the two circles added to *b*, which go to make *c*, find a symmetrical increase only in *figure f*.

What sort of reasoning is this?

By selecting analytically certain common features in the first sequence of figures (*a, b, c*), we were then able to seek the same features among the proposed continuations of the sequence. We could represent our reasoning process thus:

Premises   i)   If *a, b, c* have alternate red and white circles, and

   ii)   if *a, b, c* are constructed so that at each stage two circles are added in symmetry;

Conclusion   iii)   then *f* alone can follow on from *a, b, c*!

Note how in the mental process that takes us from *a, b, c* (premises i and ii) to *figure f* (the conclusion), we have made an arithmetical calculation, however basic. And mathematics is only one of the languages in which we express ourselves. However, the fact that any calculation, or information, formulated in any kind of "language," can be represented verbally is taken by psychologists to show the greater wholeness, versatility, and adaptability of verbal language. It is not possible to explore the very depths of the human mind; but we may be certain that it works in an integrated and integrating way, as though distinctions of language—which the process of analysis constrains us to use—did not exist.

Reasoning with figures

Here is a series of tests for anyone who wishes to exercise their faculty for deductive logic. Similar to the previous game, they are taken from intelligence tests and arranged in increasing order of difficulty. However, the reader should approach them as a game, for the sheer enjoyment of it. Thus there are no final scores—the results are solely for the reader's own benefit, to interpret as he or she wills. (The answers are given on p. 92.)

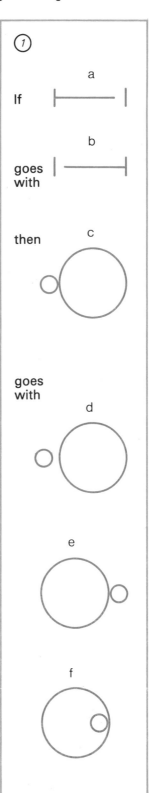

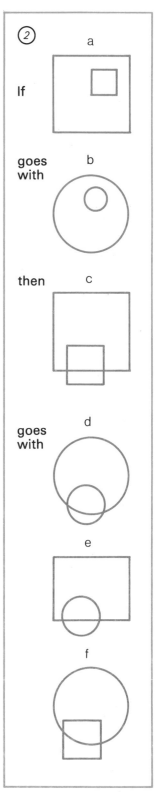

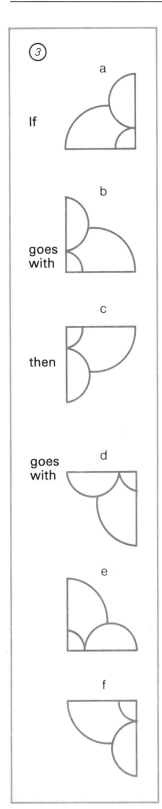

3

a

If

b

goes
with

c

then

d

goes
with

e

f

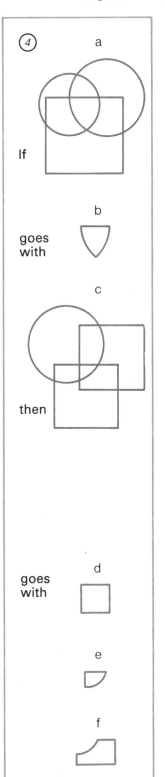

4

a

If

b

goes
with

c

then

d

goes
with

e

f

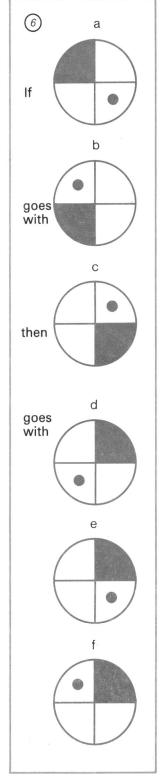

5

a

If

b

goes
with

c

then

d

goes
with

e

f

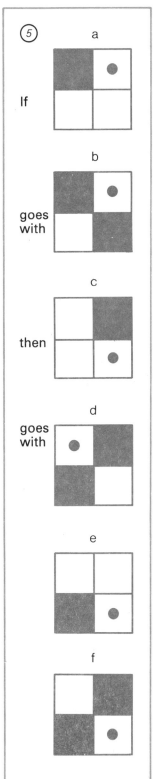

6

a

If

b

goes
with

c

then

d

goes
with

e

f

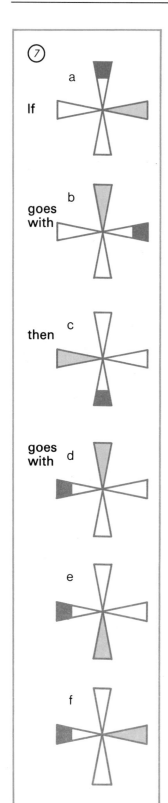

(7)

a

If

b

goes with

then c

goes with d

e

f

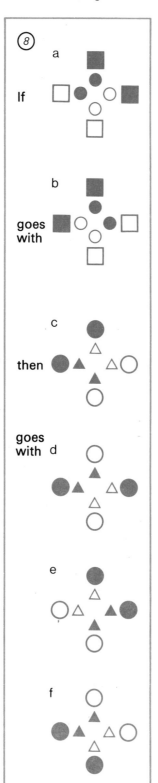

(8)

a

If

b

goes with

then c

goes with d

e

f

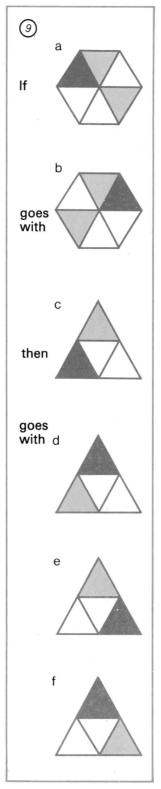

(9)

a

If

b

goes with

then c

goes with d

e

f

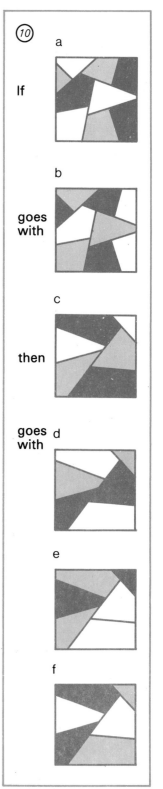

(10)

a

If

b

goes with

then c

goes with d

e

f

The game of true and false

Reasoning consists in moving from one or more premises to a conclusion. Usually such movement is undertaken in verbal language.

Here is a series of premises and optional conclusions, arranged in increasing order of difficulty. In the first ones, the solution will be fairly obvious; the later ones may require more reflection. The test is to identify which of the suggested possible conclusions must logically be the correct one. If only one conclusion is suggested, the reader must determine whether it is correct or not. True or false.

Study the following example:

Premises	I) If the stars are out this evening, tomorrow will be fine; II) the stars are out this evening.
Conclusions	III) So tomorrow will be cloudy. IV) So tomorrow evening they will be out again. V) So tomorrow will be fine.

It is not difficult to see that only conclusion V can be logically true, and that III and IV must be false.

Now you try! (Answers on p. 92.)

1

Premises	I) I am heavier than Charles. II) Charles is heavier than George.
Conclusions	III) George is heavier than me. IV) So I am heavier than George. V) So George and I are the same weight.

2

Premises	I) Ted is not yet eighteen. II) But Ted is an athlete.
Conclusion	III) So Ted will not vote in the next elections.

3

Premises	I) Nicholas lives between the stadium and the town center. II) The stadium is between the town center and the railway station.
Conclusions	III) The stadium is nearer to Nicholas's home than to the station. IV) Nicholas lives between the town center and the station. V) Nicholas lives nearer to the stadium than to the station.

4

Premises	I) Everybody in the sixth form failed their exams. II) Mary is in the sixth form.
Conclusion	III) So Mary failed her exams.

5

Premises	I) Some children have been vaccinated against German measles. II) But all have been vaccinated against polio.
Conclusions	III) So some children have been vaccinated either against German measles or against polio. IV) So some children have been vaccinated both against German measles and against polio.

6

Premises	I) All Capuchin monkeys have prehensile tails. II) This opossum has a prehensile tail.
Conclusion	III) So this opossum is a Capuchin monkey.

Correct but not true, true but incorrect!

Let us see whether the following lines of argument are true or false:

a) *Premises*   *I) All cats can fly.*
II) Fufi is a cat.

Conclusion   *III) So Fufi can fly.*

b) *Premises*   *I) Summer is the hottest season.*
II) But Atlantis never existed.

Conclusion   *III) So the Nile is the longest river in the world.*

We can start by distinguishing the two modes of reasoning: in the first, a), the conclusion is not true, because the premises are not true, even though the reasoning is impeccable. Meanwhile the second, b), has a true conclusion, but nobody could claim that the reasoning is correct. Why not?

Common sense should tell us that the validity or correctness of an argument and the truth (or falsehood) of a conclusion are distinct elements, since it is possible to reach false conclusions from correct reasoning and true conclusions from bad reasoning. Thus it is necessary to distinguish truth from "correctness": one does not necessarily imply the other. Correctness is a requisite of the "form" of any line of thought, regardless of the content (true or false) of the premises and the conclusion. Truth is what we are concerned with in the conclusion. Nevertheless truth and correctness are not totally disassociated: for the "formal structure" of an argument is correct or valid so long as true conclusions emerge from true premises.

Answers to the tests on pp. 88–90

1) e: if the line with the perpendicular section attached on the left (a) goes with the line with a perpendicular section attached on the right (b), then the larger circle with the smaller circle on its left (c) must similarly become (e)—in which the smaller circle has moved to the right of the larger one.

2) d: if the square containing a smaller square in its top right-hand corner (a) corresponds to a circle also containing a smaller version of itself in the top right (b), then a square with the bottom line intersected perpendicularly by the sides of a smaller square (c) must correspond to d—a circle intersected at the bottom on the left by a smaller circle. (Note how, in translating into verbal language the mental steps we have already taken regarding these geometrical figures, it all seems more complicated: what the eye immediately absorbs and transfers to other figures, now become ponderous descriptions of exact characteristics.)

3) f: there is symmetry between a and b, which is continued only in f.

4) e: as b is the element common to all the geometrical figures making up a (which is formed of two circles and a square), so e is to c. This test is slightly harder because it is not immediately obvious which features of a recur in b; thus some reflection is needed to discern the same correlation between c and e.

5) f: the red ball is in the same position in both a and b—as it is, too, in c and f.

6) d: while the red section moves one-quarter anticlockwise, the red ball moves 180 degrees.

7) e: the pink arm moves 90 degrees anticlockwise, the red-and-white arm moves clockwise 90 degrees.

8) f: the circles in a and b rotate clockwise, and the little outer squares anticlockwise; thus the correspondent to c must be f, in which the inner triangles have moved clockwise and the small outer circles anticlockwise. Another correct answer would be e. For b can also be seen as symmetrical with a, so it would be fair to choose e as being the mirror image of c.

9) e: if we trace a vertical line through the middle of the two hexagons, we find that a and b are symmetrical; similarly, e is symmetrical with c.

10) d: the red sections in b are where the pink were in a; the pink are in the places that were white, and white has become red!

Discussion of answers to the tests on p. 91

1) The only true conclusion is IV. The others contradict the premises. To reach the logically correct conclusion, we have applied a form of reasoning similar to that employed in mathematics: if A is greater than B, and B greater than C, then A is greater than C.

2) The suggested conclusion (III) is not necessarily correct, since premise II is irrelevant to it.

3) IV is the correct conclusion: since both III and V introduce an element of closeness/distance that is not to be found in the premises.

4) Even intuitively we can sense that the correct answer must be III: this kind of argument, which follows a typical form of "All A is B; all B is C; therefore all A is C" is known as a *syllogism*.

5) The logically correct conclusion is IV, since if all children have been vaccinated against polio and only some against German measles, it follows that some must have been vaccinated against both diseases.

6) The conclusion is not true: an opossum cannot change into a Capuchin monkey. It is a faulty syllogism.

Areas without bounds

"I should have more faith," he said; "I ought to know by this time that, when a fact appears opposed to a long train of deductions it invariably proves to be capable of bearing some other interpretation."

Sir Arthur Conan Doyle

Against the mechanical

It is easy to split the mind's capabilities into different areas, reflecting the activities by which area of ability is measured. This can be of some practical benefit: for example, someone who is good at motor-visual tests (for example, good at recognizing shapes and colours, and manipulating them) is likely to be good at jobs in which such skills are required. Similarly, a high score in word tests may suggest aptitude for work in which mastery of language and ability of verbal expression are important. However, these distinctions are somewhat artificial and limited in value. For any prognosis of this kind to be fully reliable, it is necessary to take the whole personality into consideration. The human mind is not, after all, divided into watertight compartments. Rather, the categories through which the "functioning" of the mind can be analyzed are created for the convenience of the observer (the psychologist, for example). Our daily lives are a constant interaction between present stimuli, past experience, states of anxiety or relaxation, hope, expectation, disappointment, desire for affirmation, submissiveness, and so on and so forth. And it is this continuous, complex interaction (of which we are largely unaware, albeit to greater or lesser degree sensing it through feelings—likes, dislikes, and so on—that we cannot fully explain) that deter-

mines human behaviour. Hence it is that predicting success or failure in studies, for instance, or in a job, is so often extremely difficult. And this applies to both individuals and the groups to which they belong, even when narrowly specific activities are involved. We do not of course wish to claim that predictions based on tests are unreliable; but we do wish to warn against a mechanical kind of interpretation of test results. As we have just said, it is necessary carefully to consider personality—interests, motivations, and the like—in order to understand (and predict) behaviour.

Such knowledge is only to be gained through study of areas of experience that are notoriously "fluid," such as success, love, friendship, politics, art, and ethical and religious feelings.

Mind journeys

The games, exercises, and tests that we have provided, relating to those aspects of behaviour that seem most closely related to intelligence (verbal, numerical, and visual skills), all share one common element. All concentrate the mind to find a single solution, out of a whole range of possibilities. Identifying the number with which a certain series continues, or choosing one drawing out of several that shares features in common with certain others, illustrates this point. When one thinks about it, it can be seen that the mind works upon several data, then "converges" on a single given fact, thereby "concluding" the exercise. Our use of the word "converge" was deliberate, because psychologists talk of "convergent thought" to denote one of the ways in which the mind works. An opposite way of thinking is called "divergent thought," whereby (as the term suggests) the mind works toward a certain "openness": from a small number of data, it seeks to find the greatest possible number of solutions, from the most varied and original to the oddest.

This broad distinction was first made by the American psychologist J. P. Guilford, who states that divergent thought is characteristic of creativity and the search for new and effective answers to the problems thrown up by life.

tion, continuing the genetic line of his parents and physically conditioned by work, diet, and so forth, and on the other hand the heir of a cultural heritage (the ideas, traditions, corpus of knowledge, and preconceptions of the society of which he is part). It is thus unrealistic to think of creativity as a faculty acting freely and untrammelled in the mind of the individual. Being creative involves ordering the world round about, and one's own personal experience, in a new and original way.

It is not easy to be creative. We often have to stretch our mental boundaries, direct our imaginations, and understand how to change already existent realities into new forms. And this implies the ability to step outside ourselves, away from our normal modes of thinking, to see and judge ourselves from a different perspective.

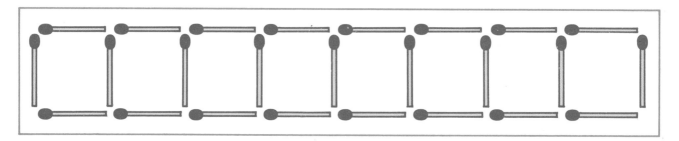

Imagination and creativity

Creativity is commonly associated with imagination. To "use one's imagination" means stepping out of the normal scheme of things and conceiving something new: work out the plot of a story, paint a picture, or even prepare a meal with friends, devise an interesting holiday, and, on a broader scale, build one's future and happiness for both ourselves and those with whom we live—all these activities demand the use of the imagination.

Usually, to "be creative" means to be inventive. Inventiveness is a faculty that takes many forms and suggests intuition, the involvement of an individual's inner life, motivations, and interests. As such it can be discerned in the most varied spheres of human activity, not only in art or at work, but even in disciplines that might appear to leave little room for imagination, such as geometry and mathematics in general. There is a common tendency to reduce creativity to mere "fancy," but to be truly creative, entails more than living in an imaginary world: it means freeing the imagination from past experiences in which it has all too often become enclosed and seeing new solutions to old problems.

An individual is a complex biologicocultural entity, on the one hand the product of natural evolu-

Two different ways of thinking: two different ways of playing

Matches are useful objects that, over and beyond the purpose for which they were invented, also make good materials for many games. This dual function can be taken to illustrate the difference between *reasoning* and *imagination*—broadly, that is, the difference between "convergent thought" and "divergent thought."

With twenty-five matches one can make eight adjacent squares, as in the figure above. A typical problem of, broadly speaking, convergent thought might be: How would it be possible to make eight squares using three fewer matches? One possible answer is shown on the opposite page.

Working above all with the imagination, divergent thought transforms cold geometrical shapes into real, colourful objects, giving them movement and life. The eight squares in the figure above can thus become the basis for a story such as that of the rabbit breeder.

The rabbit breeder. Rabbits having proved a worthwhile investment, an enterprising breeder makes eight cages (see figure above), each big enough to hold two rabbits—a male and a female.

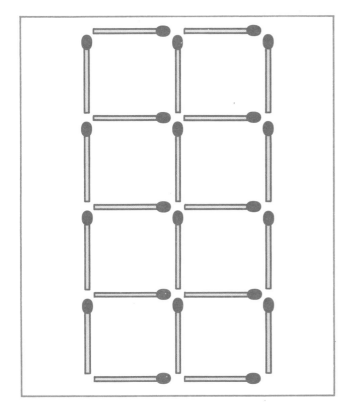

The eight cages were ready the day before market day, but during the night three sides of one were stolen. Still wishing to have eight pairs of rabbits, the breeder did not know what to do.

Was there any way he could re-create eight cages out of the remaining seven?

The solution is illustrated in the figure above.

Making up a story

The way we were educated, the values taught us at home and in school, and the experience of everyday living form a sort of "package" that we never lose. Certain ways of seeing things, of classifying and evaluating them, and our reactions to given facts, objects, and types of behaviour all owe much to past experience. As we have seen, an individual's creativity lends new significance to these preset attitudes. All too often, imagination and sensitivity lazily conform to such attitudes, at home in a world from which habit has rubbed off the "edges" of newness and peculiarity. In relationships with others, creativity means seeing the whole scope of a person's character, recognizing the variety and potential of those we meet, and always seeing them afresh.

Imagination and inventiveness can also make us see new uses for familiar things—even when very different from their intended function.

Geometrical figures such as squares and triangles, points and lines, generally evoke memories of school, mathematical formulae, and logical argument. Yet imagination can invest them with a new vitality, bringing them more immediately to life.

The story of the exclamation mark

One day Peter picked up his geometry book and began to read the first page, which the teacher had set for homework: "The point and the line are the basic concepts of geometry ...!" Often when he was doing his homework, he would be seized with

boredom and would go outdoors to escape the effort of schoolwork.

On this occasion, too, Peter at once started dreaming over his book. Then, as if awakened from a long sleep, the point and the line began to speak:

"I represent unity and perfection, and am the basis of geometry," the dot began.

"I reflect continuity, I convey a sense of the flow of time; without me geometrical figures would have no shape," the line replied defensively.

"But I give a sense of the single, fleeting moment; without me, time could not be measured," the dot went on.

"I convey the idea of infinity, of that which continues without ever stopping," retorted the line.

"But I give the idea of what is complete, the finite, I put a limit to things," the dot replied again.

"But without me no lengths could be calculated," countered the line.

"Without me, it would be impossible to count, and do calculations," insisted the dot.

This altercation was becoming rather long drawn out when Peter, admonished by his mother, began to reapply his mind to geometry. But it was so boring! Taking a pen, he started doodling on the book—and all of a sudden out came a dot and a line—an exclamation mark!

A square, a circle, and . . . a child!

Once upon a time, a square and a circle were seized with a terrible fit of boredom on their page in a geometry textbook.

"I am a perfect figure," the square began vainly. "A circle is really no more than a square blown up so the angles disappear."

"On the contrary!" replied the circle defiantly.

It was not the first quarrel between the two. And once they began, they went at each other hammer and tongs.

"I symbolize stability, solidity, and perfect symmetry," continued the square.

"I'm not impressed by your boasting," the circle retorted again. "If you want perfection, I am the most perfect curve, others are just poor imitations."

"My shape has lent stability and strength to the most enduring monuments," the square went on.

"But basically you're also the symbol of the static, the immobile, the ponderous, whereas I inspired the wheel, and we know what that invention has done for history. I symbolize movement and dynamism!"

The square had to admit that the circle was right and began to feel depressed, when curious noises were heard. It was a boy forced to study geometry, leafing through the book. As young students are often wont to do, the boy started to liven up the dull figures in his book. The square became an earnest, strong-looking man with a flowing mustache and top hat; the circle was transformed into the clear, smiling face of a pretty girl with beautiful, flowing hair and long eyelashes.

It is not hard to guess what happened once the boy abandoned his book: the square took a fancy to his attractive neighbour, and the circle in turn was not averse to the attentions of the mustachioed face with its eminently masculine conformation.

They remained happily in love for years, and even (it is rumoured) have had a child!

The long history of matches

What history can an everyday utility object like a match possibly have? We do not always realize that our acts—even those that seem most mechanical —are the outcome of a lengthy process of evolution. Daily habit has stripped them of all sense of historic or cultural significance. This is true of the simple act of lighting a match. Yet the origins of that little splint of wood, tipped with a compound that will flare into flame with the right sort of friction, goes way back. Its history is part of mankind's long endeavour to harness fire to his own uses. When documentaries show us primitive societies in which, still in the twentieth century, fires are lit from sparks caused by rubbing sticks together, we are reminded that our own ancestors once lived similarly, and that it is our experience of the effort and anxious strain (the fear of not succeeding in what one is attempting to do) of such a life-style that has stimulated our development. That is not to say that the invention of the match was the decisive answer to the problem of harnessing fire: nevertheless it did represent a considerable advance towards easier control of one of the most vital elements.

The discovery of fire opened up new possibilities of life and mastery of nature to primitive man, not just by making more food available (for instance, cooked vegetables became tastier and more digestible), but also by encouraging characteristically human behaviour—such as the sense of belonging to a group (tribe or clan), enhanced by being able to gather around the warmth of a fire.

For thousands of years, the problem was how to make fire readily available. It would take too long to trace the whole history of mankind's conquest of fire. But we should recall that, as well as rubbing two sticks together, there was another way of creating fire: from the very earliest times, flames were sparked also by knocking two flints together. The South American Incas had another highly ingenious device: with large burning mirrors they caught the rays of the sun and concentrated them onto some flammable material. For the ancient Greeks and Romans fire was considered to be sacred, a very symbol of the city. For all this, however, it was not until centuries later that a simple, quick, and safe way of "harnessing" fire was invented.

Advances in chemistry during the Industrial Revolution (late eighteenth, early nineteenth centuries) eventually led to the production of a simple sliver of wood, one end covered with a compound (of nontoxic phosphorus) that when rubbed against a rough surface burst into flame. The flame would then ignite the wood and so continue to burn.

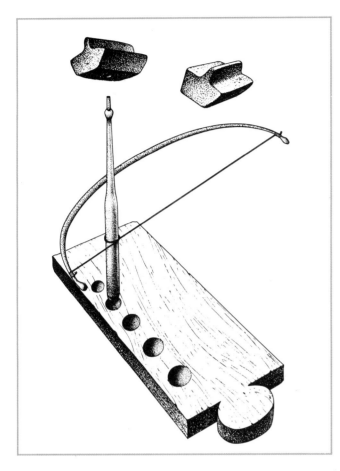

Above: component elements of the bow-type device used by the Eskimos for igniting fire. Below: the invention of matches (late eighteenth, early nineteenth centuries) not only provided an easy means of lighting a flame, but also supplied a source of materials for model making (bridges, ships, and the like).

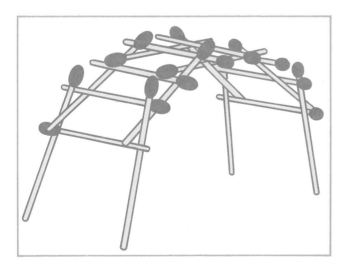

Matches: to spark the imagination!

Let us begin with a completely banal statement: some of the commonest objects lying around at man's disposal were stones. That is hardly the sort of observation that will set the Thames on fire! However, it contains an important cultural hint. Stones could be used for all kinds of things—heaps of things, literally—but they were also an aid towards abstract understanding, since they were a help in counting. The Latin *calculus* (and hence our own words "calculation" and the like) in fact meant "little stone." And of course little stones are the ancestors of the abacus, and of many games and pastimes developed therefrom.

The history of matches has much in common with that of stones: to begin with, they too were intended for practical use and have since come to be used also as aids to the imagination, in games of intelligence. This demonstrates how mankind seeks to resolve practical, material problems, yet at the same time feels an irrepressible urge to give functional objects some unfunctional significance, by playing with them.

It was above all in the twenties that games with matchsticks became widespread. Newspapers and magazines printed brainteasers, puzzles, and little figures all constructed out of matchsticks.

How did the little match girl die?

Hans Christian Andersen (the Danish writer, born of humble origins in Odense in 1805, died Copenhagen 1875) told the tale of "The Little Match Girl," who, on New Year's Eve, hungry and shivering with cold, goes to sell matches in an archway. A few people pass by, glancing at her unfeelingly. Nobody buys any matches. Time passes and it becomes colder. Unable to resist the temptation, the girl tries to warm herself by lighting her matches one after the other. Gradually she uses them all up, until eventually, as the last one burns out, she too dies.

Of cold? Well . . .

The actual history of matches perhaps provides a less moving, more prosaic explanation. To begin with, the flammable compound of the matchhead consisted of phosphorus, which gave off a lethal gas when alight. Only later were matches invented that used red phosphorus, which while it might have created a somewhat unhealthy gas, was at least not deadly. (The inventor of this was the Swede E. Pasch; further improvements also came from Sweden.) Thus we may conclude that Hans Christian Andersen's little girl probably died from a lethal dose of phosphoric gas.

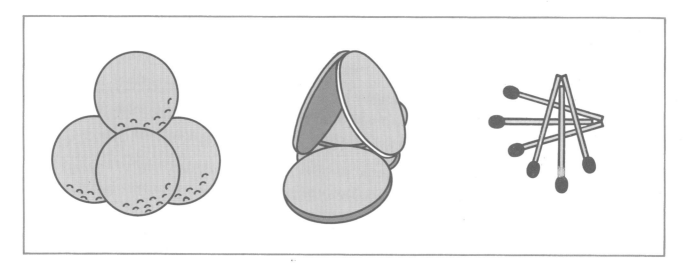

Four balls, five coins, six matches . . .

Four golfballs can be arranged in a pyramid so that they are all touching each other (see figure above left). In the same way, five coins can be so arranged that each touches all the others (figure above center).

Is it possible to arrange six matches so that each one touches the other five? (They must not be broken or bent.) The traditional solution is as shown in the right-hand figure above.

Animals and matches

From earliest times, the colourful and endlessly varied animal kingdom has stimulated man's imagination. This is hardly surprising: primitive man's very survival depended on animals, which provided raw materials (sharp bone for knives and the like, skins for clothing, bristles, and so forth) as well as food. Thus in the prehistoric era, walls of caves were covered with animal paintings. In the same way, it was perfectly natural that when people began to invent games with matches, designing formalized animal figures with them was one of the first of such games.

The top figure on the right is an attempt at portraying a stocky wild boar rooting for food. Imagine now the baying of a pack of boar hounds in the distance. . . . The boar stops and raises its snout. . . . By moving just four matches, the top figure can be altered to represent the boar sniffing the air, sensing danger.

Which matches must be moved?

The answer can be seen from the bottom figure on the right.

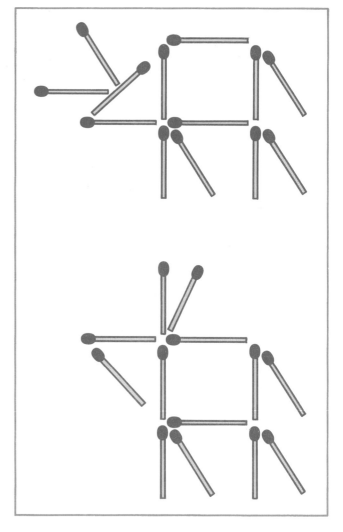

Art and creativity

A work of art is a highly complex experience, combining aesthetic taste, sensitivity, culture, vision of the world, and individual sense of being. It is often the product of hard discipline, accompanied by continuous objective, self-critical appraisal.

Artists are often thought to be "a bit mad," extroverted, sometimes rather wild, or at any rate not simply run of the mill. In fact, being an artist requires one particular quality: the development of inherent originality. The artist sees in a certain way and has the ability to order words, shapes, colours, and other perfectly normal elements of experience so as to create a unique and significant synthesis.

Scientists also exercise the creative spirit in the process of invention, of recognition of new functions and relationships, of acute observation of natural phenomena that are the common experience of all and sundry; it is present in the way new theories are expounded, and even more so in the development of advanced research programs, the evaluation of data, and the recognition of results that go beyond—or indeed sometimes actually contradict—normal experience and common sense.

Here it must be stressed that modern thought on science and the scientific method sees imagination as a fundamental component of progress.

However, it is not always possible to detect a direct relation between the spirit and scholarly achievement: it is not the case that the "intelligent" schoolboy will necessarily be the most creative adult. There are famous examples of scientists who were not "star pupils," yet turned out to be major innovators (the physicist Einstein, who revolutionized classical physics, is a supreme case). School tends to teach a ready-made culture, in which there is little call for personal imaginative contribution. Mastery of academic disciplines presupposes above all a good memory and the ability to reproduce classic notions. Individual verve, originality, and personal insight are rarely encouraged. Some research suggests that the most creative pupils are also the most independent, the ones who kick hardest against rigid restrictions of thought and conduct.

We should therefore ask ourselves: Is there some better way of fostering creativity?

Family life and school can both in different ways stimulate the creative spirit, above all by being open to the free self-expression of those growing up in them: growing up without fear of self-expression, their interest and curiosity in life will be enhanced, and they will be helped to develop faith in themselves and their own abilities.

A first exercise

The creative spirit manifests itself in the ability to synthesize old forms and structures anew.

Figures a, b, c, d, e, f, g, h, i, and *j* are each composed of one or more of the numbered figures above. The exercise is to identify the component numbered figures in each case (write the relevant numbers beside the lettered shapes). The shapes are not necessarily kept the same way around or the same way up. (Solutions below.)

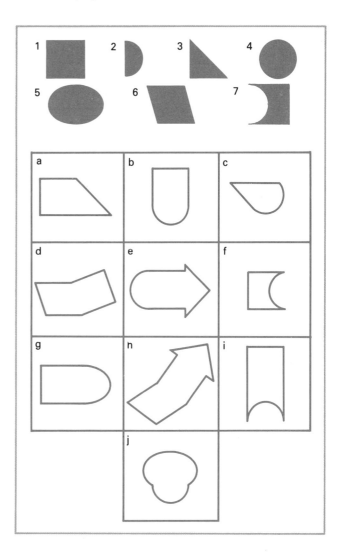

Answers

a) 1 and 3 b) 1 and 2, or 7 and 4 c) 3 and 2 d) 6 and 1 e) 2, 1, and 3 f) 7 g) 7 and 5 h) 3, 1, and 6 i) 1 and 7 j) 5 and 2

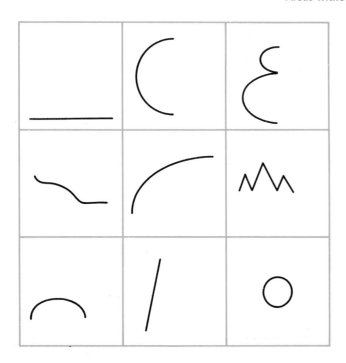

Re-creative games!

Can the creative spirit be enhanced?

It is not easy to answer this, as so many factors are involved in this aspect of "intelligence." As has already been said, imagination, motivation, im-

pulse, character, reaction to stimuli, and individual sensitivity are all fundamental. Exercises claiming to develop the creative spirit have been devised. On the other hand, it is hard to evaluate a faculty as many-sided as creativity. Such exercises consist of filling in half drawings (see figure on left) as fancy dictates.

Evaluation of the results is purely personal. Perhaps the reader would like to make some comparison between his or her own "results" with those offered below.

We suggest that the left-hand "results" below are less original than those on the right.

Success

We live in a society—or rather, a type of civilization —in which individual success is one of the key virtues. Encouragement to seek success is fed to us in various ways from our earliest childhood. Games very often are contests, with winners and losers, that make "winning" a primary aim. The mass media presentation of certain sports (football being an obvious example) promotes certain values, of which success is the greatest. Yet above all it is the educational establishment that promotes this ideal among the younger generation. Classification (for instance, in exams), scholarships, and selection procedures all in a sense give a "foretaste" of the life of adult society.

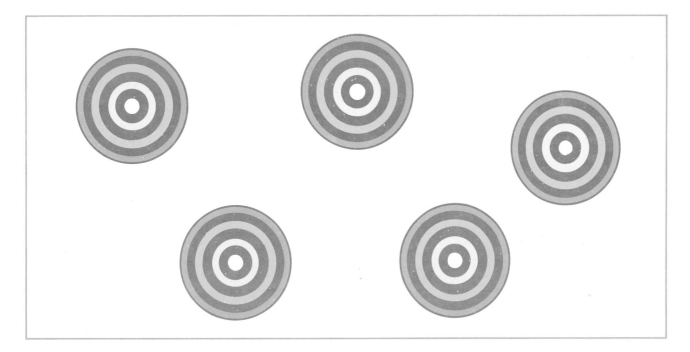

Is there an "intelligent" form of the successful life?

We have seen how individuals absorb the success ethos through various channels. Now our society is based, and survives, on the mechanics of profit making, which is an economic value. It is thus easy to identify success with economic success. The desire to be well off and aspirations to wealth are legitimate and positive goals. Yet there are ways and ways. And intelligence expresses itself in a balanced affirmation of oneself and one's abilities —"balanced" in the sense that there should be no clash with other values that contribute to human happiness, values that consist fundamentally in one's relations with one's fellow beings. An individual's instinct of self-affirmation, of self-expression at work, at leisure, and in relationships with others, can only be of positive value, a worthy means of self-fulfillment, so long as it is guided by reason and imbued with realization of true autonomy. This ideal can thus lead to individual happiness, and happiness also for others.

The game of success

To be successful in life, certain qualities are required. One of these in particular is very valuable: the following game will reveal whether you have it or not!

The figure above contains randomly positioned circles such as one sees, say, on a shooting range. Each player takes a sharp pencil and looks carefully at the circles for as long as desired, paying particular attention to their position. Then, eyes closed, and starting with the pencil raised above your head, try to pinpoint the center of each circle with the pencil, keeping your arm out straight—and your eyes of course still shut! You have five goes only, and only bull's-eyes count.

How many bull's-eyes did you manage to score out of five?

If only one, that does not prove that you lack this magical, unknown quality. If you scored more than two bull's-eyes out of five goes, this would suggest that you probably had your eyes open. To hit the very center of the target with a pencil at arm's length is so difficult that it is more a matter of chance than skill if you succeed.

It is highly likely that anyone seriously claiming to have scored more than two bull's-eyes was in fact cheating.

The most honest answer is much more likely to be no score at all. And it is this last answer that will reveal the right attitude for success. In striving for a goal, for success in one's job or an individual task, or for the highest score in any competition, there can be no justification for dishonesty, either towards oneself or towards others. Honesty will generate trust. And if we are untrustworthy, our life will be bound to prove a failure.

Work

"Less work for young people and women. . . ." "So many made redundant. . . ." "Unemployment: what is the government doing about it?" Every day we see the same headlines in the news. The economy seems to survive on the brink of crisis day by day, with unemployment, takeover bids, and redundancies affecting the lives of more and more people.

Such emphases in the news highlight, with true objectivity, at least the central importance of work in the life of the individual. There is no shortage of information on the disastrous material and moral effects of lack of work or job insecurity. All the more—since it is usually those in the weakest positions socially who are affected, thus increasing the psychological pressure—on young people seeking their first job, and women. Many experts agree that unemployment and drug abuse are closely linked among the young.

Work is clearly a vital necessity for any individual: it provides contact with others and a sense of usefulness—and hence of true participation in a given society or nation. Work provides a clear way of supporting oneself and one's family and hence is a major prerequisite for personal and familial happiness. It can both affirm an individual and be a means of self-fulfillment, and it can at the same time be humiliating, degrading, and frustrating, to such a degree that it sours existence.

Our day-to-day activities largely condition our daily "routine": a job takes up most of the daytime, determines our leisure time, and in effect sets the tone of our life. Our attitudes, our creative ability, our aspirations, indeed our whole intelligence are all directly influenced by the work we do.

Contemporary psychology sees work not merely as a means of survival, but also as a reason for living—an important way for the individual's personality to grow, through to some extent "finding itself" therein. It can afford a new satisfaction in life.

Of course, when financial necessity is the determining factor, then these other individual factors, relating to quality of life, come second. There is no longer necessarily the satisfaction that is to be derived from pursuing a career for which one has trained and in which one is interested. Those who find themselves obliged to take any job that comes along tend to end up with tedious repetitive work. Such jobs are hardly very self-fulfilling, and it is not easy to pursue them with interest, to find independence, or to become involved at personal level. Work of this kind is described as being "alienating." And if alienation of this kind is more than just a temporary experience, it becomes a sort of prison, from which any form of escape is welcome.

Capacity for synthesis

Different activities can sometimes be related to each other by means of common features. The ability to design new combinations of familiar objects, instruments, elements of a whole, figures, and even abstract concepts unites the engineer and the architect, as well as the technician, the mechanic, and the carpenter, who work at a more concrete level. The ability to recognize new forms and models, to relate parts of a whole to a different whole, to apply old solutions to new problems, and to collate information and reach coherent and substantial results, all suppose a skill in discernment, categorization, assembly, and manipulation of data.

This process can be described as *analysis and synthesis*—and is common to many human activities for example to the poet in the act of writing, and to the painter in the act of creating a picture.

Analysis-synthesis and breakdown-recomposition are thus two sides of the same process. The tests that follow below can be seen as games: the complete shapes (blank) are the product of a certain ordering (synthesis) of the (red) shapes below, which represent a breakdown (analysis) of the completed composition. With a pencil, sketch the separate (red) shapes within the blank one that go to make it up. (Answers on p. 104.)

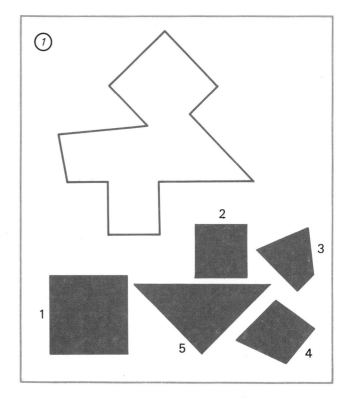

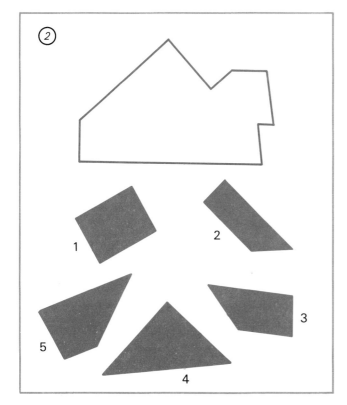

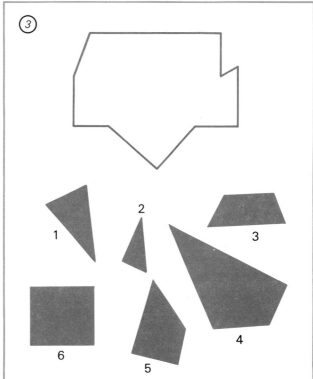

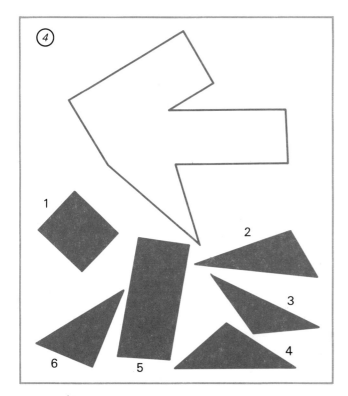

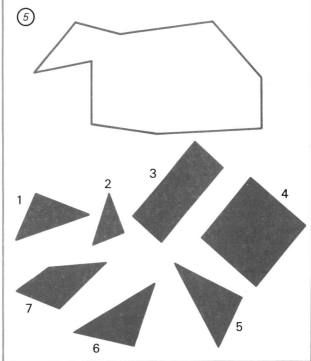

Answers

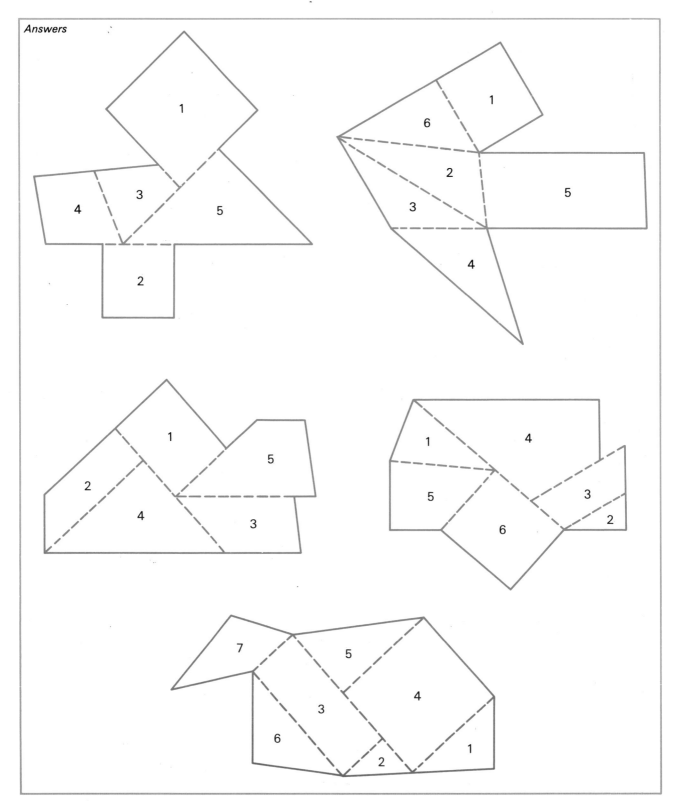

Technical aptitude

In our present society we are constantly coming into contact with the results of technological progress. Few of us live without a modern stove or refrigerator; cars, typewriters, televisions, and the like are normal features of modern life. Such inventions in some ways actually dictate our very environment. Even those who unconsciously reject them, and those who dislike "materialism," still find themselves having to face everyday tasks like tightening a screw or loosening a bolt. A certain technical ability—manual and practical—along with a mental "kit" of elementary knowledge are features of "normality" at virtually every social level. Some people, however, are vastly more competent at handling tools and mechanical instruments than others and can understand complex technology (again, a different sort of imagination is at play here) and design engines and electronic circuits that baffle most of us. Ingenuity and an ability to appreciate spatial possibilities and the play and flow of different forces are required. Not only does one need to be able to visualize but also, in one's imagination, reconstruct the component parts and the movements of engines. For example: a kind of spatial logic, of shapes and forms, is also involved.

The games below are an exercise to test your technical aptitude (that is, not just your skills with tools, but the ability to grasp the physical principles underlying all mechanics).

To start with, let us suppose that X, Y, and Z in the diagram above are cog wheels: X having twenty teeth and moving Y, which has 40 teeth and which, in turn, moves Z, which has one hundred teeth. (Assume all teeth are the same size.)

1. If X turns in the direction indicated by the arrow, Y will move:
   a) in the same direction as the arrow
   b) in the opposite direction
   c) partly in the same direction as the arrow, partly anticlockwise

2. If X turns in the direction indicated by the arrow, Z will turn:
   a) in the same direction
   b) in the opposite direction to the arrow
   c) partly in the same direction, partly anticlockwise

3. If Z does one complete turn, X will do:
   a) ⅕ of a turn
   b) 5 turns
   c) 1¼ turns

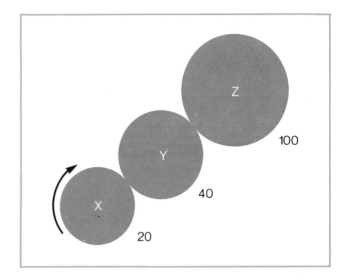

4. If X does one complete turn, Z will do:
   a) ⅕ of a turn
   b) 5 turns
   c) 1¼ turns

5. If X does one complete turn, how many turns will Y do?
   a) 2
   b) ½
   c) 20

6. If a fourth cog is inserted between X and Y, this will make Z turn:
   a) faster
   b) neither faster nor more slowly
   c) according to the size of the fourth cog

How is your mechanical skill?

To hold some types of jobs, especially in large firms, applicants are often required to take tests devised to ascertain whether they are suited to the relevant type of work. Once natural aptitude has been discovered, then of course there are other tests to find out one's level of acquired knowledge. Our exercises on the next page are simple tests of mechanical skill that nevertheless demand a certain degree of concentration and careful thinking.

Answers to the tests on this page

1) b   2) a   3) b   4) a   5) b   6) b

Answers to the tests on p. 106

1) a   2) the same   3) a   4) a   5) a   6) b   7) a   8) c

① Which pendulum swings faster?

a
b
both the same

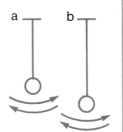

⑤ Which caterpillar track will turn quickest on this stretch of road?

a
b
both the same

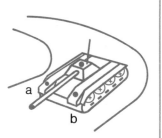

② Which section of the tightrope bears most weight?

a
b
both the same

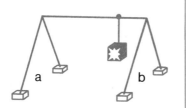

⑥ When the left-hand cog turns in the direction indicated, which way will the right-hand cog turn?

a
b

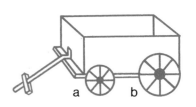

③ Which support carries the heavier load?

a
b
both the same

⑦ Which axle on the cart will turn fastest?

a
b
both the same

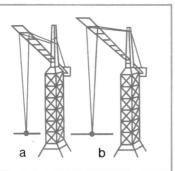

④ Which crane can lift the heaviest weight?

a
b
both the same

⑧ Which drawing correctly represents a clockface seen in a mirror?

a
b
c

GO

Considered by experts and fans of board games as the most intellectually demanding and fascinating game in the world, *go* is relatively little known in the West, where it was introduced around the twenties of the present century. (The word *"go"* is Japanese, meaning "fence game," or "control of territory.") Of very ancient origin, it was played in China under the name *wei-qi* or *wei-ch'i*, and in Korea under the name *pa-tuk*. It spread from China and Korea in the eighth century A.D. to Japan, where it became the chief pastime of the aristocracy (in fact, it was an obligatory part of the studies in the military academies that trained the young army elite). *Go* can indeed be classified as a war game (in the current jargon): but a guerrilla war game, a game of timeless tactics, unlike chess, which (if we accept that it, too, is a war game) relates specifically to medieval warfare, with its cavalry, foot-soldiers, king, queen, castellated towers, and so forth. Mao Tse-Tung, in command of the northern and central Chinese armies in the Sino-Japanese war (1937–45), wrote concerning guerrilla tactics in 1938: "Thus there are two ways of encircling the enemy, as in the game of *wei-ch'i*. The campaigns and battles of both sides resemble the way the pieces are captured;

the conquest of strongholds by the enemy and of entire areas by our guerrillas is closely similar to the moves to gain control on the *wei-ch'i* board. In fact, it is 'control of territory' that reveals the importance of the strategic role of guerrilla tactics in the enemy supply lines."

In Japan until about a century ago, the teaching of *go*, and the great *go* competitions, were financed by the state. The tradition did not then die out, but it survived in clubs and among experts who came from all social classes, no longer just the aristocracy. Still today there are many professional *go* players, some very highly admired, with their own complex ranking system to establish degrees of skill: the lowest is *kyu*, then *shodan*, then *rokudan*, *nanadan*, and so on, until we reach the top of the tree, *kudan* (a class very rarely awarded). The most famous *go* competition in recent memory was that played in 1938 between the last grand master Honimbo Shusai and the young challenger, Kitani Minoru. Shusai lost and died two years later, and some saw in this the end of an era: Minoru was the young Japan taking over the old, forcing it out, the Japan that was shortly to become involved in the Second World War and subsequently to absorb American culture, to the detriment of its own. One commentator to interpret this famous game thus was the

Japanese writer Yasunari Kawabata (born in Osaka in 1899), who committed suicide in Tokyo in 1972, four years after receiving the Nobel Prize for literature. Here he is best known for the lyrical novel *Snow Country* (Yukiguni, 1937), but the work to which he devoted most time was the novel *Meijin* (*The Master of Go*). Written between 1938 and 1954, it is a literary reevocation of the celebrated game between Shusai and Minoru. Kawabata had been present at the game, recording it and reporting it for the twin newspapers of Osaka and Tokyo (now one, *Mainichi*). He then reworked these records and transformed them into a story in which every move becomes an esoteric rite of arcane significance—mysterious as mankind himself. The old master officiates, a hieratic figure, symbolizing a mystery locked up in the mind. The spectators, breathlessly watching each move, seem caught in an ecstasy. Confucius, 2,500 years before, had already imbued *wei-ch'i* with special meaning and had recommended it to the Chinese nobility as one of the best means of keeping their minds lively and bright. Let us now look at the rules.

* *Go* is a board game for two players. The board has 19 vertical lines intersecting 19 horizontal lines, making in all 361 "points" of intersection.

Nine of these points are more strongly marked out than the others, and these are called *hoshi*, or stars (see *figure a*). In theory each player has an unlimited number of pieces, but in practice white starts off with 180 and black with 181. The pieces are placed in turn on the "points" (not in the squares), and once on the board they cannot be moved unless by being taken, in which case they disappear from the board. Black moves first (this explains why black has one extra piece).

* The aim of the game: each player tries to gain control of as much of the board as possible.

* A piece, or a group of pieces, is taken when completely surrounded by opposing pieces (see colour plate p. 109). Once taken, pieces are removed from the board and put aside (see *figure b*): at the end of the game they serve to count up the score. When encircling the "enemy," points diagonal to the "enemy" do not count: only those left and right and above and below can be used.

* If a whole group of pieces is surrounded, but 2 intersections still remain empty within the enclosed area, the group cannot be taken (see *figure c*). Cases can arise in which neither player wishes to occupy these two or more free positions, for fear of losing all their encircled pieces

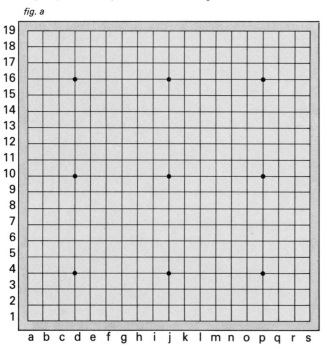

fig. a

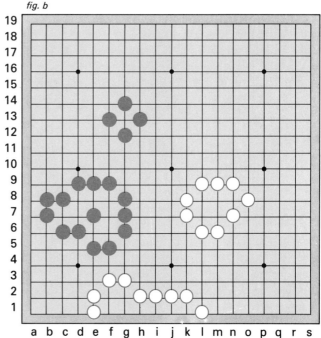

fig. b

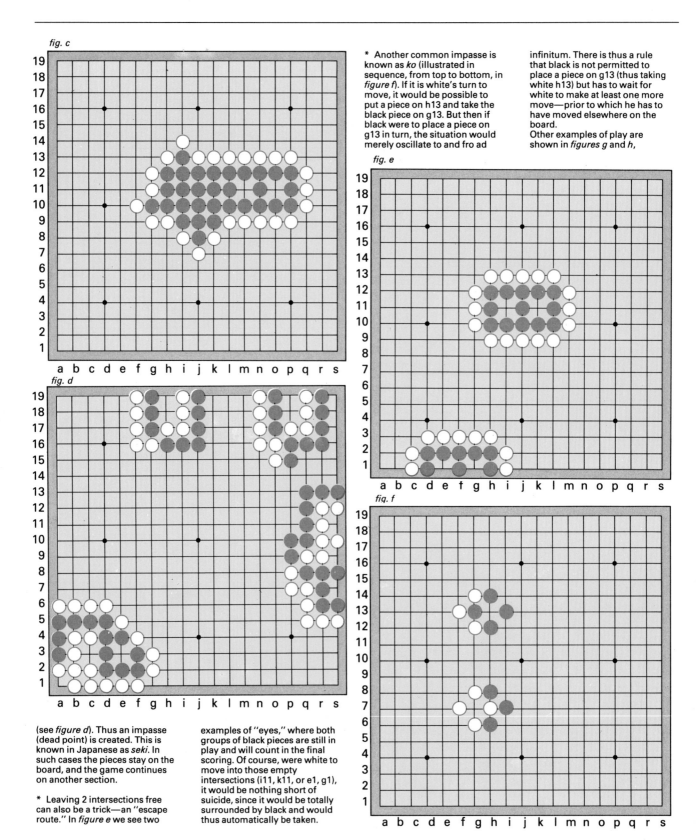

fig. c

fig. d

fig. e

fig. f

* Another common impasse is known as *ko* (illustrated in sequence, from top to bottom, in *figure f*). If it is white's turn to move, it would be possible to put a piece on h13 and take the black piece on g13. But then if black were to place a piece on g13 in turn, the situation would merely oscillate to and fro ad infinitum. There is thus a rule that black is not permitted to place a piece on g13 (thus taking white h13) but has to wait for white to make at least one more move—prior to which he has to have moved elsewhere on the board.

Other examples of play are shown in *figures g* and *h*,

(see *figure d*). Thus an impasse (dead point) is created. This is known in Japanese as *seki*. In such cases the pieces stay on the board, and the game continues on another section.

* Leaving 2 intersections free can also be a trick—an "escape route." In *figure e* we see two examples of "eyes," where both groups of black pieces are still in play and will count in the final scoring. Of course, were white to move into those empty intersections (i11, k11, or e1, g1), it would be nothing short of suicide, since it would be totally surrounded by black and would thus automatically be taken.

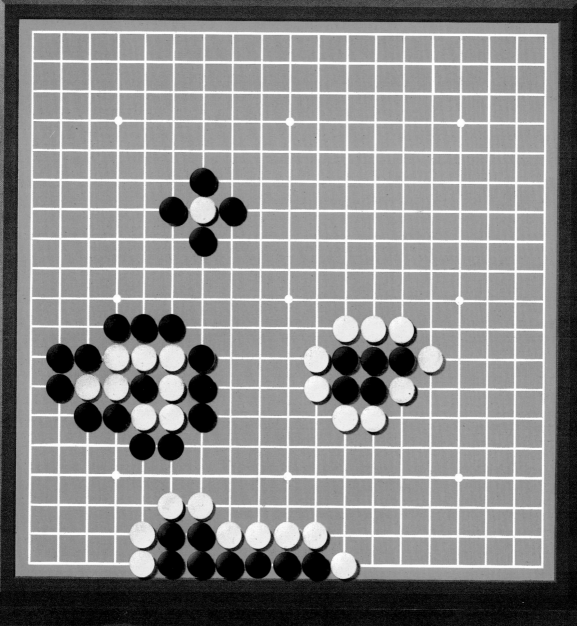

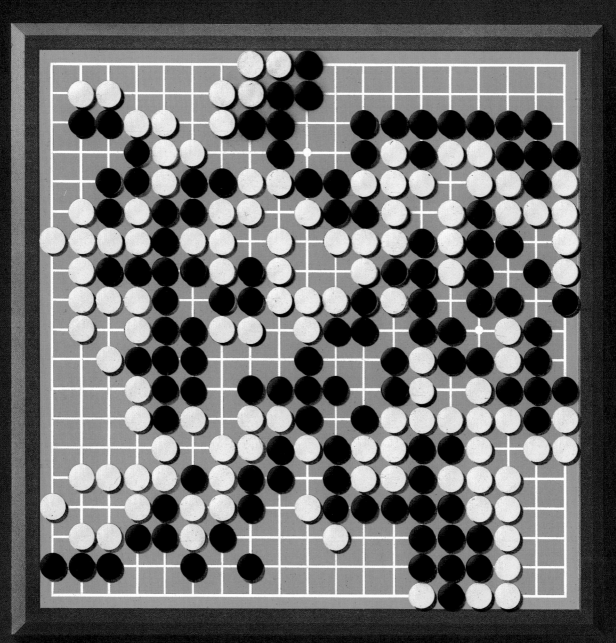

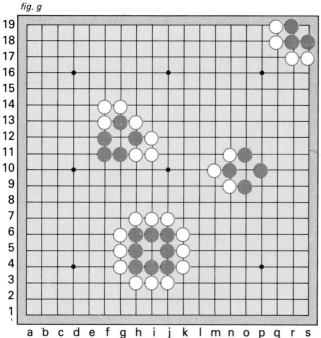

fig. g

fig. h

illustrating how a single move might be made.

The number of possible combinations in *go* is extremely high. It has been worked out as 10 to the power of 750—1 followed by 750 naughts. Here we are only trying to outline the main rules. Other rules will be readily apparent to the reader during the course of a game, as a logical consequence or corollary of what is explained here.

* The outcome of a game of *go* will depend largely on the skill and experience of the two players. If equally matched, they can fight on for a very long time and even decide to end with a truce. However, if one or the other is even slightly more skilled, the less skilled player can be completely outmatched. Thus, throughout the long history of the game, handicaps have been invented; predetermined weak positions for black to start off in, indicated on the board by the *hoshi* points previously mentioned. Black of necessity always has a disadvantage, since it makes the first move. But white's advantage can be increased by black's established scale of starting handicaps, which are as follows:

– 2 pieces on d4 and p16;
– 3 pieces on d4, p16, and p4;
– 4 pieces on d4, p16, p4, and d16;
– 5 pieces on d4, p16, p4, d16, and j10;

– 6 pieces on d4, d10, d16, p4, p10, and p16;
– 7 pieces on d4, d10, d16, p4, p10, p16, and j10;
– 8 pieces on d4, d10, d16, p4, p10, p16, j4, and j16;
– 9 pieces on d4, d10, d16, p4, p10, p16, j4, j10, and j16;
– 13 pieces on d4, d10, d16, p4, p10, p16, j4, j10, j16, g7, g13, m7, and m13;
– 17 pieces on d4, d10, d16, p4, p10, p16, j4, j10, j16, g7, g13, m7, m13, c3, c17, q3, and q17.

These positions are fixed. Only the inbuilt handicap of placing the first piece on the board (always black) enjoys freedom of choice of position. Whatever the starting position, the next move is always white's.

* The game can end whenever the players wish it to, or when all the pieces have been played, or/and when there is no more territory to be taken. The winner is the player who has encircled the largest area (the most points of intersection on the board). In counting up the score, each player takes the intersections enclosed by his or her pieces. Let us take a concrete example. In the colour plate on p. 110 we see the state of play at the end of a game of 241 moves, as described by Roger J. Girault (see bibliography at the end of this book).
The sequence of moves was listed as follows (+1, +2, and so on, indicating the number of pieces taken):

black	white	black	white
1 = R16	2 = D17	87 = N9	88 = P14
3 = Q3	4 = R5	89 = P10	90 = S16
5 = P17	6 = R10	91 = S17	92 = Q16
7 = E3	8 = D5	93 = R17	94 = P16
9 = C4	10 = C5	95 = Q17	96 = F11
11 = B4	12 = O4	97 = E10	98 = H10
13 = Q5	14 = Q4	99 = K9	100 = H14
15 = P4	16 = R4	101 = D15	102 = B13
17 = P3	18 = P5	103 = H17	104 = H18
19 = O5	20 = Q6 + 1	105 = J17	106 = J15
21 = P6	22 = R3	107 = C10	108 = B10
23 = Q5 + 1	24 = Q7	109 = J18	110 = N16
25 = N4	26 = C9	111 = L15	112 = K10
27 = C15	28 = C13	113 = L10	114 = K11
29 = C17	30 = C18	115 = F12	116 = L11
31 = D16	32 = E17	117 = M10	118 = M15
33 = B17	34 = B18	119 = K15	120 = L13
35 = E14	36 = G17	121 = N17	122 = O8
37 = E12	38 = F13	123 = N8	124 = D4
39 = C12	40 = B12	125 = D3	126 = C3
41 = D12	42 = B11	127 = C2	128 = B3
43 = M17	44 = L3	129 = B2	130 = A4 + 2
45 = L4	46 = K4	131 = M14	132 = N11
47 = L5	48 = B5	133 = Q9	134 = R9
49 = G3	50 = F4	135 = Q11	136 = N14
51 = E4	52 = F3	137 = M16	138 = N15
53 = F2	54 = E5	139 = M11	140 = M12
55 = F5	56 = G4	141 = R11	142 = R2
57 = H4	58 = G5	143 = R8	144 = P7
59 = H5	60 = G6	145 = S8	146 = L7
61 = H2	62 = H6	147 = K8	148 = N7
63 = J6	64 = J7	149 = L6	150 = O1
65 = K7	66 = K6	151 = O2	152 = R7
67 = J5	68 = E15	153 = S7	154 = S6
69 = B13	70 = B14	155 = Q13	156 = R15
71 = C14	72 = A13 + 1	157 = M7	158 = G18
73 = F14	74 = G14	159 = L14	160 = N13
75 = F15	76 = E16	161 = O12	162 = J13
77 = G15	78 = D13	163 = P1	164 = M6
79 = E13	80 = D14	165 = L8 + 1	166 = Q1
81 = J8	82 = H7	167 = P2	168 = P12
83 = H8	84 = F7	169 = O11	170 = K14
85 = F9	86 = R14	171 = J16	172 = H15

fig. i

black	white
173 = D9	174 = C11
175 = G11	176 = G10
177 = H11	178 = G12
179 = H12	180 = G13
181 = F10	182 = J11
183 = F8	184 = D8
185 = Q2	186 = R1
187 = N12	188 = M13
189 = S12	190 = Q8
191 = S10	192 = J19
193 = K19	194 = H19
195 = K18	196 = N6
197 = E8	198 = D7
199 = S15	200 = S14
201 = T16 + 1	202 = P5 + 1
203 = O6	204 = N5
205 = O3 + 1	206 = O7
207 = O4	208 = P13
209 = E7	210 = E6
211 = A2	212 = O9
213 = O10	214 = D10 + 1
215 = Q14	216 = Q15
217 = O16	218 = O15
219 = O17	220 = T14
221 = R13	222 = T15
223 = S16	224 = T12
225 = T11	226 = T13
227 = Q12	228 = T7
229 = S9	230 = J12
231 = E11 + 1	232 = M5
233 = M4	234 = F16
235 = T8	236 = T6
237 = P9	238 = Q5
239 = E9	240 = D11
241 = O13	END

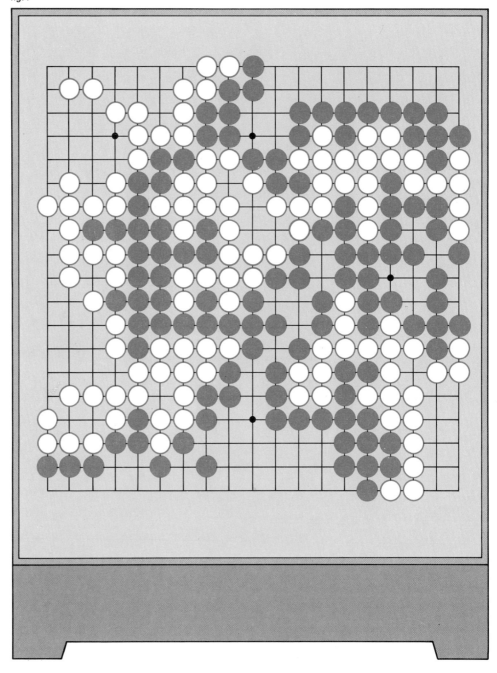

At the 241st move the players decided to stop, and as at the end of every game of *go*, they then had to "recognize" what territory each had taken, to establish who was the winner. This was agreed as follows:

– with one move at a turn, each player completed his "fences" (h13, i10, g8, g7, and so on), so that the situations of *seki* were also automatically resolved;
– then in the same way they filled up the neutral positions that neither could claim (g16, h16, n14, o11, a3, and so on);
– then they removed all the pieces that had then been "taken" (j6, j4, k3, and so on).

After this process of "recognition," the board looked as shown in *figure i*, and each player under the careful scrutiny of the other counted the number of points encircled by his pieces (that is, not the occupied positions, but—as we have already said—those inside "enclosures" of the respective colour). The result was 68 points to black and 60 to white. However, as white had taken 6 black pieces during the game, and a further 7 during the final sorting out, black had to deduct 13, to bring his score down to 55. White then had to subtract from his score of 60 the 5 pieces taken by black during the game and the 7 taken during the "mopping-up" operations, bringing his total down to 48. Black was therefore the winner. Written out like this, the game seems much more complicated than in fact it is. With familiarity, though, *go* becomes much simpler and more exciting. It is actually easy to learn, but very hard to play well. Luck has little part in the game. It is all a contest of logic and mathematical imagination, and this is what makes it such an educational exercise—helping the development and vigour of one's ability to grasp problems and see how they can be solved. According to Girault, "Only one other activity can be compared with *go*: that is, writing." Only in writing is there a similar (though indeed even more endless) complexity of combination of symbols.

Love

Intelligence as expressed in our relationships with others inevitably also includes our feelings. "Others" are those with whom we come into contact in our day-to-day dealings, but they are above all our friends, the "partner" with whom we share our life, and our family.

We have consistently described intelligence as a "unified and unifying" or "integrated and integrating" human faculty: hence it is not strange to think of it as also being at work in the sphere of feelings.

It is a widespread belief that love is one of the supreme experiences of individual existence, the climax of a whole process of physical and psychological maturation. It consists in self-giving, for self-enrichment; and as such, it might be thought to be the final stage of a long process of acquiring personal and social self-reliance.

Yet love truly means risking one's own freedom to reach full "selfhood."

The experience of love is not therefore a slight thing. Far from simply affecting one in any normal sense, or being the "final stage" of any "process," it becomes the basis for a totally new departure. When two people meet, fall in love, and decide to live together, it is as if they wished to start life from the beginning again. And this of necessity creates a dynamic of change, towards new levels of maturity, deep in the character of each person involved.

Here, intelligence takes the form of, above all, sensitivity, intuition, good sense, and balance.

A sad story

Geoff and Sally were a young couple, seemingly happy. They married a few years ago and now have a two-year-old son, John. Everything seemed well —he with a job that enabled them to live comfortably, she now having given up her job, looking after house, husband, and baby. To all outward appearances they made a happy family, yet things were not quite as they seemed. For some time Geoff had been returning from work in a bad mood, looking unwell, as if suffering from something. His relationship with

Sally had changed, there was more tension; quarrels began when Geoff started questioning Sally, almost interrogating her. Gradually the atmosphere in the home became unbearable. One sleepless night Geoff, feeling he could no longer go on like this, decided to take a drastic step: beside himself, he took a gun, shot his wife, and then killed himself.

We need only open a newspaper any day to read a similar horrific story.

Jealousy

In the story just recounted, Geoff's worries completely dominated him, to the point of deranging him and leading to a murderous and suicidal state. Jealousy in its worst forms can indeed lead to madness; reality is distorted, the person closest to one becomes the object of wild, accusatory fantasies, and the outcome is tragedy. The person suffering from jealousy has no doubts as to his sanity, there is total certainty that the beloved is unfaithful, or is at least prepared to be so. Suspicion, endless demands for proof and for oaths of faithfulness, harrying insinuations and inquiries, even obsessive supervision and, in some cases, trauma and tragedy, all can be unleashed.

One is reminded perhaps of the chastity belts that medieval crusaders used to lock their wives up in before they left for the Holy Land! Essentially it is the same defensive mentality, growing from fear of losing something or someone very dear.

A jealous person is emotionally insecure and unstable, with a need for certainty; yet unconsciously by his behaviour he renders himself impossible to love and provokes that which he most fears: separation from (abandonment, betrayal by!) the beloved. A clear contradiction underlies such behaviour. It is like somebody terrified of an approaching or even merely potential fire, who drenches his clothes with some other highly flammable substance.

In the same way as it is normal for most people to experience love, no one is wholly free of the danger of jealousy, which arises quite naturally therefrom. Just as envy is an indirect admission of the good belonging to an^ther, jealousy too is a sign of passionate and sincere love. It grows from awareness that all human good is fragile, and must be carefully protected. Kept within reason, and admitted tactfully and reservedly, jealousy can even be pleasantly flattering to the one to whom it is confessed. It can be a sign of a real love, rather than a mere abstract passion. Like other natural feelings, it can be quite healthy when thus handled: a means of more complete self-expression and self-understanding.

Othello and Desdemona in a scene from Shakespeare's tragedy. The very feelings most vulnerable to instincts of jealousy can, if intelligently expressed, be creative and fulfilling.

The following test consists of thirty questions, related to different hypothetical situations. At the end is a suggestion how one might evaluate one's own tendency to jealousy.

Who do you think is more useful?
– a road sweeper   A
– a private detective   B

Of these two characters, which do you like best?
– Othello   B
– Hamlet   A

Your cat purrs at somebody you dislike. Do you:
– like it the more for being sociable?   A
– vexed, chase it out of the room?   B

You are eating alone, and a piece of fruit falls from the plate. Do you:
– pick it up from the floor?   B
– sweep it away?   A

A friend has a terrible headache. Do you:
– try to comfort them?   A
– recommend an effective remedy?   B

Which hurts most?
– a slap on the face from the person you love?   A
– a look of admiration by the person you love to someone of the opposite sex?   B

Which would you prefer to invent?
- an invisible video camera   B
- a motor able to run on seawater   A

Do you feel happier:
- in a twosome?   B
- with nine or ten others?   A

If someone had seriously wronged you, would you prefer:
- to seek revenge?   B
- to dismiss that person from your life?   A

When you see two people of opposite sex alone together, do you assume:
- they are having a chat?   A
- they are lovers?   B

You have realized that the peach tree in your garden has a fruit-laden branch overhanging your neighbour's garden. Next year will you:
- prune the overhanging branch?   B
- suggest to your neighbour that you both share the jam?   A

A new national anthem is adopted. Do you:
- find it better suited to the modern age?   A
- rather regret it?   B

A young man or woman whom you do not know becomes your boss. Do you feel:
- that strings have been pulled?   B
- that a breath of fresh air was what was needed? A

To your mind, faithfulness is:
- a weakness?   B
- a virtue?   A

When you are introduced to someone of the same sex, does he or she appear:
- as a friend?   A
- as a rival?   B

Which would you prefer?
- a photo of your partner alone, but blurred   B
- a good photo of your partner in a group   A

If you were to go to a desert island with your partner, would you rather:
- find it peopled with helpful inhabitants?   A
- manage alone together?   B

What does the word "doubt" immediately suggest to you:
- a search?   A
- a trick?   B

If you catch someone winking at another person of the opposite sex, do you instinctively think:
- there is something between them?   B
- it is a sign of friendship?   A

As a guest in an unfamiliar house, you lose your bearings during the night. Do you:
- still try to find your own way?   B
- call for help?   A

You are invited to a card game. Do you:
- jokingly assure everyone that you will win?   A
- say you are no good?   B

Just before an important rendezvous your face acquires an unsightly pimple. Do you:
- Try to conceal it with hand gestures?   B
- confess openly that you ate too many strawberries the previous evening?   A

You have received an invitation to dine with the queen. Do you:
- phone the embassy to find out all about it?   A
- assume it is a mistake?   B

When your partner dances with somebody else, do you prefer them to:
- dance a modern dance?   B
- dance a set-figured dance?   A

A mosquito flies into the room where you are sitting. Do you:
- get up and fetch an insect spray?   A
- try to kill it with your hands while sitting?   B

You visit Napoleon's bedroom. Are your thoughts:
- of the nights he spent there with women?   B
- of his nocturnal musings upon war strategy?   A

Someone you cannot see calls you. Do you:
- respond without any sense of worry?   A
- feel a momentary fear?   B

While sunbathing on a boat, your suntan lotion falls into the sea. Do you:
- at once dive in for it?   B
- try to fish it out with a net?   A

You are on your own, looking at the moon. Do you:
- hope your distant beloved is also looking at it?   B
- wish you had a telescope to see the craters?   A

Would you prefer your partner to make a business trip alone to:
- the West Indies?   B
- the North Pole?   A

Now we come to the "answers" to this game, which will vary from individual to individual. Having finished all the questions, count the number of B answers you chose, then read the paragraph below that is appropriate to your "score."

0–5: You are not at all jealous. On the contrary you are tolerant, disinterested and unselfish. You do not believe in eternal love or grand passion. Ideas should, you feel, be flexible, never rigid, and you are not even concerned for your own comfort. It is not clear on what you base your life, and you are perhaps *too* disillusioned and cynical.

6–12: You are not overconcerned to preserve what is yours, either materially or emotionally, and this results in a certain coldness and a touch of cynicism. You are not above having a high opinion of yourself, and your own ideas are in your eyes the soundest. Everything else you consider too uncertain and vague even to be deemed a problem.

13–18: You have many doubts and uncertainties. You think one thing one moment and another thing the next. Sometimes you are a bit ingenuous, at others just indifferent and a little cynical. Jealousy comes and goes, and can flare up without real justification. You are not good at going beyond your own range, having little confidence in yourself and others. Do you try to protect your own sensitivities and do all you can not to expose yourself? By doing so, you risk concealing yourself from others and so making it impossible for others to get to know you. Even a little jealousy can be a good thing at times, as it can make us more interesting.

19–25: It would seem that your attachments are primarily to the realm of feelings and ideas rather than to material possessions. You can hardly be called altruistic, and you suffer greatly from jealousies. At times this is well concealed, while at others the slightest thing will suffice to set off the process of self-defense that renders you suspicious, greedy, or stubborn, according to the circumstances. Try to be more reasonable: it could keep you from many bouts of excess.

26–30: You appear to have an extreme sense of property, attaching yourself immoderately to the people and things in your life. This almost always distorts the way you see things and hence undermines your ability to make wise choices. You are perhaps more taken up with *keeping* than with *renewing*, and this can create a suffocating sense of anxiety—of desire for possession—that merely continues to mar your relationships with others. Remember that the first person to be hurt by jealousy is the one who has such feelings.

Games and friendship

In specialist jargon, "intelligence" is often associated with certain particular forms of behaviour relating to the ability to solve problems. We know, however, that it is fundamentally a gift of "integrity" —in that human beings are "integrated" wholes. It could even be said that there is intelligence in anything that is human: thus also in the way we get on with our fellows.

The search for happiness is common among human beings; and part of leading a happy life is enjoyment of friendships. This, however, entails a readiness to be open to others—a disposition and sensitivity that can indeed be described as intelligent. The attentiveness and love shown in the maintaining of an old friendship, the constant openness to new friendships, the personal effort of ensuring that every moment (the slightest gesture, or word, or request . . .) could potentially increase the sense of familiarity that is the basis of friendship, all these are expressions of intelligence. Of course, friendship is not wearisome in the sense that a serious problem may be, even though one's whole

being may be involved. It is more normally associated with an increased sense of freedom (we feel friendly towards those who encourage this feeling within us) and relaxedness. It cannot be other than intelligent to wish and discover how to foster the sense of harmony that makes the company of others so agreeable, to keep alive the pleasure of being together and expressing mutual happiness, and in general to create opportunities for human relationships to grow and strengthen. A meal or a drink together, or even a game played together with others, can become a special thing, involving all kinds of emotions, through which new and deeply based relationships may be formed.

Games remove obstacles, psychological barriers, uneasiness, creating among people who do not know each other very well the sense of pleasure in company that is the basis of friendship. They are also a good means of coming to know oneself and other people better, often providing a chance to understand sides of somebody's character that had previously been unexpressed. In such ways, games bring people together rather than separating them, making us wish to keep up contact and enjoy anew a form of pleasure enhanced by the presence of others.

Who is it?

Some games have the simplest imaginable rules, are easy to play, and are ideal forms of light pastime. For instance, games of question and answer: one version might be to guess the name of a famous person by means of ever more specific questions about them. To prevent the game from dragging on too long, however, there should not be too many participants. Here is one way of playing. One member of the group goes aside while the others confer about which famous person to select. When the questioner returns, he or she addresses the questions to each member of the group in turn. (The group should therefore not be too large! Otherwise, of course, it can be subdivided into smaller groups.)

The questioner usually starts by establishing certain basic facts: is the famous person male or female, alive or dead, imaginary or real-life?

It might also be worth their while writing down all the information they manage to gather.

In one game the following questions and answers came forth. (Try to guess the final answer before reading it at the end. Q = question; A = answer.)

Q: *Male or female?*
A: Female.
Q: *Real or imaginary?*
A: Half and half!
Q: *Dead or still living?*
A: Dead.
Q: *Did she die recently or centuries ago?*
A: Some centuries ago.
Q: *In the Middle Ages or the Renaissance?*
A: In the seventeenth century.
Q: *Was she English or some other nationality?*
A: Spanish.
Q: *Was she aristocratic?*
A: Yes.
Q: *Was she beautiful or ugly?*
A: Beautiful.
Q: *Did she have a happy life?*
A: No, unhappy.
Q: *Was that her own fault?*
A: No, more other people's fault.

Opposite page: good food and drink, in good company, and in due proportion, are expressions of an intelligent approach to life.

Right: a nineteenth-century print of the nun of Monza, one of the most complex characters in Manzoni's novel *The Betrothed*.

Q: Was she in the church, or was she a lady of the world?
A: In the church.
Q: Is it a character in a tragedy or a novel?
A: A novel.
Q: Was the novel written recently?
A: In the last century.
Q: The author is Alessandro Manzoni?
A: Correct.

Anyone familiar with Alessandro Manzoni will by now have gathered that the book concerned is *I Promessi Sposi*, and the half-real, half-fictional character must be the nun of Monza.

The game need not go on until the answer has been reached. It could be decided beforehand, for instance, that no more than a certain number of questions should be asked, or that no more than a certain amount of time should be allowed. Also, if the questioner suggests two wrong names, then he might be deemed to have lost. The winner would be the person to guess correctly in the shortest time or with the fewest questions.

Guess the person

There is another rather similar "famous person" game, a bit more complicated to play, in which the name is guessed through clues for each letter. One member of the group—either in turn or picked at random—goes aside for a moment, while the others agree on the name of some famous person, either from the past or in the present. The number of letters in the name should ideally be the same as the number of people in the group. The guesswork is not a matter here of moral qualities or physical details. Each player has to take an active role, taking one letter of the chosen name in order, then playing the part of some other famous character whose name began with that letter (each in turn speaking in the first person, to give the guesser a clue, as illustrated below).

The player who went aside, and who must now guess the answer, does not ask questions. He or she just writes down the initials of any names he manages to guess. If after somebody has spoken their clue he thinks he can guess who that person is pretending to speak as, he writes the initial of the name he has guessed in the appropriate place on a sheet of paper. (He has been given beforehand a sheet of paper containing a number of empty squares, corresponding to the number of letters in the name he has to guess—these letters in turn, of course, corresponding to the number of people in the group and their order of sitting.) The name

slowly becomes evident and can often be guessed before all the squares have been filled in.

In one of these games ten students had chosen the name Machiavelli, and took as their clue names Magritte, Ariosto, Caesar, Hitler . . . and so on.

The first one (Magritte) began:
– "I paint dreamlike pictures."
Then the second followed:
– "My poem was the rage at every court in Europe!"
And the third:
– "I brought my legions to the Rubicon. . . ."
The fourth:
– "I wanted to conquer the world!"
And so it went on. It is not uncommon to need to go around a second time, to give the person guessing another chance. So then "Magritte" expanded:
– ". . . like a man with an apple face. . . ."
Then "Ariosto" said:
– ". . . the main character was one of Charlemagne's paladins. . . ."
And "Caesar" continued:
– ". . . and I crossed it, saying, 'The die is cast!' . . ."
"Hitler":
– "I invaded Poland."

Part of the fun of the game is for the "actors" to portray their adopted character without saying too much. By the nature of the game, there is no limit to the amount of time it can take or to the number of clues the group might have to provide.

What is it?

Question-and-answer games are harder when the final answer is an object rather than a person: it could be an animal or anything concrete or abstract.

It is important to ask the right sort of question at the beginning, to obtain precise answers.

Here is a game played by a group of children (Q = question; A = answer).

Q: Is it concrete or abstract?
A: It's concrete.
Q: Is it natural or man-made?
A: It's man-made.
Q: Is it made of iron, or wood, or something else?
A: Of wood.
Q: Is it polished or rough?
A: It's polished.
Q: Is it ornamental or something you wear?
A: In a way, something to wear.
Q: Do you wear it above the waist or below?
A: Above the waist.

At this point the questioner stopped to think. Made of wood, polished, worn—in a way—above

the waist. . . . It must be either a piece of wooden jewelry or a small cross around the neck . . . or (why not?) a pipe!

So then he asked the decisive question:

Q: Do you wear it around your neck or put it in your mouth?
A: Usually you put it in your mouth.
 —Then it's a pipe!

The guess was right. But the group was still not fully satisfied; more details were wanted.

The questioner then continued:

Q: Is it any sort of pipe or a particular kind?
A: A particular kind.
Q: Does it belong to a famous person, either alive or dead?
A: A famous local person, alive.
Q: Is the person a public figure?
A: Yes.
Q: Is he a senior public figure?
A: He was a senior public figure.

Finally the questioner got the answer: it was the pipe the former mayor of the town was always seen smoking.

Yes, no

This game can be made more demanding by imposing another restriction: the answers can only be "yes" or "no." Since this obviously means more questions have to be asked, a time limit is set, making the game livelier and more fun.

Here is an example of this game, played by a group of boys and girls one evening:

Q: Is it a concrete object?
A: No.
Q: Is it abstract?
A: Yes.
Q: Is it an ideal?
A: No.
Q: Is it a belonging?
A: No.
Q: Is it a quality?
A: No.
Q: Is it a virtue?
A: No.
Q: Is it a defect?
A: Yes.
Q: Is it a feeling?
A: Yes.
Q: Is it normally felt for more than one person?
A: No.
Q: For one person?
A: Yes.

At this juncture the person guessing realized the feeling must either be hate or jealousy. It was important that the final questions should leave no room for ambiguity in the answers. Thus they became increasingly specific:

Q: Do you feel this feeling towards someone who has wronged you, materially or otherwise?
A: No.
Q: Towards someone you still love?
A: Yes.

So "jealousy" was the correct answer.

The hidden trick

Every now and again a little variety and novelty livens games up and stops them from becoming boring. In this game, what has to be guessed is not a person or a thing, but (at least so it is said at the start) a whole story. The fun and novelty of this game lies in an element of surprise: the whole structure of the game is crazy! How and why, we shall discover later, in the answer. One player, who obviously must not know the trick of the game, has to reconstruct the plot of a whole story. Any questions are permissible, but the only answers that can be given are again "yes" and "no." The game might start thus:

Q: Does the story have more than one character?
A: Yes.
Q: Are the characters young?
A: No.
Q: Does love come into the story?
A: Yes.
Q: Is it a contemporary story?
A: No.
Q: Is it set in the last century?
A: No.
Q: The Middle Ages?
A: Yes.
Q: Does a lot happen?
A: Yes.
Q: Is it boring?
A: No.
Q: The characters are well-known figures?
A: Yes.
Q: Are they universally famous?
A: No.
Q: Are they well known only to highly educated people?
A: No.

At this point the person trying to reconstruct the story may feel a bit confused. After a little reflection, however, he may realize that it is a "set-up job," and there is in fact no story. In fact, the group has decided together to answer "yes" to any question starting with a consonant and "no" to any that started with a vowel.

The game continues until the person asking the questions gives up or manages to grasp the principle behind the seemingly self-contradictory answers. The more imaginative and persevering the questioner, the more entertaining it is for the group —hearing a random half story emerge through the questions, from the questioner's own mind.

One player found himself faced with the following blind alley:

Q: Is there more than one character?
A: No.
Q: Is that character male?
A: No.
Q: In that case she must be female, then?
A: No.

On this occasion the questioner then went on to construct a glorious tale about a hermaphrodite, which is of course neither male nor female!

The analogy game

There are different variants of the guess-the-famous-person game. What changes is the style of the questions and answers. This version is sometimes known as the analogy game because the clues come through character analogies with plants, animals, and objects of all sorts. All the questions start, "If he/she were . . ." or, "If he/she had been . . ." and the answers, "He/she would be . . ." It is said to be particularly popular in the forces, especially where there is national service, when there are long hours of inactivity, combined with a lack of home comforts, and fantasy tends to be given free rein! Well-known film stars of the more physically alluring kind are thus ideal for this game. In the example given below, the name is that of a famous and beautiful woman:

If she were . . .	*She would be . . .*
. . . an animal?	a cat.
. . . a plant?	an orchid.
. . . a season?	a hot summer.
. . . an article of clothing?	a skimpy bikini.
. . . a colour?	a blonde.
. . . a country?	la belle France.
. . . a drink?	a soothing pint.
. . . a piece of furniture?	a luxuriant bed.
. . . a car?	a red Ferrari.

(The answer on this occasion was Brigitte Bardot; see photo.)

Who said . . .?

Friends who see a lot of each other or who live together get to know each other's good and bad points. An observation about ourselves made by a friend whom we respect and by whom we feel accepted helps us understand ourselves and improve our weaknesses, rather than irking us. Even when such observations are critical, the same applies. In fact, between good friends a game can be made out of each other's little foibles. The game we are now describing consists in a free expression of how friends see each other, or at least certain sides of each other. Everybody who plays has to answer certain questions. In turn or at random, one by one, each goes aside, so as not to hear what the others are telling each other about him or her. One member of this group acts as secretary, noting down the different comments that are made. Each member of the group has to contribute one (not more) observation on the victim's character. The secretary records all that is said and also who said what. Then the "victim" is invited to come over and listen to the secretary read out the various judgments expressed on him or her. After leaving a little time for reflection, the secretary then rereads the list slowly, item by item, and the "victim" must decide who made that particular comment in each case. For instance, the questions might go thus:

– Who said you are easily annoyed?
– Who said punctuality is not your strong point?
– Who said you have a mania about tidiness?
– Who said you are lazy at work?
– Who said you are bigoted?
– Who said you are too aggressive with women?
– Who said you never have a comfortable relationship with men?
– Who said you are a greedy pig?
– Who said you are always losing things?
– Who said you are not physically very wonderful to look at?

There are not really any winners here. It is more a game of mutual familiarity and confidence among a group of friends. However, it can be made more entertaining by imposing a penalty for every wrongly guessed name—every time the "victim" attributes an observation to the wrong person.

Also, the game can be differently organized so that everyone is actively involved. Thus, for instance, each player writes his or her name on a piece of paper, then folds it in four and hands it to the secretary (who still plays the main role). The secretary carefully mixes up all the bits of paper, then hands them around to the players again, going clockwise. Usually each member of the group gets a piece of paper with somebody else's name on it, then duly writes a comment on the character of that friend. If by chance you get your own signed piece of paper back after the shuffling, you can write some judgment on yourself. After this the secretary reads each name aloud, as it comes, with the attached comment. And again, the "victim" has to identify the author of the comment and pay a penalty if he or she is wrong.

Other variants can be dreamed up to improve the game still further and to help everyone become more involved.

Blind associations

There are many games that groups of friends can play. Here is one of the most amusing. Everyone sits in a circle, each person with a sheet of paper and something to write with, and simply writes the first thing that comes into their head—even if it makes

no sense. All that bits of paper are then folded, just to cover what has been written, and passed to the right-hand neighbour. Everybody thus receives from their left-hand neighbour a similarly folded piece of paper. Without reading the covered-up words written by the neighbour on their left, each player then once again writes whatever comes into his head. This continues until the sheets of paper are folded up completely. Obviously, at no stage should anyone read what has already been written. It is usual to stop after the sheets of paper have been around the whole circle. They are then thrown together, jumbled up, and redistributed, after which each player reads out all that is written on his or her sheet. Some of the associations of words and phrases can be extremely funny. But since everyone contributed to each sheet, there cannot be said to be any winners.

The sort of randomness produced can be hilarious:

– Will you come and have a meal with me?
– The moon is blue!
– Like a cabbage . . .
– Two's company, three's a crowd!
– She sells seashells . . .
– Why?
– . . .

A love story

Different things can be written on the sheets of paper—descriptions of an event, a meeting, an exchange of wit, and so on. The game then has to be carefully arranged. First of all, each player is given a sheet of paper and told to write on the top, "The . . ." plus some suitable adjective to refer to a man (handsome, charming, stumpy, audacious, timid, and so forth). Then the paper is folded, so that the words are invisible, and passed on to the next player, who (without looking at the adjective written by his or her neighbour) adds a man's name. It can be all the merrier if the name is that of one of the people playing the game! Other possibilities might be some common acquaintance or a name of some famous person. The third writer then adds the verb "meets," followed by an article and an adjective suitable for a woman (beautiful, attractive, hideous, alluring, and so on). The fourth step is to write a woman's name—again, of course, without seeing what has been written beforehand. And here, too, if the name is that of one of the people taking part in the game, it can be all the more entertaining. In general, the more players there are, the livelier the game is. The story need by no means stop here:

other actions can be introduced (such as they greet each other, they shake hands, they turn their backs on each other, they insult each other, and so forth); then "he said to her" and "she replied," and so on. If there are more than seven players, it is not hard to think up further ways of continuing the story. One small group of girls and boys came up with the following "love story," which prompted much laughter:

"The handsome Anthony met the clubfooted Bertha. They kissed. 'Did you bring the money?' asked handsome Anthony. 'I smashed the plates this morning!' replied clubfooted Bertha."

In itself it is not that funny, but it was far funnier in context: for one of the group happened to be the local priest—whose name was Anthony!

A macabre game

You only need two people with pencil and paper for this type of game. One person thinks of the most obscure word possible and writes the first and last letters, leaving blank spaces for the others. The other player tries to fill in the blanks, letter by letter. If he guesses correctly, the first player duly writes the letter down in the correct space. If his guess was wrong, however, his opponent starts to draw a crude diagrammatic sketch of a man on a gallows. (This game is often, in fact, called "hangman.") Thus the game continues until either the word has

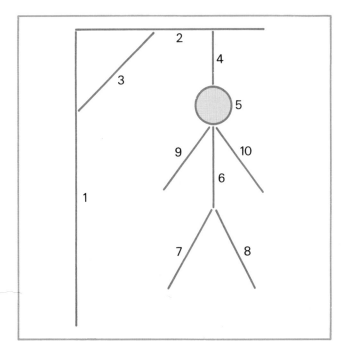

D	**O**	**W**			
.	.	.	.	.	.

C A R P E T	= nil
C O R D O N	= two
B U R D E N	= one
S H A D O W	= three

been guessed or the drawing of the gallows (see figure below) is finished. Hours can be wasted playing this game! And to establish a winner, it is worth keeping track of how many times each player is successful. On each occasion it is the winner of the previous bout who thinks up the next word. As the drawing can easily have fewer or more stages, you can agree on a maximum or minimum length for the word to be guessed. If the same letter occurs twice in the same word, it need not be guessed twice.

The same-letter game

The important thing in this game is to work out how to win, and then follow one's strategy through to the end. It is possible to play with many participants. Each player has a sheet of paper and a pen. One thinks of a word—either selected beforehand or picked at random—and tells the others how many letters it has. Each of the others in turn then suggests a word with the same number of letters. If in these suggested words one or more letters coincide (for example, if the same letter occurs in the same position as in the word to be guessed), this has to be declared—though only the number of "same letters" is declared.

To illustrate this, let us start an imaginary game.

Imagine that the first player has thought of the word "window" and thus told the others that there are six letters. Each of the other players then writes six blank spaces on their sheets of paper (see figure above). Then they begin to suggest other words of six letters: the first, "carpet," to which the response is nil, since there are no same letters. Each player writes "carpet" and crosses out the letters with a line. The second player then suggests, say, "cordon": this time the answer is two (the *d* and *o*—not *n*, since the *n* in "window" comes third rather than last). Now, since "carpet" resulted in a nil response, we can immediately eliminate the *c* and *r* of "cordon" as well, since they correspond to the *c* and *r* in "carpet," which we know are wrong. The task remains to discover which of the other letters of "cordon" are the two correct ones. The following player

should pick a word as close as possible to "cordon." "Burden" brings a response of one—which is probably either the *d* or the *n* (since "cordon" and "burden" share *r*, *d* and *n* in common, and *r* has already been eliminated). We can now try another word. If the next suggestion is "shadow," the response will be three: and since the only same letter between "burden" and "shadow" is the *d*, the fourth blank space at the top is probably *d*.

Usually, once one letter has been discovered, the game becomes easier. It is important, however, to try to identify a cluster of letters, rather than individual ones separated from each other. In our example, the *o* ("cordon"–"shadow") is a likely candidate for the blank after *d*. The word will in fact often be guessed before all the letters have been discovered.

Various different approaches can be adopted, but the basic principle remains that each player benefits from the words suggested by those before him. The winner is the first one to guess the word, and it is he or she who then thinks up the next.

A meal in company

You are having dinner with friends. Some of the other guests you know well, others little or not at all.

As the meal progresses and the mood relaxes, conversation turns to familiar themes, and the usual opinions and feelings are aired. Then a member of the opposite sex, who you hardly know says something—nothing very remarkable, perhaps—that for some reason attracts your attention. Their mere manner has somehow become more "interesting" in the context of a friendly evening with good food and good wine. You feel a wish to cultivate this acquaintance, to dedicate your time to following up these feelings. It is the start of a relationship. . . .

Probably many will recognize in this description the beginning of a friendship or love. Human relationships, whether close friendship or companionship, thrive on casual, relaxed occasions, when food and conversation are shared and time spent together. Games can certainly strengthen friendship, but a meal shared can introduce a new warmth and new interest into a friendship.

An invitation to a meal can be a good way of ending a job of work together, a friendly way of repaying some debt or obligation, a means of strengthening new ties, and an auspicious start to a new undertaking. Careful preparation and taste, an element of surprise, good food and wine all work together to create an occasion when all our tact, sensitivity, and intelligence come into full play.

An ancient remedy

Games, good company, and shared meals all help to make our life on this earth more agreeable. However, it is worth devoting some attention to one of the traditional vital ingredients of enjoyable relaxation—wine.

Two thousand years ago, the poet Horace observed that wine makes everybody more eloquent. The ancients well knew the liberating effect of wine and its importance in developing human relationships. During feasts and banquets (at which Romans reclined on couches—the *triclinium*), friendship burgeoned in an atmosphere at once warm and lively, with fine food and wine, singing and dancing. Reclining on a couch was also a good symbolic expression of relaxation from the pressures of daily affairs.

Horace once again extols the pleasures of "freeing the spirit . . . with sweet Lyæus" (Lyæus being another name for Bacchus, the god of wine, son of Jupiter and Semele, the inspirer of poets and the dispeller of care).

Horace's work continued in a tradition dear to the Greeks—evoking the delights of feasting, with wine having special human significance.

Wine drinking goes back to the dawn of history. Christianity, continuing the Judaic tradition, confirmed the ritual importance of wine and thus encouraged the spread of viticulture. Indeed, we read in the Bible how Noah was the first to plant vines, drink wine, and get drunk.

Most people speak more freely and are more at ease physically after a glass or so of wine.

Obviously we are talking here about moderate consumption. It is commonly accepted that when wine becomes a means of escaping the worries and tensions arising from serious problems, when one starts desiring to drink more and more, and to drink on one's own, then it becomes a destructive drug and starts to cause serious problems. Once an individual ceases to be in control of his or her own cravings, wine drinking ceases to be an "intelligent" occupation.

Wine and good food, as the ancients realized, help to make life happier and more pleasant, halting —momentarily, at least—the race of "time's winged chariot" that bears us inexorably towards our end.

At the "Full Moon" inn

In the great Italian novel *I Promessi Sposi*, one of the characters, Renzo, stays at the Hostelry of the Full Moon in Milan. It had been an action-packed, exhausting day, and the young man was hot and

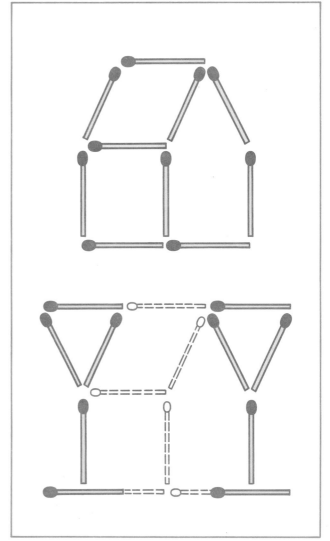

thirsty. Summoning the innkeeper, he ordered something to drink. One glass followed another, and not surprisingly Renzo became drunk. Growing somewhat boisterous, he was taken to bed, where he slept soundly. The following morning he was awakened by loud knocking at the door.

To his astonishment he found himself in police custody, handcuffed and about to be led to prison. He manages to escape, but nevertheless those glasses of wine proved more than he had bargained for!

Illustrating this story, we might imagine that the top shape in the figure above represents the inn: can you now change the arrangement, by moving six matches, to represent two of the wineglasses Renzo emptied? (The solution is shown in the lower figure.) (Similar arrangements are possible by moving just four matches.)

SEEGA—DERRAH

After *mancala* (*wari*; see p. 129), the best known of African board games, there are many others that reveal in their simplicity how different tribes exercised their wits in devising pastimes. The class of games with which we are concerned here does not use a board of alternating dark and light squares, such as is used for chess or checkers. The board in this case consists of a number of plain sections alone. Anthropologists have established that up until the last century many Africans played a game called *seega*, using a board of 25 plain sections. This is a game for two players, each having 12 pieces, either white or black. Turn by turn they place 2 pieces at a time in any 2 sections, though not the central one. After all the pieces are on the board (see drawing on opposite page), the last player to have placed a pair in position makes the first move. (It is thus important to agree at the outset, by lot, who starts.) Pieces can be moved one at a time, from one section to a neighbouring one, though not diagonally, in an attempt to "trap" the opponent. An enemy piece is taken (and removed from the board) by bringing 2 of your own pieces alongside it, 1 either side—rather as if it were a suspect being arrested by two

policemen (see *figure a*). If a piece moves to a space between 2 opponent pieces, however, it is not taken, since it has (so to speak) declared that it is not guilty by placing itself between the two "police."
If the player who has the first move cannot make a move, he has the right to remove whichever of his opponent's pieces he likes. (In a variant rule, his opponent must take a second turn.) It is then his opponent's turn. During the game, whenever a piece takes an enemy, it can move again if it is able thereby to take another enemy, any number of times. The winner is the player who manages to capture all of his opponent's pieces or, if there is an impasse (excluding the start of the game), the one with most pieces on the board.

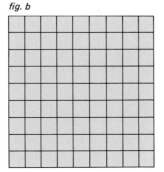

fig. b

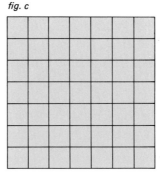

fig. c

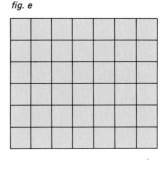

fig. e

More demanding variants of this game can be played on boards of either 49 or 81 sections (see *figures b* and *c*), with 24 or 40 pieces per player respectively.

"Block"
One version of *seega* still played in Africa is called "block" or "jump," which starts with the pieces set out as in *figure d*. They are moved singly, one space at a time, and never diagonally. Opposing pieces are taken in single or multiple jumps—rather as was explained for *alquerque* (see p. 34)—but it is not obligatory to take a piece whenever possible.

Derrah
Derrah is still played today in Nigeria and North Africa, on a similar board, though with 42 sections (see *figure e*). It cannot

really be considered a version of *seega*: it might more fittingly be considered an ancestor of tic-tac-toe (see p. 37). Played by two people, there are 12 pieces per player, each player having a different colour. Having decided who shall begin, they then in turn place on piece at a time until all are in play. Then the first player continues, moving a single piece one space (not diagonally). The idea is to form rows of three, either horizontally or vertically (again, not diagonally), removing an enemy piece each time such a row is achieved. However, rows formed during the initial placing of the pieces do not count; nor do rows of other than 3 pieces. The winner is the player who first makes it impossible for his or her opponent to make another row of three.

fig. a

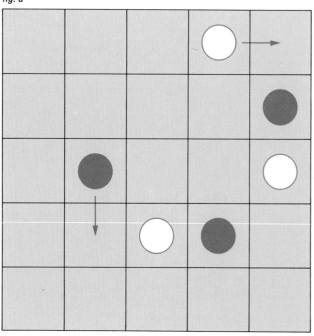

fig. d

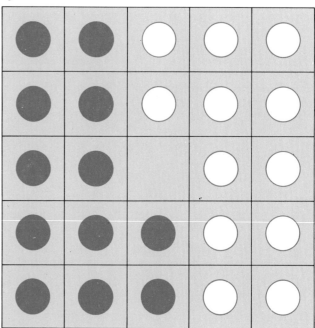

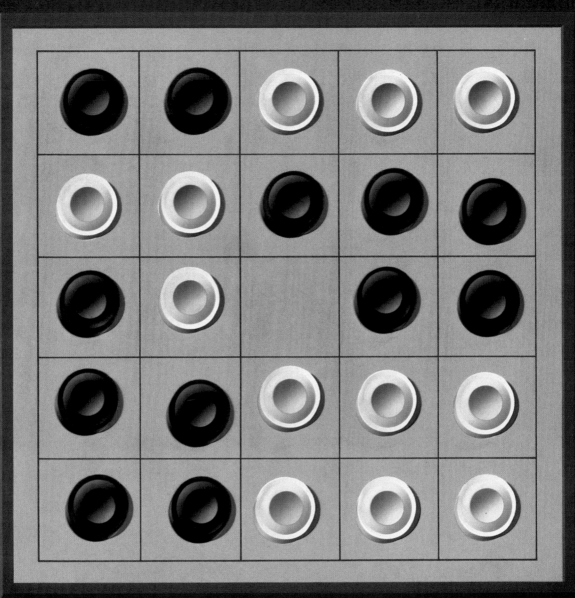

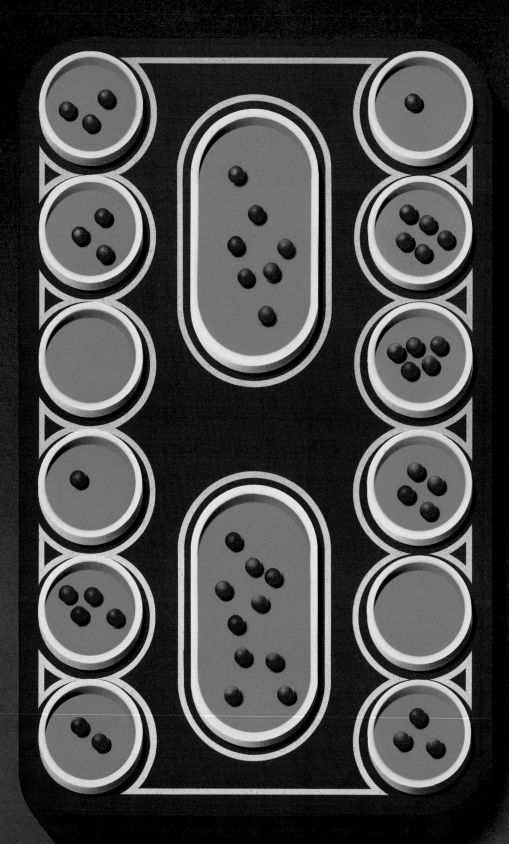

WARI

Wari is a highly entertaining and very subtle game played by two people, like chess or checkers. It is also known by various other names and is widespread in equatorial Africa. In certain areas it still retains its old sacred status and is reserved for the priestly and noble castes. We have chosen to use the name *wari* because this is the most familiar in Europe (especially Britain), as well as in Florida and some islands of the West Indies (such as Antigua). It is a game for both adults and children. Other names for the same game are *awelè* (W. Africa), *gabata* (Ethiopia), *suba* or *wuri* (the black communities in the United States), and most commonly *mancala* (*màncala* in Syria, *mancàla* in Egypt, *mancalà* in France).

Like chess and checkers, *wari* is a game of pure skill, with no room for chance. Though it may at first appear simple, it will soon be apparent how absorbing it can become, demanding skill, quick reasoning, and tactical ability. And it retains these qualities even when reduced to the most basic form (when instead of the board, simple wooden or plastic bowls, broken shards of pottery, or even—as African children make do with—holes in the earth are used, with berries, small shells, or pebbles as pieces). As was noted above, *wari* is a game for two players, the aim being (as we shall see) to take as many of the opponent's pieces as possible. The board lies between the two players such that each has a row of 6 bowls or troughs in front of him. Troughs a–f (*figure a*) belong to player S (South), and g–l to N (North). To start, each player places 4 balls or pieces in each of the troughs on his (or her) side. It must then be decided one way or another who shall make the first move. At each move, *all the balls* in one of your own troughs are *distributed* around the board, one per trough, starting at the next-door one, in a counterclockwise direction (see the arrows in *figure a* and *figure c*), *without missing any trough*, thus frequently landing in the opponent's territory. (In the illustrations, the balls being distributed are red, the ones already in each trough black.) When there is only one ball to move (when there is only one ball in the trough), it is simply dropped into the neighbouring trough—which may well be an enemy one, as for example in *figure b*, f–g. Examples: if S

starts from trough d, he will go e, then f, then over to the opponent's side, around to h. At this point, N could take the 5 balls in g and distribute them around to l, without going into enemy territory (*figures c* and *d*). By now the basic principle of the game should be clear: the balls in troughs a–f can only be moved by S (South), and those in g–l by N (North).

To take balls, the last one of the relevant distribution must have landed in the enemy camp. At each move there are *four* possibilities: a) the distribution can finish on the distributor's *own territory*, in which case no balls are taken; b) it can finish in enemy territory, in a trough with either *1 or 2 balls already in it* (thus bringing the total in that trough to 2 or 3 respectively)—in this case, *all* the balls in that trough are then taken, the rule being that when the last trough to be filled in any go ends up with *2* or *3* balls in it (no more and no less), then those balls can be taken; c) the final trough of any distribution may be *empty* or may already have *3 or more* balls in it, in which case the balls are not taken (according to the rule just stated); d) when the last ball of a move brings the total in that trough to 2 or 3, those balls are all taken—but this is not necessarily the end of the move: if there are also 2 or 3 balls in the previous troughs, the player who has just moved *continues to take balls* until there is a trough containing either only 1 ball or more than 3 (see *figures e* and *f*). *Figure e* gives an example in which S sets off from e and takes 9 balls (2+3+2+2), namely those in g, h, i, and j. *Figure f* shows two less fortunate examples: if S plays the 6 balls in f, he or she will be stopped by k; or if the 4 balls in e, by h. It will only be possible to take the balls in l and i (3) respectively.

There are three forms of defense when threatened:
a) *flight*—when your opponent is threatening the ball or balls in a trough on your side, the trough in question can be *emptied* (*figure g*: in this example, S is under threat from trough j, so empties d, transferring those 2 balls to e and f);
b) *reinforcement*—when a trough containing 2 balls is threatened (*figure h*: here S reinforces d, which is threatened by N's trough k, by moving the 3 balls in b, thus augmenting d to 3 balls, thereby making it secure); c) *overkill*—a threatening trough on the enemy side can be rendered harmless by a kind of "overkill" tactic, by increasing the number

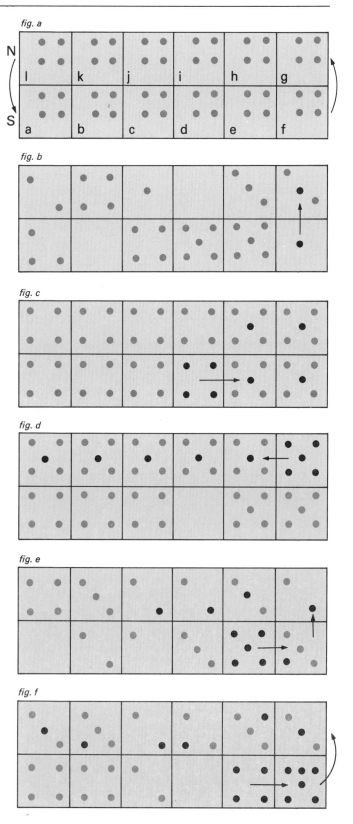

fig. a

fig. b

fig. c

fig. d

fig. e

fig. f

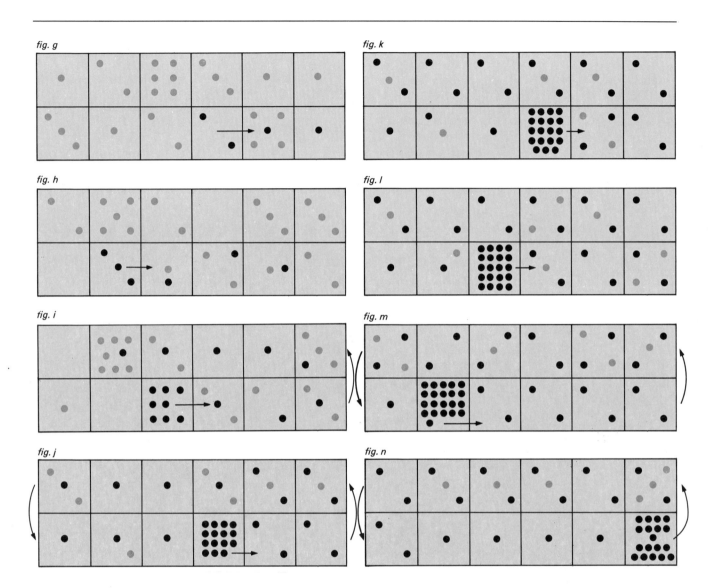

fig. g

fig. h

fig. i

fig. j

fig. k

fig. l

fig. m

fig. n

of balls in it (*figure i*). In this example, N's offensive, represented by the 7 balls in k, is defused by S distributing the 8 balls in c (k thus ends up with 8 balls, which would mean it would end up in its own territory, in g).

One important rule should be observed: When there are enough balls in any one trough to do a round of the whole board and beyond the trough again, *that trough must be missed out* (this being an exception to the general rule given at the beginning). Moving the 15 balls in d (*figure j*), S will then jump from c to e, and end the move in h, taking 6 balls (1+1+1 in h, and 1+1+1 in g).

"Building a house" means having enough balls in a single

trough to do the round of the board, continue beyond the first trough, and end up back in enemy territory. Such a maneuver is not necessarily advantageous: a) *complete success*—S distributes the 19 balls in d (*figure k*), finds the opponent side almost finished (all the troughs either empty or containing only one ball) and ends the game by taking 15 balls, thus emptying the enemy territory; b) *middling success*—S moves the 20 balls in c (*figure l*), reaching l, but is halted by i, so can take only 7 balls (3+2+2); c) *complete failure*—unable to make any other move, S distributes (*figure m*) the 21 balls in b, and finishes in l, where, since there are now 4 balls there (2+1+1), the move

ends; d) *complete failure*—unable to do otherwise, S moves the 18 balls in f (*figure n*), so ending up in a, which is his own territory, hence no balls can be taken.

The game ends when one player's territory becomes completely *empty*. However, that player is not necessarily the loser. The winner is the one who has taken the most balls by the time one or other side ends up empty. (Balls still remaining in troughs do not count either way in the final scoring.)

To understand the real attraction of this game it is necessary to play it often. You should not be discouraged if at first it seems inconclusive, or if it is difficult to decide how to move.

Remember, it is vital to have a

plan of action (this requires much practice) and to see each move (each distribution of balls from any one trough) in the light of this strategy, anticipating as far as possible your opponent's strategy.

In the same way as *go* (see pp. 107–112), *wari* is intellectually stimulating and tests one's powers of strategic thinking.

The point: numbers and imagination

I have often admired the mystical way of Pythagoras, and the secret magic of numbers.

Sir Thomas Browne

Mathematics and reality

Numbers evoke a feeling of exactness and precision. "Two plus two equals four" is a universal way of suggesting that there are some incontestable certainties. However, this is in a sense a "biased" view, when considering arithmetic, algebra, analysis, and mathematics in general.

In fact, numbers have always been rooted in the traditions, the technology, and the trade of different human societies down the ages.

Sacred symbolism (such as the symbolic perfection of the numbers 3 or 7, or the "golden section" —a certain precise ratio of the different lengths of the sides of a rectangle) often underlies the architecture of temples and other holy places. Trade and cultural contact with the East led eventually to the abandonment of Roman numerals in favour of the Arabic system. There are indeed many examples of how, far from being a remote abstract realm, mathematics is essentially bound up with the world of concrete reality.

Here it is necessary to draw a parallel between the common misconception of mathematics and the way that intelligence and creativity, and motivation, feelings, and desires are commonly related. We tend often to separate reality into neat compartments. But to do so is as misguided as to separate mathematics from the human contexts in which they have evolved.

The world of the psyche (in its broadest sense, including mind and soul, as well as "psyche" in the usual meaning) does not have precise lines of demarcation. Just as we are all "intelligent" to some degree or other, we are also all "creative," each with our own rich world of impressions and feelings. The various elements of our being interpenetrate and interact, and it is this process of inner working that creates an individual personality, with all its great store of potential.

A synthesis

Ingrained habits, the stimuli of the environment, the teaching and example of important individuals in one's life (parents, relatives, school and university teachers, for example), and relations with friends all combine in any one person, along with genetic traits (inherited through one's parents), to create that person's "essential" character. It is hardly deniable that "character" as such exists. And there is undoubtedly a certain correlation between one's own intellectual ability and that of one's forebears. However, the argument as to whether intelligence is inherited or cultivated has been long and bitter. It is of course not possible to determine the "structure" of a child's intellectual capacity after the moment of birth. On the other hand, genetic and biological engineering is still at an early stage—and its use is already raising fundamental ethical problems.

Thus we can only discuss the way things are at present, using the present to develop as far as possible every individual's capacity for profound motivation (towards success, friendship, cultural and professional achievement, family life, and so on) and interest in life. For these constitute personality. And personality is always changing. Certain aspects predominante at certain times, others at other times.

Human behaviour is predictable only to a limited degree. Very many people "make up for" poor education or what might be termed average intelligence by sheer force of will and dedication to the achieving of a fixed goal. Others perhaps solve their problems by "stepping beyond themselves," so to speak, in a sort of creative act that sets everything in a new and more "workable" order.

Yet it is somewhat artificial to separate the various aspects of a person's being (whether one does so professionally or as an amateur). They are in fact too intimately linked—just as the history of a single individual is bound with that of the social group to which he or she belongs, just as myth can stimulate science, and just as the intellectual process of analysis and synthesis goes hand in hand with creativity.

Thus it is that the number stories in the following paragraphs involve myth, imagination, and cultural and economic facts of history.

The intelligent crow

Medieval man had much greater contact with animals than we have today. Hunting had its own laws, and of course there were no guns, so the survival of whole species was not endangered. The castles of feudal lords would also have been full of animals —the lower floors were often overrun with rats and mice, while crows and other birds nested in the towers.

One day one of these lords decided to try and get rid of a particularly noisy crow that was nesting in his castle watchtower. On a number of occasions he had attempted to creep up on it and take it by surprise, but the wretched creature's hearing was too sensitive; it heard him coming and flew to a nearby tree, from where it could safely observe the proceedings. Once the man had left, it simply returned to its former place. For the lord, it was no longer just a question of disposing of an irritating bird pest: it had

become a battle of wits. He thus thought up a plan that would test the crow's counting ability. He sent two men up the tower. The crow immediately flew off to its safe perch in the tree. Then one of the men left the tower, in full view of the bird. It was not to be deceived, however, and only returned to its nest once the second man had also left. The lord then tried with three men, two leaving together first. Again, the crow was not taken in. Wishing to discover how far the crow could count, the lord then sent four men, but once again with negative results. Only when five men went into the tower and four came out did the bird lose count and so finally fell into the trap.

From this story it emerges that crows are intelligent birds, with, however, only a limited ability to count!

Counting: a human faculty!

One mode of behaviour we can unhesitatingly call typically human is the use of language. All animals seem to have some form of communication—signs, postures, and sounds—that represent messages. In mankind, however, language has evolved such a variety and multiplicity of meanings, and a capacity for conveying such subtle nuances, that it is unlike any other form of communication. But there is one language in particular that man uses and has developed to a supreme degree, clearly distinguishing the human species from the other animals: that of numbers. Whether true or not, the anecdote of the crow is based on the observation that certain animals have some sense of numbers. There are animals that clearly possess elementary perception of concrete quantities. Yet this is very different from an ability to count. Rather, it is an ability to distinguish between groups of objects of the same nature. In many species of animal, for instance, mothers become agitated if one or two of their young are missing.

The tools of counting

It would appear that no human community, however primitive, has been without some basic form of counting.

The "tools" used in counting are numbers, symbols representing abstract concepts, in that they can stand for any object whatever without having any direct relation to it. Different civilizations in the course of history have used different systems and codes to represent numbers and numerical calculations.

Even the most primitive peoples now alive, with the most crude counting systems, have words for numerical concepts such as "one" and "two," then "two and one" to mean three, and "two and two" to mean four: numbers above four being simply "many."

Numerical bases and systems

Linked with the concept of number is that of *system of enumeration*, which denotes all the symbols (necessarily a finite quantity) used to enlarge the range of use of those same symbols. What we call Arabic numerals (0, 1, 2, 3, 4, 5, 6, 7, 8, 9) are merely the symbols relating to the system of enumeration that the West has used for centuries. Other cultures, both past and present, had and have different systems. Numbers are thus simple sequences of symbols arranged according to the rules of a certain system. The *base* of a system of enumeration indicates how many units of a certain order are needed to make one unit of the next higher order. The base of our own counting system is decimal. That is, we change to a higher order every ten figures: hence, starting from ten (11, 12, 13 . . . 17, 18, 19, 20), we

come to the next higher order (in this case, 20) after ten units (20 being the tenth figure after 10, which is the first unit of a higher order). Generally the basis for the counting systems that employ our figures is denoted by 0.

If, for instance, we had taken six as base, we would then switch to a higher order every six figures. In such a system, the numbers would go 0, 1, 2, 3, 4, 5, and 6 would be symbolically represented as 10 (11 representing 7, and so on).

Let us now end with a little problem: To which number in the decimal system would 20 correspond if we knew that it was in base 6—for example, $20_{(6)} = ?_{(10)}$?

One simply needs some familiarity with natural numbers and perhaps a certain aptitude for solving this kind of problem. Thus:

$$(2 \times 6^1) + (0 \times 6^0) \times 12$$

The number 20 in base 6 therefore corresponds to 12 in the decimal system. This result can be symbolically represented as $20_{(6)} = 12_{(10)}$.

How many hands?

Our counting system—the decimal, possessing ten figures—is neither the only nor the best possible system. The philosopher Aristotle observed many centuries ago that the reasoning behind his statements lay in the fact that man has ten fingers divided between two hands and finds it convenient to count in tens. For this same reason numerical systems based on twenty were not uncommon: it was not difficult to include toes with fingers, to create four sets of five!

It is told how one day a team of anthropologists wishing to make a close study of an ancient tribe in a remote corner of the world encountered a bizarre mode of arithmetical reasoning. Written on a large dried leaf they found the following calculations:

1) 140 + 323 = 1013;
2) 2223 + 4123 = 11401.

Immediately they pondered this problem: if counting systems developed historically from the fact that man has ten fingers, distributed between two hands, how many hands would the members of this obscure tribe have had to have to result in this counting system?

The answer can be obtained by identifying exactly what that system was. First, note that there are no figures higher than 4; then 3 plus 3, carrying 1, can apply only in a system in which the move to the higher order occurs every 5 units—that is, in a system of base 5. We must conclude, then, that the inhabitants of that far part of the earth had only one hand!

It would in fact appear that numerical systems in base 5 were the most widespread. Clear proof of this can be found in certain cultures in which the words for "hand" and for "five" are identical. In ancient Persian, to say "hand" one would use the word *pentcha*, corresponding etymologically with the Greek *penté* (Latin *quinque*), meaning five—equivalent also to the Sanscrit *pança*. Greek also has a word *pampàxein*, which in the classical era was used to mean "count"—the strict etymological meaning being "to count in fives": "quindrise," one might now say. The South American Tamanacos tribe had a quinary counting system. Their word for five also meant "a whole hand"; for higher numbers, they would say "one on the other hand," "two on the other hand" (six, seven . . .), and so forth.

We know, too, that the ancient Aztecs divided the months into weeks of five days. And many other similar examples could be cited.

The planet of the one-handed

Life on earth had long been impossible. As the forests and grassland were killed off by acid rain and

the seas became irreversibly polluted, more and more humans travelled to other planets to seek a new existence.

One such group voyaged to the planet of the one-handed (so-called because prior exploration, mainly by satellite, had revealed that its inhabitants had only one hand). Having landed the spaceship without any problems, the captain and crew, then all the passengers, cautiously disembarked and began to explore. Soon their attention was attracted by strange inscriptions carved on a rockface (see figure below).

Various features, the arrangement of the symbols, and the results themselves indicated that these made up a mathematical sum. Earlier surveys had established that the planet's numbering system followed roughly the same rules as our own, and that it was based on the number of fingers on the inhabitants' single hands.

The problem can be expressed thus: Supposing that the numbers in the example below do not start at zero, how many fingers did each inhabitant of this curious planet have on their one hand?

To obtain the answer, it is necessary to find the base of their numbering system. Remembering how we have defined any such base, this should not be hard. The base of any numerical system tells us how many units of a certain order are needed to bring us to the next higher order. Let us examine the example carefully and work it out normally, as though it were written in our own system. Two figures added together★★ suffice to take us to a higher order, which is indicated as ☆. This means that the system must be ternary, in base 3.

Thus the planet's inhabitants have just one hand, with three fingers. Having identified the numerical system, we should now be able to tell what the left-hand figures should come to in our own decimal system. The only possible solution is

$$12 + 12 = 101.$$

And that "translated" into decimal is

$$5 + 5 = 10$$

Three times one-five = five-one

"If three times one-five equals five-one, how much is six times one-three?"

The formulation of the problem makes it seem more complex than it actually is. However, it does conceal one interesting feature. The way the number 15 is represented (as one-five) should tell us that we are not dealing with the decimal system but are in another base, which we must discover if we are to obtain the correct answer in our system. If we read 15 as "fifteen," we would be confusing it with the decimal base; in fact, "15" merely tells us that, reading from right to left, there are five units of the first order and one of the second. To identify the base of unknown numbers, there are various empirical methods of procedure (note, for instance, that in $3 \times 15 = 51$ the highest figure is 5), but the safest is to resort to an algebraic equation. Representing the unknown base as B, we can establish:

$$(3 \times B^0) \times (1 \times B^1 + 5 \times b^0) = (5 \times B^1 + 1 \times B^0)$$
$$(3 \times 1) \times (B + 5 \times 1) = 5B + 1$$
$$3 \times (B + 5) = 5B + 1$$
$$3(B + 5) = 5B + 1$$
$$3B + 15 = 5B + 1$$
$$5B - 3B = 15 - 1$$
$$2B = 14 \quad B = 14/2 = 7$$

The base of this system is thus 7.

Having discovered this, we can then answer the original problem, thrown up at the start: What is six times one-three?

It is advisable to do this problem as it stands, without translating it into decimal, working it out and then translating it back into base 7. Let us rationally try to work in the same numerical system, even though this is different from ours (the Latin word *ratio*, from which "rational" stems, in fact means both reason and, specifically, "counting" and "calculation"). To do this we need only remember that every seven units we need to pass to the next order above:

$$
\begin{array}{r}
13 \times \\
6 \\
\hline
114
\end{array}
$$

Thus we can write:

$$13_{(7)} \times 6_{(7)} = 114_{(7)}$$

We can check this result by transposing the whole operation into decimal and ensuring that all is correct:

$$13_{(7)} = (1 \times 7^1) + (3 \times 7^0) = 7 + 3 = 10_{(10)}$$
$$6_{(7)} = (6 \times 7^0) = 6 \times 1 = 6_{(10)}$$
$$114_{(7)} = (1 \times 7^2) + (1 \times 7^1) + (4 \times 7^0) =$$
$$= 49 + 7 + 4 = 60_{(10)}$$

In effect:

$$10_{(10)} \times 6_{(10)} = 60_{(10)}$$

The "Black Cat" Society

The Black Cat Society had been implicated in some serious crimes. Its members were mostly ex-convicts who sought obscure compensation for their past in secret rites and ceremonies and mysterious practices that in the end led back to the same crimes as before. The police had decided the organization should be outlawed. However, the crimes still continued. It thus seemed probable that the society was still operating clandestinely. A message was received that they would be meeting in a cellar on a certain night, and the police duly descended on the place that evening—to find it deserted! Everyone had vanished. Nevertheless there were signs that they had been there shortly before. Some odd mathematical scribblings on a blackboard caught the attention of the police inspector:

$$16 \times 253 = 5104$$

He examined this for a while, then exclaimed, *"The Black Cat Society uses a different base!"*

What base did the society use for their mathematical calculations?

Let us proceed by trial and error. Note first that there are no figures higher than 6: thus the base must necessarily be higher $(7, 8, 9 \ldots)$.

So let us begin by imagining that the base was 7; this would mean that when multiplying, a new order is reached after every seven units:

$$
\begin{array}{r}
253 \times \\
16 \\
\hline
2244 \\
2530 \\
\hline
5104
\end{array}
$$

Luck is with us: the base indeed is 7.

By way of example, let us go over the way we worked: six times three is eighteen, but since we are in base 7 we have to base ourselves on the first multiple of seven before eighteen, namely "fourteen"; this being four less than eighteen, we write four and carry two. Continuing on, we come to six times five = thirty, plus two carried = thirty-two. Here again, we need to return to the first multiple of seven—which is twenty-eight. This is four short of thirty-two, so again we write four, and this time carry four. Finally six times two = twelve, but sixteen = two times seven plus two, so we need to write "two-two," and so on.

Try out some other calculations using different numerical bases.

I	II	III	III,ΛΙ	Λ	ΙΛ	X,+	↑,↓,↙	⬖,⊕,⬗	≷,⧸	≦,⧹,8
1	2	3	4	5	6	10	50	100	500	1000

The origins of indigitation

The Romans were a remarkably inventive lot, able most importantly to enrich their own civilization by adopting the cultural and technical "know-how" of the various peoples with whom they had contact, adapting and evolving them according to their own requirements. We know, for instance, that from the Greeks they took their alphabet, with only slight modifications. However, the civilization that had the profoundest influence on them initially (in every domain—arts, sciences, technology, religion, and so forth) was the Etruscan. And it was from their Etruscan neighbours, in fact, that they took their decimal-base numbering system. (See figure above.)

If the arrangement of these figures seems odd (6, IΛ, and more strikingly the four, ΛΙ), it should be remembered that Etruscan writings were read from right to left. Identical methods of counting were in use among other Italic peoples, such as the Osci, the Umbri, the Sanniti, and so on.

The Romans took over the Etruscan numerical symbols but turned them around, to read from left to right and upside down (thus Etruscan 6, IΛ, became VI, and Etruscan 4, ΛΙ, became IV).

What were the characteristics of these symbols? At first sight, especially in their original Etruscan form, they seem merely to be the simplest kinds of symbols to write or carve—so much so that they continue to be used even today, albeit not for calculations.

Several authorities have seen in them traces of a primitive numerical system in base 5 (a "quinary" system).

And it is not too far fetched to suppose that number systems were evolved from earlier modes of "indigitation"—the use of one's fingers to indicate quantity (deriving from the Latin *digitum*, meaning "finger"). Following on from this, it is hardly surprising that the first symbol used to indicate classes of objects (sheep, trees, people, and so on) did indeed represent five. According to Theodor Mommsen (1817–1903), the great German jurist and philologist, and one of the greatest historians of ancient Rome, the symbol for five, common to all the peoples of central Italy, was a highly simplified and stylized picture of a hand. It is surely not impossible that this symbol of a numerical unit ("I") should represent one finger, "II" two fingers, "III"

three fingers, and "IV" a hand less one finger. It would then seem not unreasonable that "VI" should represent a hand plus one finger, "VII" a hand plus two fingers, and so on. Ten ("X") can perhaps be understood as two "V"s, one inverted below the other: in which case, nine ("IX") is simply two hands less one finger. Logically, then, the symbol "XX" would be used to mean four hands.

The Roman numbering system is thus clearly quinary in origin. And it was no great step to go from that to a decimal system: a human after all has ten fingers, on two hands, and five is a multiple of ten.

The oldest mode of calculation

There are still people living in what we might term "primitive" stages of cultural evolution, who generally have no names for numbers. For counting, they often have codes of gestures. In practice, numbers are conveyed for religious or commercial purposes by means of a series of established signs, frequently using different parts of the body.

Once names are given to numbers, a certain degree of abstraction has been attained: a separation has occurred—what was mere indistinct plurality has become a single, precise, concept, quite separate from any originally concrete reality.

Mankind evolved as the "cultural animal" that we now are by virtue of having hands. Once we were able to walk on two feet only, our hands were left free, as highly flexible and adaptable "tools" of evolution. First and foremost they were invaluable in building and in the use of ever more powerful and efficient functional instruments: and this remains true in our own day, when the inventions we use are capable of radically changing the world in which we live. As well as being useful for making things, our hands were also ideal for counting and making mathematical calculations. The supply of ten fingers in a row, so "ready to hand," made the notion of cardinal and ordinal numbers a wholly natural one.

True, there are all sorts of means of counting (with stones, shells, blocks of wood, and so on), but there can surely be no simpler method than using one's own fingers. Most children, when they learn to count, learn on their fingers. And, as we have already observed, our ten fingers are an extremely practical base for mathematical calculation.

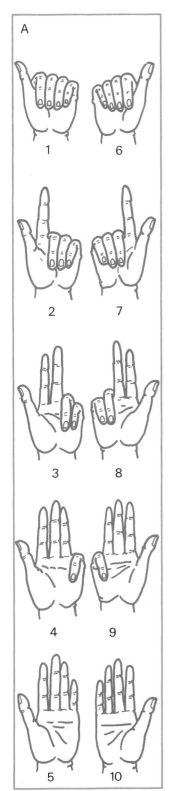

A

1 6

2 7

3 8

4 9

5 10

B

1 6

2 7

3 8

4 9

5 10

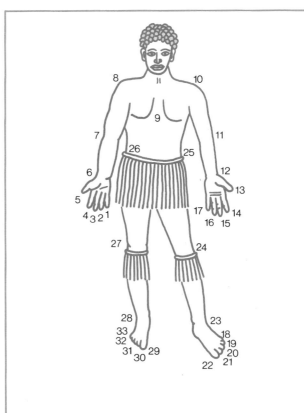

Body numbering—a system used by some of the islanders of the Torres Strait in the South Pacific: 1, right-hand little finger; 2, right ring finger; 3, right middle finger; 4, right index finger; 5, right thumb; 6, right wrist; 7, right elbow; 8, right shoulder; 9, breast; 10, left shoulder; 11, left elbow; 12, left wrist; 13, left thumb; 14, left index finger; 15, left middle finger; 16, left ring finger; 17, left little finger; 18, left little toe; 19, left annular; 20, left middle toe; 21, left second toe; 22, left big toe; 23, left ankle; 24, left knee; 25, left hip; 26, right hip; 27, right knee; 28, right ankle; 29, right big toe; 30, right second toe; 31, right middle toe; 32, right annular; 33, right little toe.

One, two, three . . . ten: on your fingers!

Ever since he started using numbers, man has found it "handy" to represent them by means of his own fingers, giving each one a whole numerical value within the regular series.

In *figure A* left, all the fingers start off folded; then for "one," the thumb of the left hand is extended; for "two," the adjacent index finger is also raised; and so on until, with the little finger on the right hand, we reach "ten."

This could be done equally well in reverse, by starting off with the hands fully extended and folding the fingers one by one, beginning with the

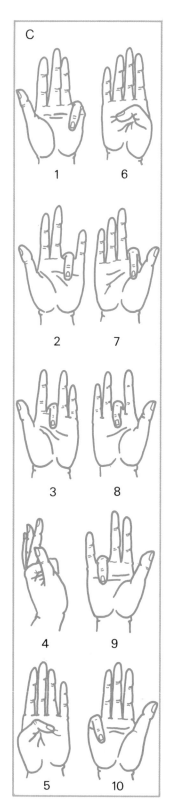

C

1	6
2	7
3	8
4	9
5	10

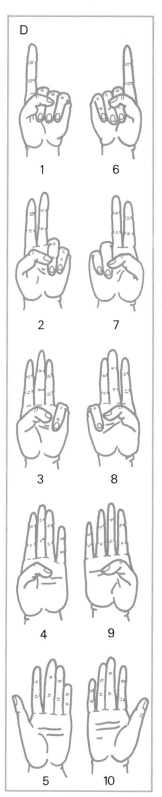

D

1	6
2	7
3	8
4	9
5	10

left-hand little finger for "one," then the ring finger for "two," and so on, until we reach the right-hand thumb (see *figure B* left) or the right-hand little finger (see *figure C*). Also of interest is the system used by Arabs in North Africa—starting with all ten fingers folded and extending the left- or right-hand index finger for "one" (see *figure D* left).

It is true to say that digital calculation, which still survives today in areas of Europe and Russia, dates back to earliest times.

Below: the famous *"mano guidiana"* ("guide hand") conceived by Guido of Arezzo to help singers in reading music.

Opposite page: hand gestures from a book on chiromancy by J. Bulwer.

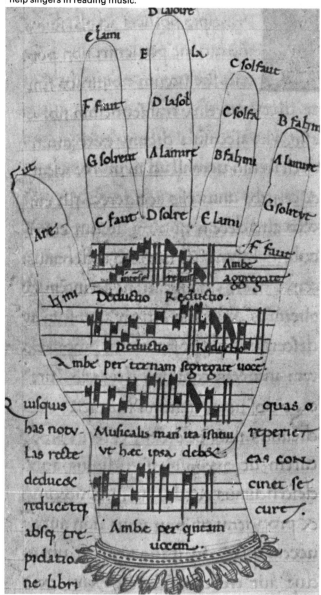

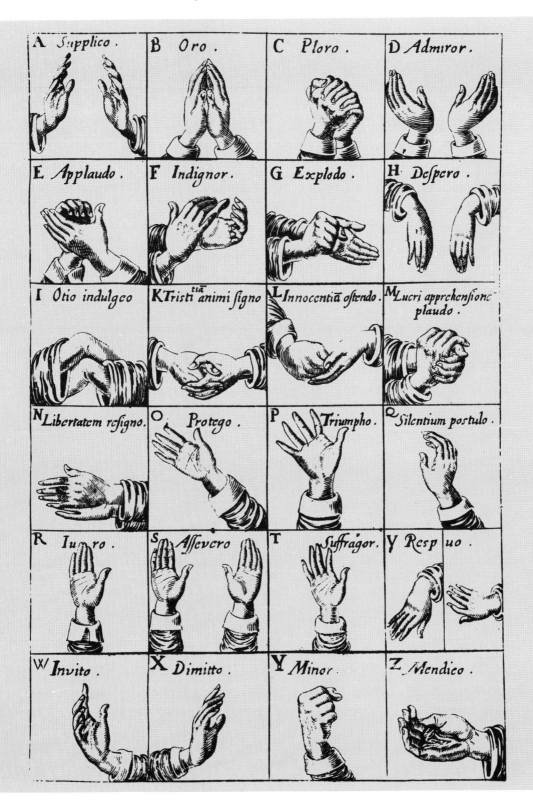

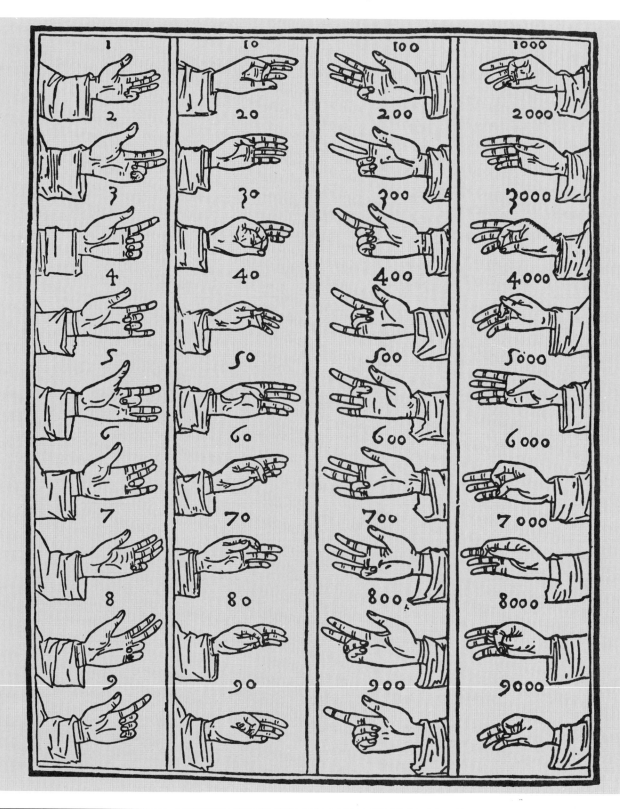

"Mathematics gives a V sign"

This remark is attributed to the celebrated Italian physicist G. Battista Venturi (1746–1822). He was referring to the similarity between certain forms of numerical representation with fingers and the insulting gesture (the suggestive V sign), which is still used in various mutations today!

The rules of "indigitation" (reckoning by the fingers) were widely followed all around the Mediterranean, especially in the Middle Ages and during the Renaissance. The habit of counting on one's fingers had become so instinctive that digital representation came to be used even in music (see illustration on page 138).

One name worth mentioning at this point is Luca Pacioli (1450?–?1520), a mathematician who studied in Venice and then became a Franciscan friar. With his friend Leonardo da Vinci, he worked in the service of Ludovico Maria Sforza in Milan. In 1494 he published in Venice his *Summa de aritmetica, geometria, proportioni et proportionalità*—the first general treatise on practical arithmetic and algebra to appear in print. In this book he illustrates one of the commonest forms of finger counting (see illustration opposite).

The practise of counting on one's fingers continued so long that for centuries arithmetic was thought of in terms of finger counting. Clear signs of this can be seen in paintings and sculptures; and certain passages in old books and manuscripts only make sense when one remembers the conventions of "indigitation," the act of reckoning by the fingers.

"Happy is he indeed who can count his years on his right hand," declared the satirist Juvenal (*c.* 55–130 A.D.). And as we can see from the illustration from Pacioli's book (opposite), the years that were counted on the right hand started at one hundred. The poet was therefore saying, "You're happy if you live to over a hundred!"

Important dates and events are sometimes referred to in medieval texts in such a way that they would be indecipherable if one did not know the code of finger counting that was being used. Still in use in the medieval schools as an arithmetical textbook was the *Liber de loquela per gestum digitorum* (*Book on the Language of Finger Gestures*) by the Venerable Bede.

Hand calculations

It was during the Middle Ages and the Renaissance especially that systems of doing calculations on one's fingers became widespread—probably because only a few people had abacuses or multiplica-

Opposite page: a system for making calculations on one's fingers, from a book on mathematics by Luca Pacioli, published in Venice in 1494. People continued to count on their fingers in later centuries, as we discover, for instance, from the *Theatrum Arithmetico-Geometricum* by Jacob Leupold, published in Germany in 1727.

tion tables beyond 5 × 5. One very simple system, known as the "old rule," employed the concept of the complement to ten: if n is a number, its complement is $10 - n$. Then, if we want to multiply, say, 8 × 9, we start by finding the complements (2 for 8, 1 for 9); next, subtract either complement from the number of which it is not the complement (hence $8 - 1 = 7$, or $9 - 2 = 7$). This tells us the "10"s digit in the final result—namely, 7. The product of the two complements ($2 \times 1 = 2$) then gives the final digit: placed in the correct order, 72 indeed emerges as the result of 8 × 9.

This same principle was applied to calculations worked out on fingers. Keeping our example of 8×9: each finger is assigned a number from 6 to 10 (see figure below); to multiply 8 by 9, one finger called "8" has to be placed against one called "9."

It can be seen that the complement of 8 is represented by the two top fingers of the left hand (above

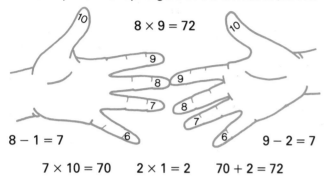

$8 \times 9 = 72$

$8 - 1 = 7$ $9 - 2 = 7$

$7 \times 10 = 70$ $2 \times 1 = 2$ $70 + 2 = 72$

the two that are touching), and that of 9 by the single finger (referring to thumbs as "fingers"!) on the right hand. The number of the "touching" finger on one hand, less the complement represented by the upper fingers on the other totals 7: this is the "10"s digit. The product of the upper fingers, namely 2 (2 $\times$ 1) gives the units: 7 and 2 are 72. The figures below show multiplications of 6×6 and 7×10.

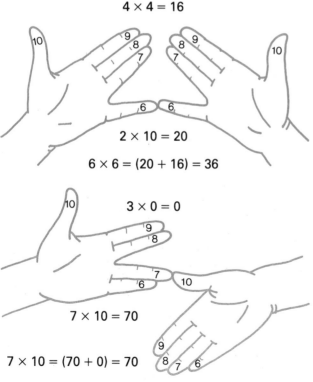

$4 \times 4 = 16$

$2 \times 10 = 20$

$6 \times 6 = (20 + 16) = 36$

$3 \times 0 = 0$

$7 \times 10 = 70$

$7 \times 10 = (70 + 0) = 70$

This method of multiplying on fingers can be applied to all the "10"s above 10 itself, though with slight modification. Suppose, for example, we wish to multiply 13×15: the fingers are then numbered 11 to 15 (see figure below), and finger "13" will be placed against finger "15." We then multiply the eight fingers below (representing the last digits) by 10: $(5 + 3) \times 10 = 80$. Taking the lower fingers again, we multiply the two hands ($5 \times 3 = 15$), and this product is then added to the previous total ($15 + 80 = 95$). And the final step is to add the constant, 100. Thus:

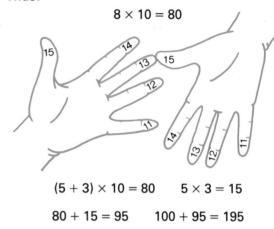

$8 \times 10 = 80$

$(5 + 3) \times 10 = 80$ $5 \times 3 = 15$

$80 + 15 = 95$ $100 + 95 = 195$

The disadvantage of this method is that it is too slow, however, it has considerable value as a teaching method. First, children are entertained by discovering new ways of producing the same results in arithmetic. Second, the device of using complements to ten is a concrete example of the algebraic multiplication of binomials. Glancing back to the example of 8×9, we could express the same process in terms of the relation of each figure to 5—$(5 + 3)$ and $(5 + 4)$—and multiplying them in a different way:

$$
\begin{array}{r}
5 + 3 \\
5 + 4 \\
\hline
25 + 15 \\
20 + 12 \\
\hline
25 + 35 + 12 = 72
\end{array}
$$

Finding out how certain calculations were made and problems of arithmetic solved in the past is not mere idle curiosity. Sometimes examining methods that have been dropped in favour of faster and more efficient processes brings into relief or reveals new and interesting properties of numbers and relations between them that all too often pass unnoticed.

What is XLVIII by CCLXXXVIII?

Most of us are familiar with the ancient Roman numerals, although we no longer use them to calculate with. In fact, they remained in use throughout the West up until the fourteenth and fifteenth centuries, when they were replaced by the quicker and more economical Indo-Arabic system. (And it should be pointed out that even then the adoption of this latter system by Western Europe was hindered by a general prejudice against anything deriving from the world of Islam.)

To bring home the great advantages of the Arabic system, let us see how long it takes to multiply XLVIII by CCLXXXVIII in comparison with 48 to 288. No documents or accounts illustrating how the ancient Romans coped survive. It must have been quite complicated!

One way of proceeding might be as set out in the figure below:

XLVIII × CCLXXXVIII

```
XL × C    = M M M M
XL × C    = M M M M
XL × L    =     M M
XL × X    =           C C C C
XL × X    =           C C C C
XL × X    =           C C C C
XL × V    =             C C
XL × III  =             C X X
 V × C    =         C C C C C
 V × C    =         C C C C C
 V × L    =             C C L
 V × X    =               L
 V × X    =               L
 V × X    =               L
 V × V    =                 X X V
 V × III  =                 X V
III × C   =         C C C
III × C   =         C C C
III × L   =             C L
III × X   =                 X X X
III × X   =                 X X X
III × X   =                 X X X
III × V   =                   X V
III × III =                   I X
```

```
M M M M M M M M M M C C C C C C C C C C C
C C C C C C C C C C C C C C C C C C C C L L L L
L X X X X X X X X X X X X X X X X I V = M M M
M D C C C X X I V
```

Roman numerals with matches

Ancient Romans had no matchsticks: to light a fire, they used a flint (*lapis ignarius* or *pyrites*), which produced sparks when struck with either another stone or a piece of iron. These sparks would fall onto tinder (*igniarium*)—some easily flammable material, usually dry wood. It is not easy to imagine how much time this rather crude system of creating five took. How much effort must have been wasted in damp or rainy weather. Doubtless no one ever dreamed of a day when a flame on the end of a little stick of wood was a perfectly normal and easily attainable thing. Ironically, then, these same "miraculous" little bits of wood are now ideal for us to use to represent ancient Roman numerals.

Below are some examples of Roman numbers. However, the sums are not quite correct. By moving a single match in each case, is it possible to obtain correct mathematical expressions?

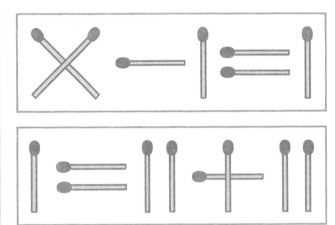

The solutions are as follow:

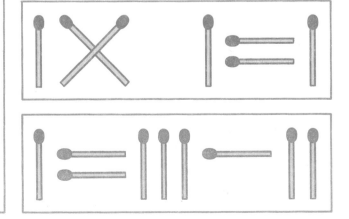

A system for the human brain

As we saw when we tried to multiply 48 × 288, even the simplest calculations are laborious when using Roman numerals. As time went on, it became increasingly uneconomical to retain them, and when in the thirteenth century the decimal-based Indo-Arabic system was introduced to the West by Leonardo Pisano (better known as Fibonacci), the Roman system was slowly discarded. The success of the new system was due entirely to its great simplicity: any number could be expressed in terms of the ten figures 0, 1, 2, 3, 4, 5, 6, 7, 8, 9. The *position* of each figure in any given number was what mattered: the quantity represented by each digit was determined by its position in the number as conventionally written down. For instance, taking the number 2222, the 2 second on the right represents the tens, the third from the right the hundreds, the fourth (the first 2 on the left) the thousands, and so on. The criterion here, therefore, is one of *position*, whereas in the Roman system it is mostly a matter of *addition*—that is, each symbol always has the same value regardless of its position: a symbol is merely added to the previous one when it is of lower value, or subtracted from the following symbol when it is of a higher value. Where symbols are repeated they are simply added together, but no symbol is repeated more than three times.

Despite early opposition the new decimal-base Indo-Arabic system, was so clearly superior that it eventually won the day. Its superiority lay not in its having ten figures, however, but in the advantages of a *positional* system over an *additional* system.

The "farmer's system of multiplication"

In the long history of mathematics many different ways of doing calculations have been evolved, and we never learn the less common ones. An example of such a case is the so-called farmer's system of multiplication, which in fact does have considerable interest and works according to its own logic. See if you can identify the underlying principle in the example below. Let us suppose we are to multiply 14 × 24.

14	24		14 ×
7	48		24 =
3	96		———
1	192		56
	——		280
	336		———
			336

If we multiply the same figures in the normal way (see right-hand calculation), we can check that the result is indeed correct. How does the "farmer's system" work?

A look at the left-hand figures will show that the "14" column numbers are just divisions by two, forgetting the remainders (2 into 14 goes exactly seven times, into 7, three times, and into 3, once: and here the division by two stops), while those in the "24" column are a progressive multiplication by two (2 × 24 = 48; 2 × 48 = 96; 2 × 96 = 192).

The total of 336 is made up of the sum of all the numbers opposite odd numbers in the "14" column: 48 + 96 + 192 = 336. Note, too, that the same answer would be given if the factors were reversed:

24	14
12	28
6	56
3	112
1	224
——	
	336

We deliberately took two even numbers as an example, but in fact the same method can be applied equally to odd numbers.

This curious way of multiplying offers the one advantage of enabling us to forget about remainders. On the other hand, it is somewhat cumbersome and slow. Hence it is rarely used, and the method normally taught at school proves quicker and more reliable. The "farmer's system" is interesting as a relic of an ancient use of the binary system, using only two figures.

Let us now look more closely at the chief features of this.

Only two symbols

Initially, the binary system of numbering, in which any number can be expressed by means of only two symbols, "0" and "1," appears the simplest. Yet it is important here to consider what we mean by "simple." Although it does only have two symbols, in practice it works less neatly and quickly than other systems.

Let us examine some examples of binary mathematics, for it is always useful to have some acquaintance with it. (Incidentally, the word "binary" comes from the Latin *bis*, meaning "twice.") Take the number $101_{(2)}$, which would read "one-naught-one" (in this sort of exercise it is advisable to indicate the base) in order not to confuse it with the normal decimal "one hundred and one." This number tells us that—reading from right to left—there is one unit of the first order, no units of the second, and one of the third. With only a few, and simple, calculations, it is possible to move from the binary number to the corresponding decimal, or a number in any other base.

For example, to find the equivalent in the decimal system of the binary number $11001_{(2)}$, we need only make a quick calculation:

$$11001_{(2)} = (1 \times 2^4) + (1 \times 2^3) + (0 \times 2^2) + (0 \times 2^1) + (1 \times 2^0) =$$
$$= 16 + 8 + 0 + 0 + 1 = 25$$

One could thus write: $11001_{(2)} = 25_{(10)}$

It does not matter which numerical system one uses, the actual mathematics is not affected. This indicates that the rules of arithmetic are independent of whatever particular base may be used.

Though there is a variety of bases, then, it may be said that they are all just different ways of symbolizing and presenting the same "argument." Numbers and the activity of counting must always obey the same laws, regardless of whether the person counting is a top boffin or a wild Amazonian Indian!

Is there a reason?

Is there a reason why, whatever the base, if one multiplies a number by 10 (which, remember, we read in decimal as "ten," but which in binary is "one-naught," and in yet other numerical systems will be different again), the result will always be the simple addition of a naught?

Consider. Adding a naught in a "positional" system means passing to the next higher order: and this process is expressed by moving all the other figures one place to the left.

Anyone with any familiarity with the abacus knows this from physical action: for on an abacus, to multiply by ten involves moving everything one space to the left and leaving the right-hand end space empty, to indicate naught.

The hidden binary principle

What is the principle behind the curious method of handling numbers, which previously we referred to as the "farmer's system"?

Having now given some explanations of the formal features of the binary system, we are in a position to identify that principle. Let us take two numbers—not too high, say, 35 and 11—and multiply them as already illustrated: divide the number at the top of the left-hand column (35 in the table

following) by two, disregarding the remainder, and at the same time multiply that at the top of the right-hand column (11) by two. Then cross out the lines that consist of even numbers in the left-hand column and add up the remaining numbers in the right-hand column. Note that it does not matter which number is on the top of the right-hand columns. The important thing is that the lines crossed out are those that correspond with the even numbers on the left.

1	35	×	11
1	17		22
0	8		44
0	4		88
0	2		176
1	1		352
			——
			385

Let us now convert 35 into binary (in other words, do the reverse of what we did earlier).

$$35 \begin{array}{|c} 2 \end{array}$$

Thus $35_{(10)} = 100011_{(2)}$.

Now place these binary figures beside the column headed "35," with the first figure at the top—and observe how the naughts correspond to the crossed-out even numbers. Similarly, the final answer to the multiplication, it can be seen, was reached by totalling the numbers of the right-hand column corresponding to the binary "1"s.

By now it should be fairly easy to see the principle underlying the "farmer's system" of multiplication. When the binary version of the number at the top of the left-hand column is written vertically beside it, the right-hand-column numbers corresponding to the binary naughts are crossed out. (Incidentally, it is perhaps worth recalling that any number multiplied by naught equals naught.)

A system for a computer "brain"

In order to understand what numbers really are, it is useful to compare different numerical systems. The symbols by which we represent numbers, and which form the different bases, are purely conventional. Various factors may result in one system being more practical than another, but there is one in particular that makes a vital difference: "positional" systems prove far more effective than those that are essentially just a chain of additions. "Positional" systems are all in fact equally good; and as we heard from Aristotle earlier, the adoption of a ten-scale system as the norm is really due to the way our own bodies are made. However, the binary system can also in its own way become "quite complex," because it alone is applicable in modern digital computer work. Most of us have at least a rough idea of what a computer is: a fairly intricate arrangement of various basic components. These components (circuits and elements that can be used inside the computer) are such as can exist in two states: in any given circuit, current may pass or not pass (open/closed); an electronic tube may be either alive or dead, a certain material may be magnetized in one direction or in the opposite direction, and so on. It can be helpful to think of these two states as "0" (for the "off" state—when current does not pass) and "1" (for the opposite state). It is in general true that the binary system is positional, but nobody would ever dream of doing normal calculations in that mode; it would take far too long. We should realize, though, that what is a limitation for us is an advantage for an electronic machine (such machines operate at the speed of electric current—which for everyday purposes we can think of as instantaneous).

How to count in binary on your fingers

Human fingers are eminently suitable for counting with "0" and "1"—curved for the former, perhaps, and outstretched for the latter. In this way one can count from 1 to $1111111111_{(5)}$ corresponding to $1023_{(10)}$. Start by folding all your fingers, thus forming two fists, with the back of your hands upwards. For "1" extend the little finger on your right hand; for "2" (written $10_{(2)}$), fold back the little finger and extend the ring finger of the right hand; for "3" extend both the little and the ring fingers . . . and so on.

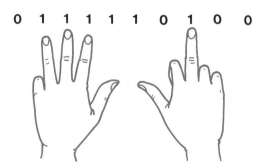

0 1 1 1 1 1 0 1 0 0

How could one represent $0111110100_{(2)}$? The left-hand figure below suggests a way.

With a little practice it is possible to do binary calculations. Whether we do them on our fingers or on paper, however, they are still slow, crude, and tedious. Such drawbacks cease to matter, though, when a machine like a computer is involved—for as we have already seen, they work at the speed at which electric current travels.

A game of strategy in binary

There is a game called *Nim* (probably Chinese in origin), which is based on a binary concept. It is for two players, and the rules are as follows: Piles of matches are placed on a table, and each player in turn removes as many matches as he or she wishes from any one pile—the whole pile if so desired. The winner is the player who removes the last match.

Try this game out, and you will find it is not as simple as it sounds, especially in the early moves, as knowing how many matches to take away each turn, in order to be the last to remove one, requires some cunning.

Let us imagine we have four piles, one with 7 matches, another with 5, the third with 3, and the last with just 1 match.

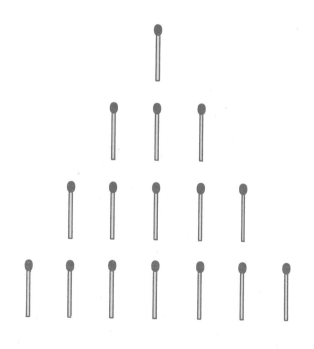

Say we kindly agree to let the reader start: he removes 2 matches from the pile of 5:

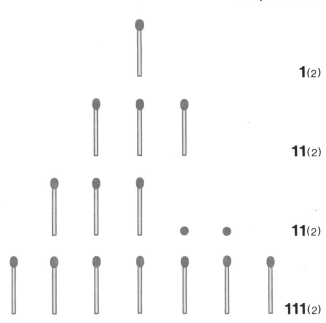

1(2)

11(2)

11(2)

111(2)

It is now our turn, and we take 6 from the pile of 7, thus leaving only 1 match in that pile. After the first round, the table is therefore, 1, 3, 3, and 1.

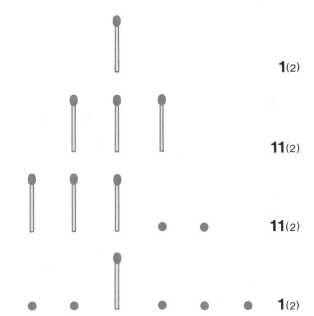

1(2)

11(2)

11(2)

1(2)

Let us then suppose that the reader removes one of the two piles of 3 matches. We then take the second pile of 3. The following diagram illustrates the state of play at this stage.

1(2)

1(2)

1(2)

What can the reader do? Does he yield victory?

Nim has a secret inbuilt binary strategy that can be used right from the start. Letting the reader begin was not such a polite or kind thing after all: in fact, if we had had to start, it would have been hard for us to win. What is this hidden strategy?

Let us transcribe the numbers of the four piles (7, 5, 3, and 1) into binary:

$$1_{(10)} \qquad 1_{(2)}$$
$$3_{(10)} \qquad 11_{(2)}$$
$$5_{(10)} \qquad 101_{(2)}$$
$$7_{(10)} \qquad 111_{(2)}$$

In the first column, from left to right, there are two units, in the second, again two, and in the third, four. When this situation arises it is impossible for the player who starts to beat a knowledgeable player. All that is needed is an even number of units in each column. And our game had this from the outset (see calculation below left); thus, in letting the reader start, we were actually giving ourselves the victory. Whatever our reader did, he or she was bound to create an odd number of units in some column.

Knowing this, let us look more closely at what happens when the reader removes 2 matches from the pile of 5 (see calculation below, right): there remain piles of 1, 3, 3, and 7, which in binary would be $1_{(2)}$, $11_{(2)}$, $11_{(2)}$, and $111_{(2)}$.

$$1_{(2)} \qquad\qquad 1_{(2)}$$
$$11_{(2)} \qquad\qquad 11_{(2)}$$
$$101_{(2)} \qquad\qquad 11_{(2)}$$
$$111_{(2)} \qquad\qquad 111_{(2)}$$
$$\overline{} \qquad\qquad \overline{}$$
$$224_{(10)} \qquad\qquad 134_{(10)}$$

There are therefore two columns with an odd number of units. Our move (taking 6 matches from the pile of 7) restored each column to an even number of units.

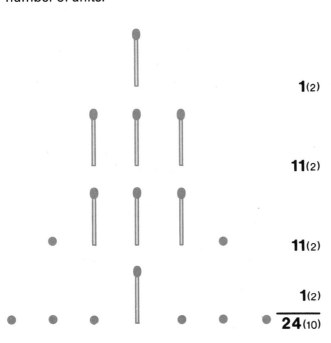

1(2)

11(2)

11(2)

1(2)
24(10)

The reader's next move (taking away one of the piles of 3) inevitably once again created an odd number in either one of the two columns, or both:

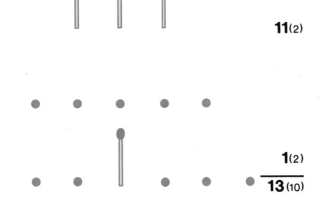

1(2)

11(2)

1(2)
13(10)

Finally, we have also removed the other pile of 3:

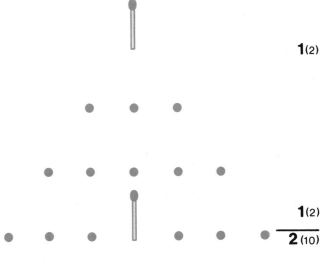

1(2)

1(2)
2 (10)

The end came when only two piles of one match each remained, and it was the reader's turn to move.

Another problem

Would the opening player win if the piles consisted of 10, 4, 7, and 2 matches respectively?

First, change these numbers into binary, then total the units in each column (in decimal):

$$
\begin{aligned}
10_{(10)} &= 1010_{(2)} \\
4_{(10)} &= 100_{(2)} \\
7_{(10)} &= 111_{(2)} \\
2_{(10)} &= 10_{(2)} \\
\hline
& 1231
\end{aligned}
$$

This gives us two columns with an odd number of units. So the opening player can win, as long as he makes no mistakes during the game.

Is it possible for the reader's first move to result in an even number of units in each column? (Suggestion: try removing 9 matches from the first pile. . . .)

Logic and mathematics: false/true—naught/one

We have already said that arithmetic is essentially a language—a convention of symbols with no par-

Computers use binary logic, as the mass of electronic circuits of which they are constructed exist only in two modes: either they allow current to pass, or they do not. These circuits can thus be referred to as *logical circuits*, or *logical gates*. There are six basic types, shown here on the right with the symbols conventionally used to denote them. As can be seen, each has one or two input elements (A, B) and an output (U), and in the explanatory table, "1" represents a passage of electric current and "0" a blocked current. For our present purposes we have just shown a few examples of logical gates, but readers who wish to learn more should consult the bibliography at the end of this book for books on mathematical logic. In an AND gate (corresponding to mathematical addition and a conjunction between propositions), there must be two input impulses (1, 1) to produce an output of (1); otherwise the output will be (0). In an OR gate on the other hand, only one input impulse is needed to produce an output of (1): 1, 0; or 0, 1. A NOT gate simply reverses the input, and so the logic of the gates develops. As the explanatory table shows, 1 and 0 are the "building bricks" of computer logic.

LOGICAL GATES		EXPLANATORY TABLE		
CLASS	SYMBOL			
conjunction **AND**		A	B	U
		1	1	1
		1	0	0
		0	1	0
		0	0	0
non exclusive disjunction **OR**		A	B	U
		1	1	1
		1	0	1
		0	1	1
		0	0	0
negation **NOT**		A		U
		1		0
		0		1
NOR ("not or")		A	B	U
		1	1	0
		1	0	0
		0	1	0
		0	0	1
NAND ("not and")		A	B	U
		1	1	0
		1	0	1
		0	1	1
		0	0	1
exclusive disjunction **XOR**		A	B	U
		0	0	0
		0	1	1
		1	0	1
		1	1	0

ticular concrete referents: the natural number 3, for instance, can mean three apples, eggs, or even ideas. Arithmetic is thus a code of rules and indications for setting these symbols in relation with each other (addition, subtraction, multiplication, and division), while the significance we find in the results is essentially that which we attribute to them. There is thus nothing to stop us from thinking of the number "1" as "true," and of naught as "false." Now, these two figures are the symbols of binary arithmetic: hence we are now ready to transform logic into a process of logical calculation.

Modern computer language is also based on the digits "0" and "1." Thus the underlying logic of this new technology remains purely mathematical.

Appendix of games with numerical systems

In line with the rather discursive style in which we dealt with the origins of numbers and arithmetic,

here is a series of problems presented as games, in which we can all try out our facility with numbers —or rather, our ability to master the language of numbers. There is one thing to bear in mind, however: these numbers are not given in a decimal base. Thus you will have to vary your numerical "points of reference" and your normal sense of "home territory" in simple calculations, and free yourself of habits of mathematical reasoning that are less than absolute. Sometimes stepping outside our usual acquired mental habits and trying to do calculations by methods with which we are not familiar can be not only entertaining but also helpful in giving us a better mastery of mathematical reasoning. It enables us to see numbers, and the relations between them, in a new light.

Some of the tests relate to concepts discussed in this section and are similar to the examples used as illustrations. Others require more individual "input." Even these, however, can easily be worked out with some concentration and straight thinking.

①

How does the series continue?

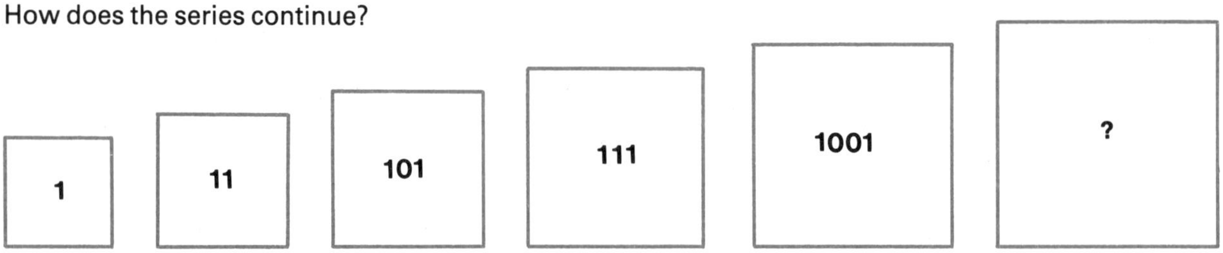

| 1 | 11 | 101 | 111 | 1001 | ? |

②

Using the "farmer's system" of multiplication, work out the following:

a) **37 × 9**   b) **28 × 13**   c) **49 × 7**

③

What is the missing number, bearing in mind that the squares have an operative purpose?

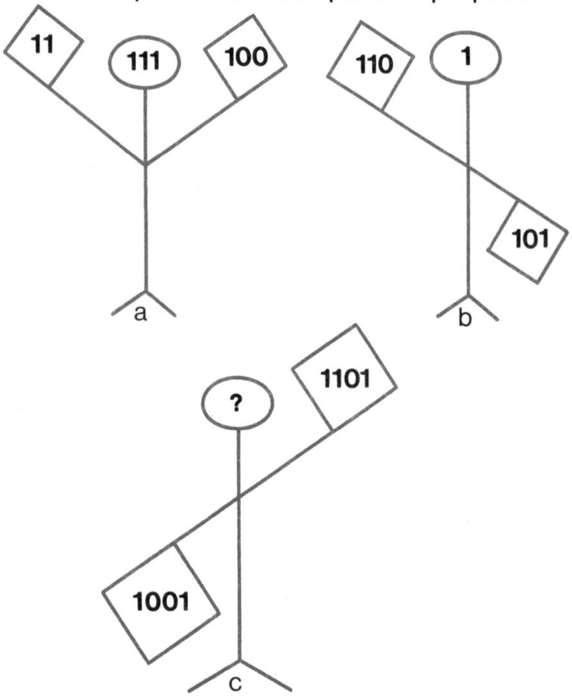

11   111   100

110   1   101

a

b

?   1101

1001

c

④

Supply the missing number.

a)

1	11
11011	1001

b)

?	110
110110	10010

⑤

Supply the missing number.

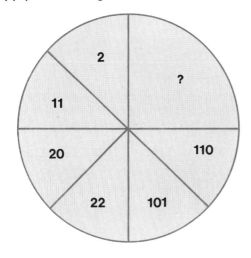

⑥

How does the series continue?

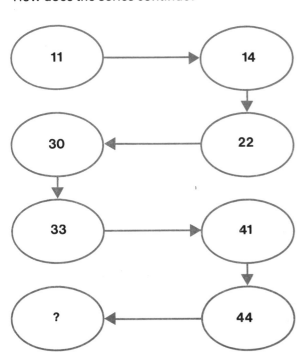

⑦

Insert the missing numbers.

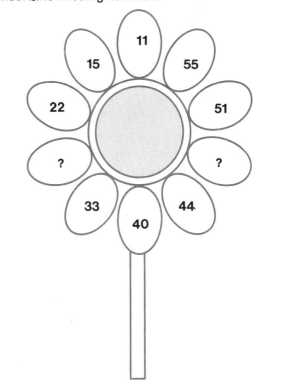

⑧

Which of the following numbers are even, and which odd?

a) **110**(2)

b) **1011**(2)

c) **2012**(3)

d) **1021**(3)

e) **2013**(4)

f) **112**(4)

g) **42**(5)

h) **103**(5)

Tests 1–8 on pages 150–1: answers and explanations

1) 1011. As we can see, in this first exercise the numbers are expressed in binary form, and each is the sum of the previous one plus 10: thus $11 = 1 + 10$, $101 = 11 + 10$. Since

$$\begin{array}{r} 11\,+ \\ 10 \\ \hline 101 \end{array} \qquad \text{hence } 1001 = \begin{array}{r} 111\,+ \\ 10 \\ \hline 1001. \end{array}$$

Thus, to establish the number that continues the series, we need simply add 10 to 1001: $1001 + 10 = 1011$; the answer, therefore, is 1011.

At this point we might, for interest's sake, work out what this corresponds to in decimal. Remember that 10 in the binary system equals 2 in the decimal system, while 1 equals one factor in both systems. Thus the number that continues the series is 11: 1 (+2), 3 (+2), 5 (+2), 7 (+2), 9 (+2), 11.

2) Answer 333, 364, 343.

a) 37 ×	9	b) 28 ×	13	c) 49 ×	7
18	18	14	26	24	14
9	36	7	52	12	28
4	72	3	104	6	56
2	144	1	208	3	112
1	288		—	1	224
	—		364		—
	333				343

3) 100. A careful examination of *a* will show that the "head" figure 111 represents $11 + 100$. The two flaglike squares emanating from *a* indicate an addition. In *b*, however, if the number in the "head" (1) is the result of some calculation between the two numbers in the flags, we can hazard that the lower number has been subtracted from the higher, since 1 is less than both 110 and 101. Therefore:

$$\begin{array}{r} 110\,- \\ 101 = \\ \hline 1 \end{array}$$

It is therefore probable that in *c*, too, the relative positions of the flags indicate a subtraction ($1101 - 1001 = 100$). Hence the missing number in *c* is 100. It is not difficult to see that here, too, we are working in binary and so can establish that $1101_{(2)} = 13_{(10)}$ and $1001_{(2)} = 9_{(10)}$, and hence $13_{(10)} - 9_{(10)} = 4_{(10)} = 100_{(2)}$.

4) 1. In square *a* the series goes $1 \times 11 = 11$, then $11 \times 11 = 1001$ since

$$\begin{array}{r} 11\,\times \\ 11 = \\ \hline 11 \\ 11\,- \\ \hline 1001 \end{array}$$

and then $1001 \times 11 = 11011$; in *b* it is not too hard to see that a similar principle has been followed, with simply an extra naught. The missing number is thus 10. We can check this by switching all the numbers into decimal: thus in *a* $1_{(2)} = 1_{(10)}$, $11_{(2)} = 3_{(10)}$, $1001_{(2)} = 9_{(10)}$, $11011_{(2)} = 27_{(10)}$; while in *b*, however, $10_{(2)} = 2_{(10)}$, $110_{(2)} = 6_{(10)}$, $10010_{(2)} = 18_{(10)}$, $110110_{(2)} = 54_{(10)}$.

5) 112 or 0. First we must identify the numerical system—which, since the highest figure is 2, we suspect is ternary. The series proceeds by the addition of 2 at each stage. Thus: $2_{(3)} + 2_{(3)} = 11_{(3)}$ and $22_{(3)} + 2_{(3)} = 101_{(3)}$. Hence $110_{(3)} + 2_{(3)} = 112_{(3)}$. In the decimal system this corresponds to 2, 4, 6, 8, 12, 14; thus the final number is 14 and the first number (before 2) is zero.

6) 102. It will be noticed first of all that the highest figure among these numbers is 4; we are thus involved with a system whose base is at least higher than 4. Already in the first step—from 11 to 14—we see that 3 units have been added. Now let us reflect: in what numerical system would we, by the addition of 3, end up with this result, $33 + 3 = 41$? Clearly, if 3 plus 3 equals 6 and is written carrying 1 (which, added to the 3, gives the 4 in 41), we can only be in a quinary system (in base 5). Thus to supply the number that continues the series, we need only calculate $44_{(5)} + 3_{(5)}$—giving the result $102_{(5)}$. Transcribed in the decimal system, the series would go 6, 9, 12, 15, 18, 21, 24, 27.

7) 26 and 51. Here let us first note how the series develops: 11–15–22.... While 11 to 15 leaves a difference of 4 units, 15 to 22 is more. So in what system could $15 + 4 = 22$? A short calculation ($5 + 4 = 9 - 2 = 7$) will tell us that we are in base 7. Let us then confirm this discovery by looking at the following numbers: $33_{(7)} + 4_{(7)} = 40_{(7)}$ and this coincides; $40_{(7)} + 4_{(7)} = 44_{(7)}$; thus the two missing numbers are given by $22_{(7)} + 4_{(7)} = 26_{(7)}$ and $44_{(7)} + 4_{(7)} = 51_{(7)}$.

The reader may transpose this into decimal if he or she so wishes.

8) We might answer this problem by transcribing all the numbers into decimal:

a) $110_{(2)} = 1 \times 2^2 + 1 \times 2^1 + 0 \times 2^0 = 4 + 2 = 6_{(10)}$;

b) $1011_{(2)} = 1 \times 2^3 + 1 \times 2^1 + 1 \times 2^0 = 8 + 3 = 11_{(10)}$.

This much can be said regarding the binary system: if the last figure of the number in question is a 1, then it must be an odd number; and if a naught, then the number is even.

c) $2012_{(3)} = 2 \times 3^3 + 0 \times 3^2 + 1 \times 3^1 + 2 \times 3^0 = 54 + 3 + 2 = 59_{(10)}$;

d) $1021_{(3)} = 1 \times 3^3 + 0 \times 3^2 + 2 \times 3^1 + 1 \times 3^0 = 27 + 7 = 34_{(10)}$.

Note how in *c* the number ended with an even number but came out odd, while the reverse happened in *d*.

e) $2013_{(4)} = 2 \times 4^3 + 0 \times 4^2 + 1 \times 4^1 + 3 \times 1 = 64 + 4 + 3 = 71_{(10)}$;

f) $112_{(4)} = 1 \times 4^2 + 1 \times 4^1 + 2 \times 4^0 = 16 + 4 + 2 = 22_{(10)}$.

In *e* the number was odd in base 4 and also came out odd in decimal; and the same also occurred in *f*. Let us examine the numbers in base 5.

g) $42_{(5)} = 4 \times 5^1 + 2 \times 5^0 = 20 + 2 = 22_{(10)}$.

h) $103_{(5)} = 4 \times 5^2 + 0 \times 5^1 + 3 \times 5^0 = 29 + 3 = 32_{(10)}$.

The final figure of the quinary number in *g* is even, and so too is the corresponding figure in decimal; whereas the last figure in *h* is odd, but the decimal equivalent is even. As the reader may have gathered, the last figure is not a reliable criterion for establishing whether numbers written in a numerical system with an odd-number base are even or odd.

Is it possible to find a criterion for telling whether a number expressed in any base is even or odd? We shall attempt to formulate one: if the base is given by an even number, then a number is identifiable as even if the unitary digit is even, and as odd if the unitary digit is odd. However, if the base is given by an odd number, then the number in question is even (or odd) if the sum of the values of each digit, counted in decimal, is (respectively) even or odd.

Pick your own games

And still it is not finished. How well I know it, the whole book is like that! I have wasted a lot of time on it: a perfect contradiction remains mysterious to wise and foolish alike. This art, friend, is both old and new.
Mephistopheles' reflections in Goethe's *Faust*

A brilliant solution

Some years ago, Omar Fadhami, the emir of a small state in the Persian Gulf which until the oil boom had been poor and little known, but which had since become rich and great in world esteem, paid a visit to a certain European country. Naturally he was accompanied by a retinue of wives, advisers, ministers, children, and servants.

One day he decided to give his court presents, and at the head of a kind of procession he went into the smartest and biggest store in the capital. The courtiers swarmed around the laden counters.

The emir was very satisfied, until he noticed that the children were squabbling over toys, sweets, and picture books. An equable man, however, he did not think it appropriate to intervene. But he began to be annoyed when he observed that his wives and the ladies of his retinue were behaving in a similar fashion, fighting over lengths of material, makeup and perfumes. Solima, usually so sweet-natured, hit out at young Iris, who had "robbed" her of a little vanity case. Things were hardly much better among the servants: arguments became louder, faces more flushed. Omar, pensive as ever, reflected on the irrationality of the situation. Everybody was choosing in a hurry, without bothering to think whether what they were becoming enraged over was really either necessary or useful. A moment of reflection would quieten everyone down.

At this point he made a decision. Clapping his hands three times, he obtained sudden silence, as if by magic. Then he turned to the store manager and said: "Pack everything for me, and send it to me. At home, in the quiet of the palace, everyone will see what they really want."

The emir's order was speedily carried out by the delighted manager and the affair was widely publicized by the media. Everyone was so happy to receive everything in the store because now Solima, Iris, the children, and all the courtiers had time to sort things out.

And it is in the same spirit that we offer the following "pick" of games—for each reader to choose from, to classify, and to evaluate as he or she wills.

Geometrical figures with matches

Two fundamental concepts of geometry are the point and the straight line. Upon these—which are given, rather than defined by means of other concepts—the whole structure of the discipline rests.

What, in geometrical terms, does a match remind us of? Despite the slight bulge of the sulfur cap at the end, it can be seen as a short straight line; or better, as one of an infinite number of possible embodiments of the abstract notion of a "section of a

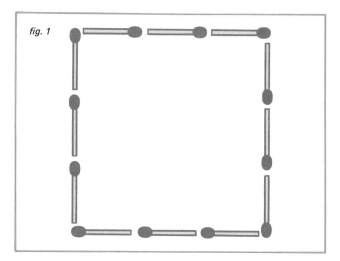

fig. 1

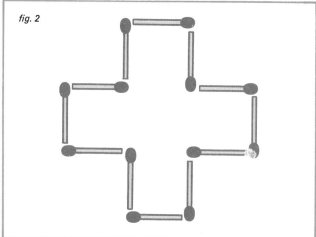

fig. 2

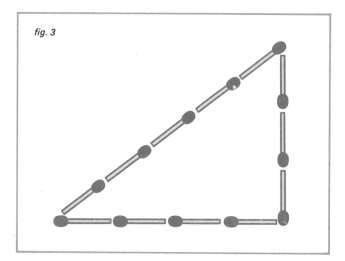

fig. 3

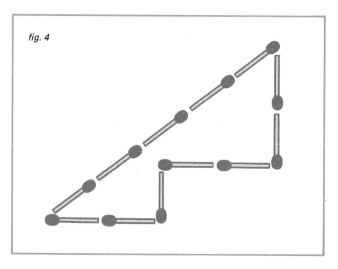

fig. 4

straight line." This perhaps explains why, ever since they were invented, matches have been used for creating geometrical figures to "kill time." Their unvarying size and shape, rather than being a drawback, in fact proves a spur to devising ever more unusual and curious geometrical patterns. There is, too, a less obvious advantage—though it is for all that no less potentially fruitful: since each match is identical, they can be used as units of measurements for the figures formed from them. This means that in the games that follow, mathematical concepts and calculations are necessarily also involved.

If, for example, we have twelve matches, we can form various types of polygon all with sides representing a whole number. A square is a polygon with four equal sides, and twelve is exactly divisible by four—three times, as we all know. So let us take three matches at a time and make a square with sides of three units (using the concept of matches rather than inches, centimeters, and the like). The result will be a square divisible into nine smaller squares with one-match-long sides (*figure 1*).

Taking this figure and modifying it slightly, we can form (*figure 2*) a cross made up of five smaller squares. In other words, four of the small squares out of the total of nine in the first figure were removed, leaving five.

Let us now consider the following problem: Is it possible to construct a polygon consisting of four smaller squares, using all twelve matches?

One solution might be the following. First, make a right-angled triangle, as in *figure 3*.

The surface of this triangle consists of six square units: $4 \times 3 \div 2 = 6$! Thus the problem now is to modify this six-unit figure to achieve one of four units. The solution is shown in *figure 4*.

BACKGAMMON

Many games developed from the classical "royal table"—a game known to the Romans as *tabula*, which was played throughout the Middle Ages and into more recent times in Italy. One of the best known of these developments is the English game of *backgammon* which uses the same characteristic board, and the rules of which relate quite closely to the original form of "royal table." The name "backgammon" comes from "back game"—for, as we shall see, a single man (piece), known as a "Blot," resting on a point, and hit by his opponent, has to go back to the "Bar" and start all over again (two or more Blots may be hit in one play).

Today backgammon is very popular as a game all over the world. A game for two players—although there is a version, *chouette*, for up to five players or more—it has a distinctive board (see *figure a*),

with 12 wedge-shaped points of one colour and 12 of a different colour. There are 15 white or light-coloured men and 15 red or dark ones. The board is divided into four tables, each player having an "inner table" and "outer table." Each table has 6 points, those in the inner table are numbered from 1 to 6, those on the outer from 7 to 12. Each player has 2 six-face dice numbering 1–6; there is also another die for double scoring, also six-faced, numbering 2. 4, 8, 16, 32, and 64, usually used when the game is played for high stakes.

* The men are distributed on the board as shown in *figure b* (overleaf). Starting from this layout, which may at first seem odd but which in fact is designed to make the game quicker and more interesting, white moves from his opponent's inner table to the far side of the board, across to his own outer table into his inner table. Red moves in the opposite direction. The dividing space of the two tables

(inner and outer) is called the "Bar." Each player moves his men according to the throw of the two dice into his inner table, and when all are there, he throws or bears them off (starts to throw off men from points corresponding to dice thrown). The first player to remove all his men wins.

* To decide which player starts the game, a single die is cast, the higher throw deciding the issue; ties are rethrown. For each move, both dice are thrown. The count begins on the point next to the one on which the man is resting. Numbers on both dice must be played if possible. Two men are moved according to the score of each die (one score per die), or a single man can move based on the score of one die, then continue on the score of the second die, but the two numbers cannot be added and played as one move. In the event of a double score (4 + 4), each counts twice, so the number of moves also doubles. The moves may be effected by the same

man (four times), or by two, three, even four.
If, having thrown the two dice, a player can only use one of the two scores, it is the higher score that must be used—that is, so long as such a move is possible; otherwise the lower score must be used. In all other cases players must use both scores. In other words, a player must play one or other score.

* Other basic rules of the game are as follows:
A point with two or more men on it is *blocked* against an opponent, although it may be jumped, and when a player cannot move because of blocked points, he loses the move. There is no limit to the number of men either player may have on one point.
A Blot, hit by his opponent and sent to the Bar, must reenter in his opponent's inner table and travel all around the board to his own inner table before more men can be moved or taken off. Thus a man "sent off" can only come back into play when one or

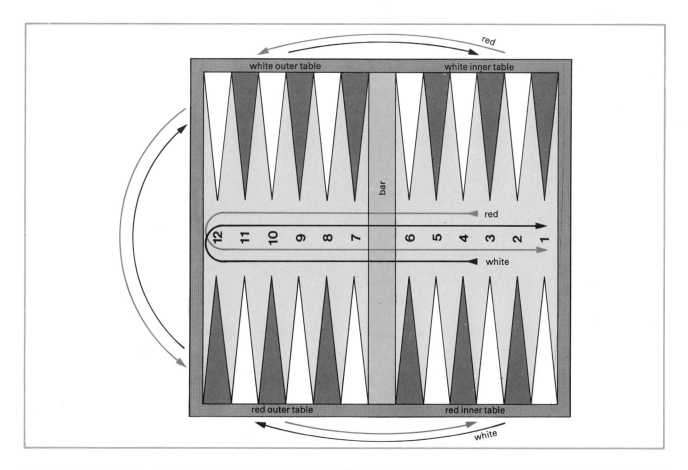

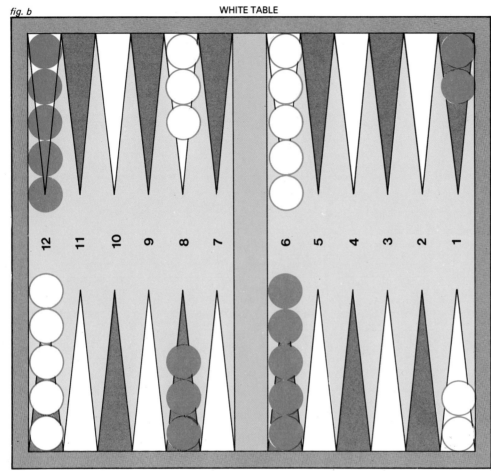

12 11 10 9 8 7 6 5 4 3 2 1

RED TABLE

* The skill in this absorbing game lies in impeding the opponent's progress as much as possible, hitting Blots and building up "houses," which make it difficult or impossible for the other player to proceed or to reenter from the Bar. At this point it should also be mentioned that if one manages to build "houses" (to group at least two) on points 7 and 5—so-called key points—one's opponent becomes greatly handicapped (and even more so, the more houses one forms on the opponent's outer table). What requires most skill is gauging how safe or otherwise it is to leave one's own men exposed as Blots. In fact, there are manuals that list exhaustively the various possible permutations of the moves during a game, giving the probabilities for and against creating a Blot in any situation.

* There are three types of victory: a) single win, when one's opponent has also begun the process of removing his men from the board, having already removed at least one; b) *gammon*, when the opponent has not yet removed any of his men; and c) *backgammon*, when the opponent still has one or more men in the other player's territory or at the Bar. In the event of a single win, the winner takes the straight stake; with a *gammon*, double the stake; and with a *backgammon*, triple the stake.

* The single die (already mentioned) for the doubling version of the game is only used when the game is played for money (and thus a stake has been fixed). A player who feels he or she has the upper hand at any point can set this die to 2, thereby doubling the stake; if the other player at any time during the course of play thinks he has the upper hand, he can set the die to 4 (double the already doubled stake). This can continue up to 24 times the stake—though alternating each time between the two players (thus, A, 2; B, 4; A, 8; B, 16; and so on). A player can refuse a double at any point: in which case, he pays the stake already reached, and a new game is begun.

other of the die scores puts it on a free point in the opponent's inner table (a point that does not have two or more enemy men on it, in which case it would be blocked). If the enemy point has one man on it, it is a Blot and goes to the Bar in turn. The returned man (or any other on the board) is then moved according to the score of the second die, but only *provided* the player does not have any other men at the Bar.

* As mentioned, the final stages of the game consist of the removing of men from one's inner table. This can only happen when *all* the men still in

play are assembled together in one's inner table. Two kinds of moves are possible:

1) One can remove one or two men from the board, depending on the throw of the dice, for example, if one of the numbers thrown is higher than the highest-numbered point on which a man is resting, the next highest can be removed (for example, if one die scores 6, and the highest man is on 5, it can be removed from the board.) One can, if one wishes, take the lower score first (for example, in the event of a 5 + 6 score, one could remove the single man on 5, then that—or one, if there are

several—on 4, to make up the 6 score).

2) On the other hand, one might wish to reduce the number of men on the higher points of one's inner table (5 and 6), or to turn a Blot into a "house" (two or more men on a single point). This is most important when one's opponent has a man at the Bar—for on reentering the game, he could force an enemy Blot back to the Bar in turn, from where it would have to go around the whole course again. As long as every point in one's inner table has a "house," it is impossible for an opponent to move from the Bar.

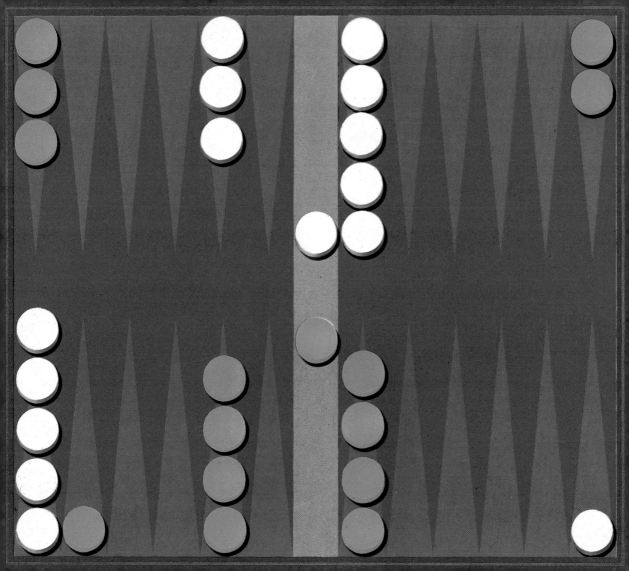

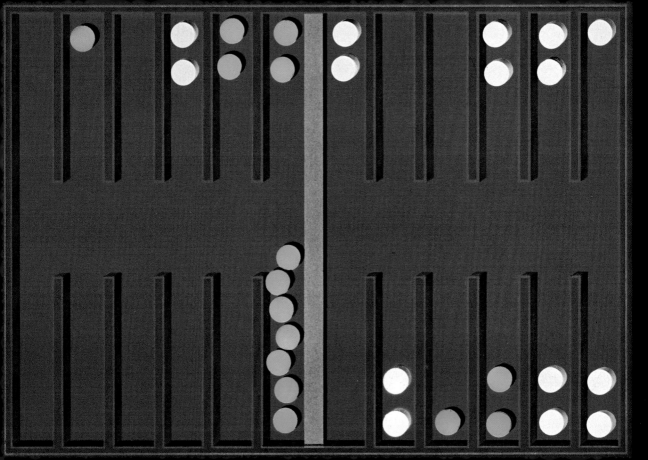

PUFF—ALEA OR TABULA

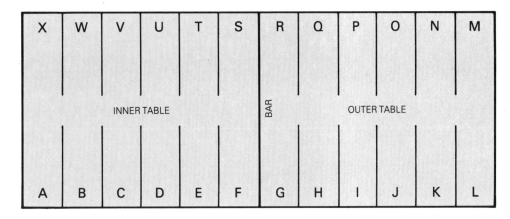

Puff

When a game becomes established in the "heritage" of a society, an indication of its vitality is the way it fragments, so to speak, into all sorts of variants. This happened, for instance, with the ancient and very widely played game of backgammon (see pp. 155–157). One quite common version of backgammon, played in England and Germany, is generally known as puff. Anyone familiar with the rules of backgammon will easily grasp the rules of this variant. It is always played by two people, with 15 pieces each: one set white (or some other light colour), the other black (or any dark colour); two dice are needed. Basically the same as for backgammon, the board, on right, has spaces, marked with capital letters, corresponding to the arrows. Puff is a less flexible game than backgammon. This does not make it any slower, however: games can sometimes be short, but they can equally be long drawn out.

Puff is related closely to other games besides backgammon: for instance, to the French *tric-trac*, which acquired a certain notoriety after it was played by Niccolo Machiavelli (1469–1527) during his enforced leisure in San Casciano; and to an extremely ancient game, known in Roman times as *alea* and very widespread throughout medieval Europe. Puff has basically the same rules as this latter game.

Alea or tabula

"Alea sive tabula" ("the dice game or the game board"): this reference comes from late Roman times, concerning a game that has rightly been seen as the ancestor of a number of games using a board and dice. Board games were already common in Greece and the East before the Romans conquered there and began to adopt both the culture and the everyday customs and activities they encountered.

It is not known when the score obtained from thrown dice was first used to determine the moves of objects on a board. What we do know, though, is that by classical times *alea* (literally, "a die") also meant a board game played with dice. Referring to this game, the famous historian Suetonius (70–140 A.D.), author of the popular *Lives of the Caesars*,

used the term *alea* and nothing else.

In the hurly-burly of life in Republican Rome, there were people who earned their living as professional dice players, called *aleatores*. By Cicero's day it was considered a somewhat disreputable profession, although by all accounts it was mostly old men who played games of this kind, since they required little physical strength. Times must have changed considerably, then, by the age of the Emperor Claudius (45–54 A.D.)—who, Suetonius tells us, was so fond of *alea* that he had it fitted into his carriage, to play during long journeys. Claudius was indeed so expert at the game that (still according to Suetonius) he was able to write a treatise on it. Unfortunately this book, which would have been of no small interest, has been lost. The game spread throughout the empire and is in fact played even today in the area around the Aegean, under the name *tàvli*. Anyone who saw the film *Topkapi* (a successful film of the 1960s, starring Melina Mercouri and Maximilian Schell) will probably remember the scene in which two people are seen playing *tàvli*. We have no direct detailed account of the rules of *tabula* or *alea*. But from the scraps of information we do have, we are able to more or less reconstruct the game, filling in the gaps with rules that seem pragmatically necessary.

* *Basic facts.* There were two players and three dice (while today, puff is played with two only). Each player had 15 pieces, one set black, the other white, and these were arranged on a board that, though it may not have had 24 wedge-shaped markings, would have had 12 + 12 = 24 spaces of some kind, similar to backgammon.

* *The dice.* The ancient Romans used two sorts of dice: *tesserae*, which had six sides, marked I, II, III, IV, V, and VI; and *tali*, which were oblong in shape (usually made of joint bones), rounded at either end, and marked only on the other four sides. On one side was a dot, called *unio* (in Latin, "one"), an ace known as "the dog," *canis*; on the opposite side were six dots (*senio* = "six"); on the remaining two sides, three and four, *ternio* and *quaternio*. During the game, four *tali* and three *tesserae* were used. And from this we can guess fairly safely that *alea* was played with *tesserae* rather than *tali*. Normally, the dice were shaken inside a small tower-shaped box, known as the *fritillus* or *turricula*, and thrown onto the board. The luckiest throw was called *Venus*, *jactus venereus*, or *basilicus* and consisted of 3 sixes (if *tesserae*) or the score of the *tali* when each landed with a different face up. The unluckiest throw, known as *jactus pessimus* or *damnosus*, or also *canis* or *canicula*, was three aces (with *tesserae*) or when all the *tali* fell the same way up. The other throws were worth what the numbers added up to. If one of the *tali* landed end up, it was "cock dice," and the throw was repeated. When throwing dice, the custom was to express a wish, say the name of one's true love, and the like.

* *How to play.* Alea was a sort of race in which each player started in turn at space A and proceeded anticlockwise, according to the dice throw, towards X, obeying certain rules. The winner was the first to remove the last of his or her pieces from space X. The *score* for each throw would be worked out roughly as follows:
– all scores from any dice throw were valid;
– *a piece* could be moved as many spaces as the total of the

points scored by the three dice;
– *two pieces* could be moved in one go, one as many spaces as the total of two dice scores and the other the number of spaces of the third die score;
– or similarly, *three pieces* could be moved, according to the scores, respectively, of each individual die.

* *Important rules.*
1) If one player has two or more pieces on a single space, the other cannot use that space.
2) If the fall of the dice lands a player's piece onto a space already occupied by one opponent piece, this latter may be removed and put on the central bar. This means that his opponent must bring that piece back into the game, starting at A again, before moving any other pieces.
3) No player may go beyond space L until all his or her pieces are in play.
4) No piece can be taken from X until all that player's pieces have passed R.
5) All points scored must be used, as we have described: it is not permitted to use part of the score of one die to move a piece. Points that cannot be used (for example, because of spaces occupied by enemy pieces) are lost.

Another keen player of *alea*, so tradition has it, was the Byzantine Emperor Zeno (474–491 A.D.). The colour plate, opposite page, reproduces the state of play during one game: Zeno was playing the dark pieces: his next score was 2, 5, and 6.

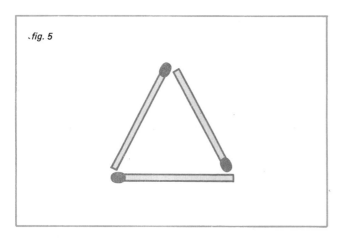

fig. 5

Adding three matches . . .

I) *Figure 5* is of an equilateral triangle formed by three matches: by adding another three, it is possible to form three triangles that, taken together with the first, make four in all! How!

The answer is illustrated in *figure 6*.

II) *Figure 7* is also of an equilateral triangle—though this time each side consists of two matches. If three are added, how many triangles will there be?

Normally the following answer is offered: The extra matches are laid inside the triangle, so as to form four small triangles; the answer therefore would be four. In fact, though, there are five, since the arrangement of the four is such as to form a fifth. A complete answer would thus be: By adding three matches, one would make five in all—four small and one large (*figure 8*).

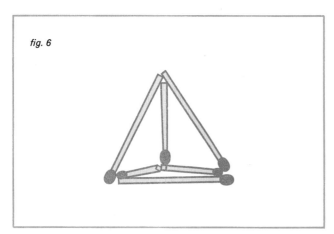

fig. 6

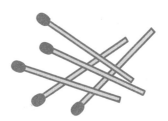

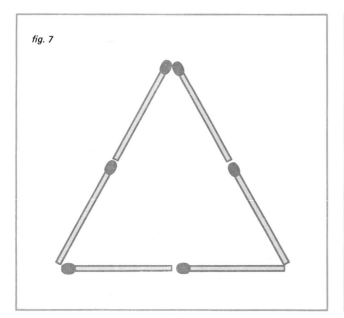

fig. 7

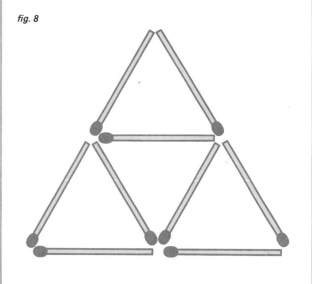

fig. 8

Removing three matches . . .

Four squares together form a single larger square (see *figure 9*); with three fewer matches, we can make three diamonds! How?

The solution is shown below (*figure 10*).

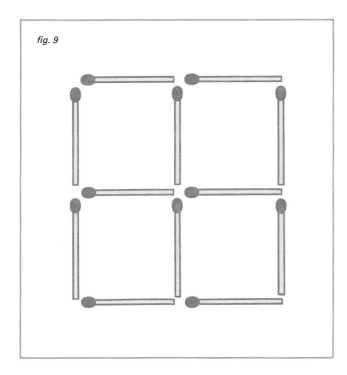

fig. 9

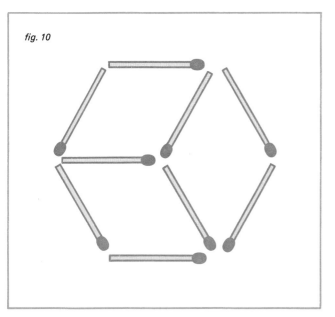

fig. 10

Let's play with squares

With twenty-two matches we should be able to devise all kinds of quite complex geometrical figures. But let us take one of the very simplest, the common square. How many squares with sides of

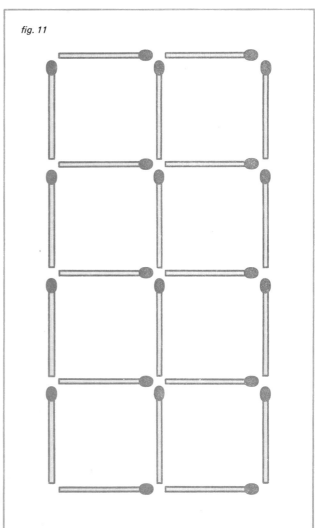

fig. 11

one match length can be made with twenty-two matches? After various combinations, we have ended up with a maximum of eight (*figure 11*). However, we shall not be surprised to hear that our maximum has been beaten: we are very willing to recognize our limitations. By constructing two 3-dimensional cubes with twenty matchsticks we can obtain eleven squares.

Other games with squares can also be tried. For

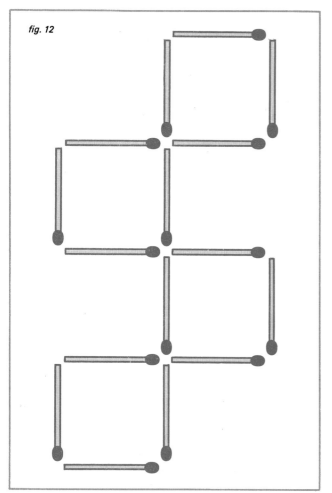

fig. 12

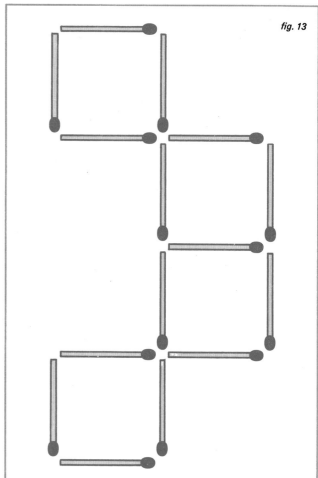

fig. 13

instance, what is the most number of matches we can remove and still be left with four squares? Let us proceed methodically. If we take away six, sixteen remain—more than enough for four squares (see *figure 12*).

Even if seven or eight matches are removed, there are still easily enough for four squares (*figures 13* and *14* show this quite clearly).

With nine or ten matches less, we are left with fewer options; however, it is still possible to form four squares with sides of one match length (*figures 15* and *16*).

Abandoning any restriction on the length of the sides of the squares, what is the minimum number of matches needed to make four squares?

Figure 17 illustrates our solution, using only six matches.

The number of squares can increase to infinity, but obviously the number of matches needed to subdivide the available space will similarly increase.

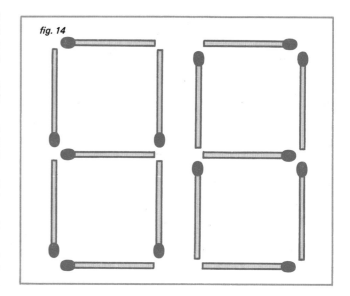

fig. 14

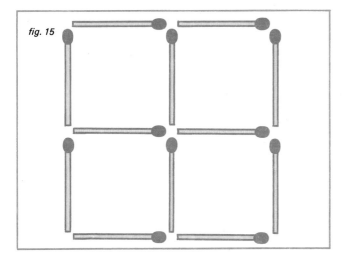

fig. 15

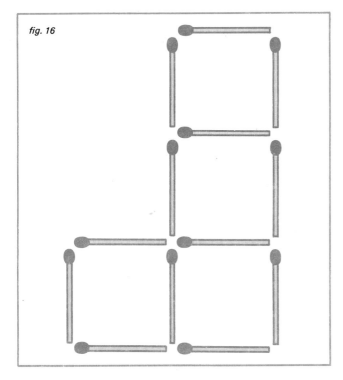

fig. 16

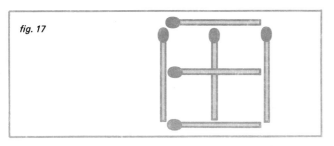

fig. 17

What are the coins in Peter's pocket?

"I have two coins in my pocket, totalling 30 cents," Peter told his friend. "But one of them is not a nickel. What are the two coins?"

The friend answered that he must have two coins of 15 cents, in that case!

"Don't be stupid!" Peter laughed.

The friend's answer was in fact along completely the wrong lines—though perhaps many of us would have thought similarly. Let us look more closely at the trick question.

Some problems are simple enough in themselves, yet become problematic because of the way they are expressed. And this is a case in point. Let us reread it carefully and analyze the language trap in which Peter successfully caught his friend. First of all, we are told, "I have two coins in my pocket, totalling 30 cents"; then comes the second piece of information, ("But one of them is not a nickel").

Wrong answers are often common in such problems because we are not really listening to that negative bit of information: here we are informed that *one* of the two coins is not a nickel—it does not say that *neither* is!

So a correct answer would be: The coins in Peter's pocket are a quarter and a nickel. As we were told, *one* of them was not a nickel: and that was the quarter.

How many horses has the farmer got?

A farmer owns ten cows, three horses, and twenty sheep. How many horses does he own, if we also call cows horses? The quick answer would, of course, be thirteen (the three horses + the ten cows, which we are calling horses). However, thirteen is incorrect.

Here we are dealing with the nature of language: for even though we have agreed to call a cow "horse," that does not actually make it a horse.

Language is only a system of symbols that we use to designate things, but the system itself is quite arbitrary. If we call a horse "an ox," the creature does not suddenly become an ox. Hence the answer to the question is the straight fact: the farmer has three horses, not thirteen at all.

We take language so much for granted that we sometimes confuse the object and the word signifying it and therefore fail to distinguish between two different levels of reality.

A square and a triangle

Sometimes the game is to visualize a certain geometrical figure without adding or removing any matches but simply altering the position of one or two, in order to create a very different shape.

For instance, the six matches in *figure 18* make a fairly conventional matchstick house shape: now, can you make four triangles just by moving three matches?

Figure 19 shows how this can be done by placing over the triangular house roof another triangle, the points of which rest on the midpoints of the original triangle's sides.

The ocean liner

World-famous buildings, churches, towers, monuments, old sailing boats and ships, galleys, modern vessels of all kinds are frequently taken as subjects for matchstick models.

Figure 20 gives us in outline a representation of the prow of a big oceangoing liner, seen from the front. It is made up from nine matches.

Now, by moving just five of these matches, can you create a pattern of five triangles?

The solution is given in the diagram in the middle of the opposite page (*figure 21*).

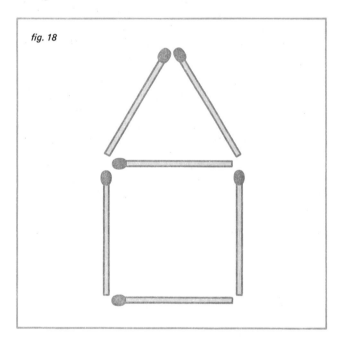

fig. 18

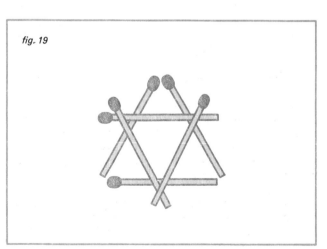

fig. 19

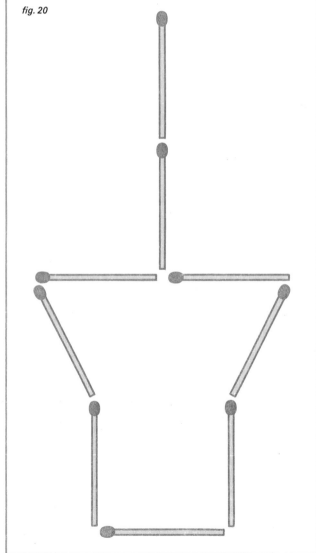

fig. 20

How old was Livy?

The historian Livy was born in Padua in 59 B.C. and spent most of his life in the capital, Rome. However, as age crept upon him he returned to his beloved native city, where he died in 17 A.D.

A Latin teacher familiar with the life and works of Livy asked his class the following question:

"How old was Livy when he died?"

At once the answer came back, "Seventy-six."

"Wrong," the teacher replied. "He was seventy-five." Why seventy-five? The pupil who had answered had added 59 + 17 = 76, without allowing

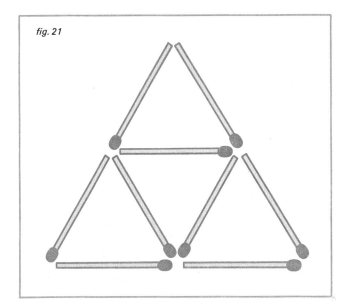

fig. 21

for the fact that the year naught (0) does not exist. Hence he should have calculated: 59 + 17 − 1 = 75.

"Trick questions" like this rely on never having considered the nonexistence of a year naught! Thus, when we need to calculate the age of somebody born before the birth of Christ, who died afterwards, in an *anno Domini*, we tend mistakenly just to add the two numbers. Normally, such questions would be phrased a little more cunningly.

Let us, for instance, imagine that Gaius was born on the ides of April in 25 B.C. and died on the same day, the ides of April, in the year 25 A.D. How old was he at his death?

We would be tempted to answer fifty. Yet that would be wrong. He would of course have been forty-nine, since the year 0 cannot be included.

To understand this better, try to envisage the lifespan of an individual as a straight line divided into short stretches: from 3 B.C. to 3 A.D., for example,

the first year of life goes from 3 to 2, the second from 2 to 1 B.C., then the third—since there is no year 0—from 1 B.C. to 1 A.D., the fourth from 1 A.D. to 2 A.D., and the fifth finally from 2 to 3 A.D. Hence one year seems to have disappeared, but in fact the actual number of years lived was five and not six.

Tony's socks

Tony was somewhat lackadaisical by nature and more than once went out with his girlfriend wearing odd socks. In the rush of going out, he would fail to notice that they were of different colours. This particularly irritated Prudence, his fiancée, who was a stickler for neatness and smart clothes.

Although it had not in fact been the cause of too much disagreement, Tony had nevertheless resolved to pay more attention to these little matters. As he was getting ready to go to a party that evening, there was a power cut, and he found he had to put on his socks in the dark (typically, he had no candles in the house and trying to find matches in the chaos in which he lived was hopeless). So he sat down and thought about it. In the drawer he knew there were ten brown socks and ten light gray ones. How many, then, should he take to be sure of having two of the same colour?

Answer: three.

There were two possibilities: either all three would be the same colour, or two would be the same and one different. In either case he would be sure of having a pair of the same colour.

. . . and Prudence's gloves

Meanwhile, Prudence had been about to look for her gloves as the power cut occurred. The thought of arriving at the party with odd gloves was not to be countenanced! In her drawer she had five pairs of black ones (ten gloves in all) and five pairs of white (ten white gloves in all).

Prudence's problem was rather harder than Tony's, for half of the gloves she had to choose from were right-handed and the other half left-handed. After a moment's thought, she took out eleven gloves, confident that among them there would be at least one pair—both a right-hand and a left-hand glove of the same colour.

Now, had she really found a solution? Should she have taken either more or fewer?

Answer: She had indeed taken the minimum necessary. If she had taken one fewer, she might have found herself with ten right-hand gloves, five black and five white.

The mill

Most of the energy used by the ancient Greeks and Romans was human- or animal-powered. Water energy (the principle of water turning a wheel by

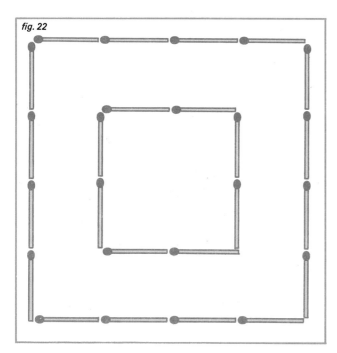

fig. 22

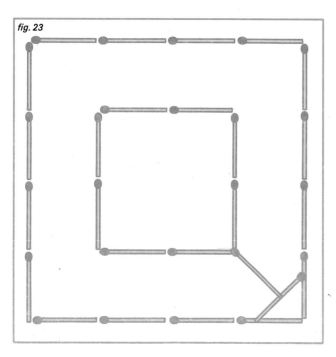

fig. 23

falling onto jutting-out paddles) was known, but slaves were so easy to come by that they were used even for such crude tasks as raising water and grinding corn.

In the Middle Ages, when slavery as it had been known in antiquity no longer existed, water mills were built throughout Europe, replacing the manual machines used by the Romans. For centuries the structure of these mills remained the same, although they did change in size and came to be built in different materials and used for a wider variety of purposes. Ever better and strong gearing systems enabled the simple rotating motion of the paddled wheels to drive many different kinds of machine, from hammers to looms, so that the word "mill" itself came to mean a factory (at least in certain areas).

The very existence of Holland is largely due to the windmill: with tireless application, they won land from the sea by digging drainage dikes, through which stagnant water was pushed out to sea by means of energy harnessed by windmills.

The bridge to the island

Figure 22 represents an island in the sea. Years back, the Dutch built a windmill on it.

It makes an ideal site, for a wind is always blowing off the nearby sea. Unfortunately, the one road linking it with the mainland has been destroyed by rough seas, and the mill is now cut off.

Is it possible, with two matches, to build a temporary bridge to reestablish the link with the mainland? One complication is that if we align two matches perpendicularly, we shall find they are not long enough to reach both sides. *Figure 23* offers an ingenious solution.

A wheel with paddles

The most basic element of any mill is the wheel, turned by some form of energy (animal, hydraulic, or wind), which is linked to a gearing mechanism in order to turn other wheels, for various purposes; not just the grinding of corn. In the eighteenth century, for instance, machines built on this principle pumped water out of mines, thus enabling shafts to be dug deeper. In water mills, the principal wheel is fitted with paddles, onto which the water falls, thereby pushing it around.

Take the sixteen matches used in *figure 22* to separate terra firma from the sea, and see if you can "construct" a water wheel with the necessary paddles. *Figure 24* shows how this can be done.

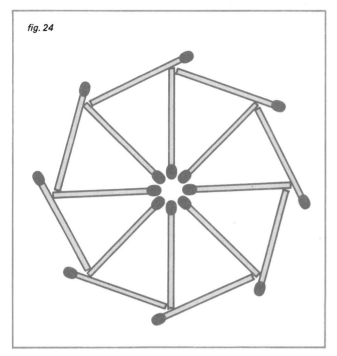

fig. 24

The hidden square

Now for a rather unusual game: set out four matches in a cross, as in *figure 25*.

Is it possible to create a square by moving just one match?

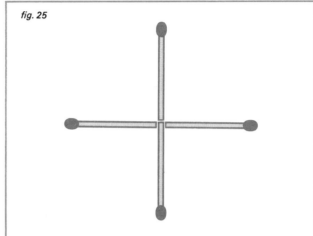

fig. 25

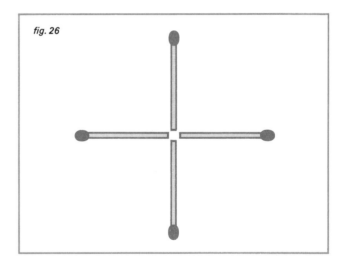

fig. 26

Claustrophobia

Patricia was an oversensitive girl who was not always able to control her fears and anxieties and see her own weaknesses in perspective. Among other things, she became agitated when she found herself in closed spaces: to put it bluntly, she was a bit claustrophobic. In certain situations she had the feeling of being trapped and unable to escape. For her work she often had to travel by train to visit a firm in a nearby town. Shortly before this particular occasion, a bomb had exploded as a train was going through a tunnel. Now just outside the station where Patricia took her train there was a long tunnel. And even before getting on board, she could feel mounting terror. She feared she would not be able to bear it once she was in the train.

What could she do? She could at least make sure she was in the quickest carriage, so as to spend as short a time as possible in the tunnel.

So she asked a guard if there was a carriage that would take her through the tunnel more quickly than the others. The guard said yes, there was one. Which one was it?

Answer: The guard recommended that she sit in the back carriage; since the tunnel came immediately outside the station, and as the train would still be accelerating, the tail carriage would thus traverse it faster than the others.

Initially, the reader will probably try to think of the matches as forming the sides of a square—in part, no doubt, because this was the case in previous games. Here, however, the solution is in itself a bit crude, but it does stretch one's imaginative abilities, forcing them to think of the problem in a slightly different way.

The only answer is to lower the bottom match until a little square is formed by the ends of all four matches (see *figure 26*).

Games with clocks

①

If   goes with   then   goes with

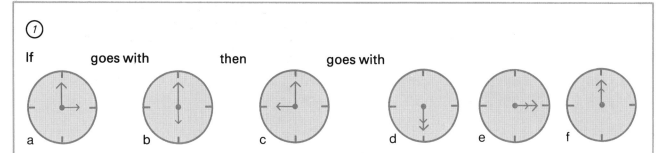

②

If   goes with   then   goes with

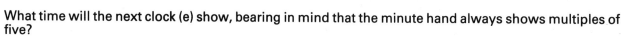
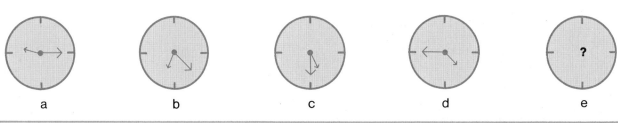

③

What time will the next clock (e) show, bearing in mind that the minute hand always shows multiples of five?

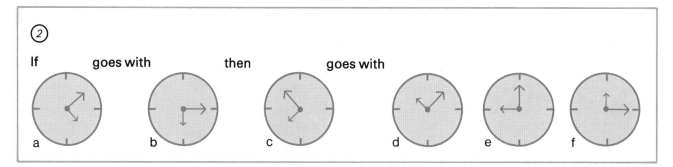

④

What time will the next clock (e) show, bearing in mind that the minute hand always shows multiples of five, while the dotted line represents the seconds?

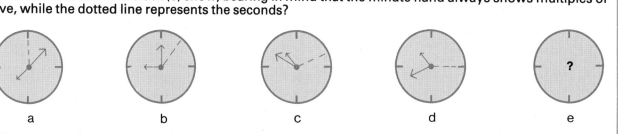

(see answers on p. 175)

MAGIC SQUARES

Are you feeling depressed, even downright melancholy? See if the following game helps raise your spirits. *Figures a, b,* and *c* are of magic squares; the sum of the numbers in the boxes is always 15, whether added along horizontal, vertical, or diagonal lines. The reader can check this personally. In all three examples, *a, b,* and *c,* the same ''magic'' works! *Figure d* is a square of the same sort, but two of the numbers have been swapped, so that in some lines and some columns the answer is no longer 15. The object of the game is to detect the misplaced numbers and put them back in the right boxes to re-create a ''magic'' square. A careful examination of *figure d* will show that by moving the 6 from the top left-hand box and swapping it with the bottom right-hand 4, we can make a square with the same ''magic'' as *a, b,* and *c.* Perhaps you are still feeling melancholy, despite this little exercise? Never mind. We were simply suggesting a remedy advocated by sixteenth-century artists and scientists to stimulate the human intellectual faculties.

Their strange allure
Magic squares are very ancient geometrical and arithmetical figures. It would appear that the Chinese were the first to discover them: the *lu shu* (*figure c*), to which particular religious and mystic significance was attached, is recorded as early as the fourth century B.C. Similar squares were known very early on in India, whence the Arabs brought them to the West, to be made known to Christian thinkers in the fourteenth century by a Greek monk called Moscopulos. The peculiar mathematical properties of these geometrical figures caught people's imaginations, so much so that mysterious magic powers were attributed to them—hence their name. At various times they have been a source of artistic inspiration, equally fascinating both to the learned and to the ignorant. Worth mentioning from the time of the Renaissance are the mathematician Cornelius Agrippa (1486–1535), who had an unflagging passion for magic squares, and the German painter Albrecht Dürer (who featured one in his famous print *Melancholia*, 1514). More recently, too, men's imaginations have been stirred by the mysterious relationships of numbers in magic squares. Benjamin Franklin was only too happy to be able to devote himself to them, and his works contain complex examples together with comments. In the present century, the American architect Claude Fayette Bragdon has based some of his buildings on geometrical models inspired by magic circles. Superstitious belief in their magic properties still survives: it is said that during the war in Cambodia, local women drew such squares on their scarves for protection against bombs; and in certain areas of the East it is still common to find them made of bone or wood and worn as amulets. This aura of magic and power is not so surprising once one becomes aware of their geometrical and arithmetical properties. Let us now look briefly at these.

Definition and properties
A magic square is an arrangement of whole positive numbers, without repetition, in a regular pattern of adjacent squares, such that each line (from left to right, or vice versa), each column (from top to bottom, or vice versa), and both diagonals all add up to the same figure. The figure *n* determines the *order* (or *base*, or *module*) of the magic square.

Figures a, b, and *c,* are all of the third order, because each side consists of three squares with three numbers. *Figure e* is also of the third order: what is different is the total for each line, column, and diagonal. This is now 21 rather than 15. Looking at the colour plate on page 171, what will the number on the central ball be? We are dealing with a third-order magic square and know from the complete rows that the total to attain is 21: hence we simply subtract (9 + 5) from 21 = 21 − 14 = 7. The missing number, then, is 7. Squares can also be devised of the fourth and fifth—and even higher—orders. The first order is not really worth considering—a simple square with one number in it! It is curious, however, that no second-order squares exist, but perhaps if you try to make one, you'll discover why.

fig. d

6	9	2
3	5	7
8	1	4

fig. e

10	5	6
3	7	11
8	9	4

fig. a

2	7	6
9	5	1
4	3	8

fig. b

6	1	8
7	5	3
2	9	4

fig. c

8	3	4
1	5	9
6	7	2

fig. f

7	12	1	14
2	13	8	11
16	3	10	5
9	6	15	4

fig. g

1	15	14	4
12	6	7	9
8	10	11	5
13	3	2	16

fig. h

2	15	5	16
9	12	6	11
14	3	17	4
13	8	10	7

More complex squares
The higher the order of the square, the more taxing, yet at the same time more satisfying, the game. Try to make a magic square of the fourth order with whole numbers from 1 to 16, such that the total for each row of four figures (horizontal, vertical, and diagonal) is 34. *Figure f* is one suggestion; *figure g* is another.
Some squares have other remarkable properties. In *figure g*, for instance, the required 34 can be found not only by adding the numbers in the outside squares each side (1 + 12 + 8 + 13 = 34), but also by taking the four corner numbers (1 + 16 + 4 + 13 = 34), or again the center 4 squares: 6 + 7 + 10 + 11 = 34. *Figure h* is a fourth-order square with similar properties, while *figure i* is a square of the fifth order. (Note: The broken diagonals also total 65—23 + 15 + 6 + 19 + 2 = 65; 1 + 14 + 22 + 10 + 18 = 65.) Then there are other yet more complicated and extraordinary squares, the "satanic" and the "cabalistic," which require considerable mental effort to understand.

Some variants
Many variants have evolved from magic squares. Here are two, which can be played as games with friends.

1) Draw seven circles as in *figure j* and number them from 1 to 7 such that the total of every row of three circles linked by straight lines is 12 (the numbers printed here are the answer).
2) Make a pattern as in *figure k* and number each circle such that every row of three linked by straight lines totals the same (a solution, in *figure k*, always gives a total of 18 for each row). The first person to produce a correct result is the winner.

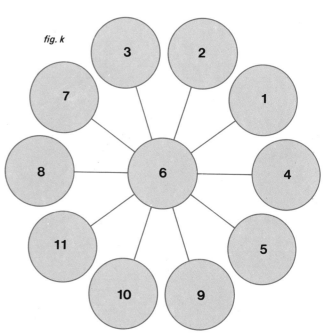
fig. j

fig. k

fig. i

1	15	24	8	17
23	7	16	5	14
20	4	13	22	6
12	21	10	19	3
9	18	2	11	25

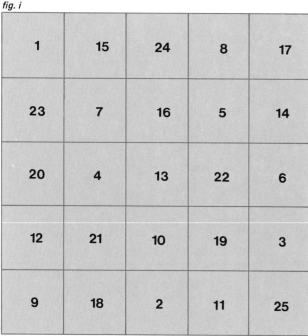

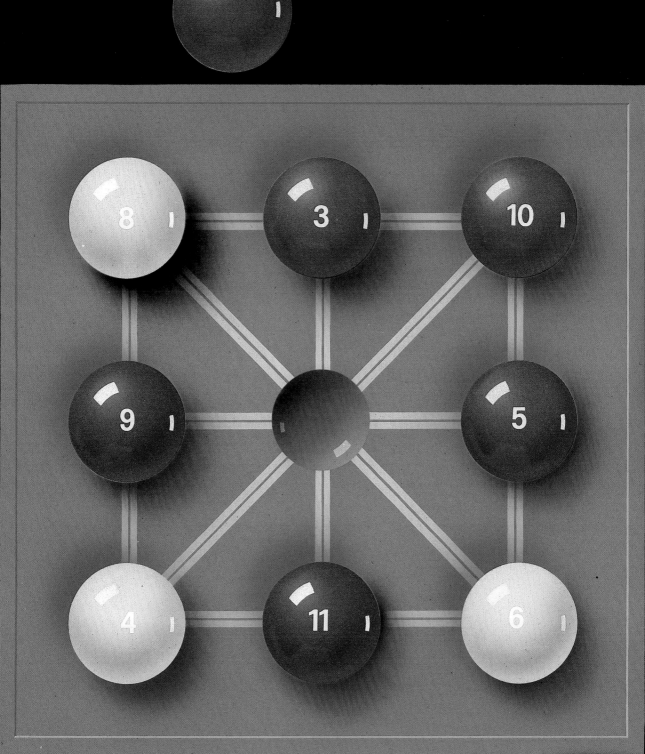

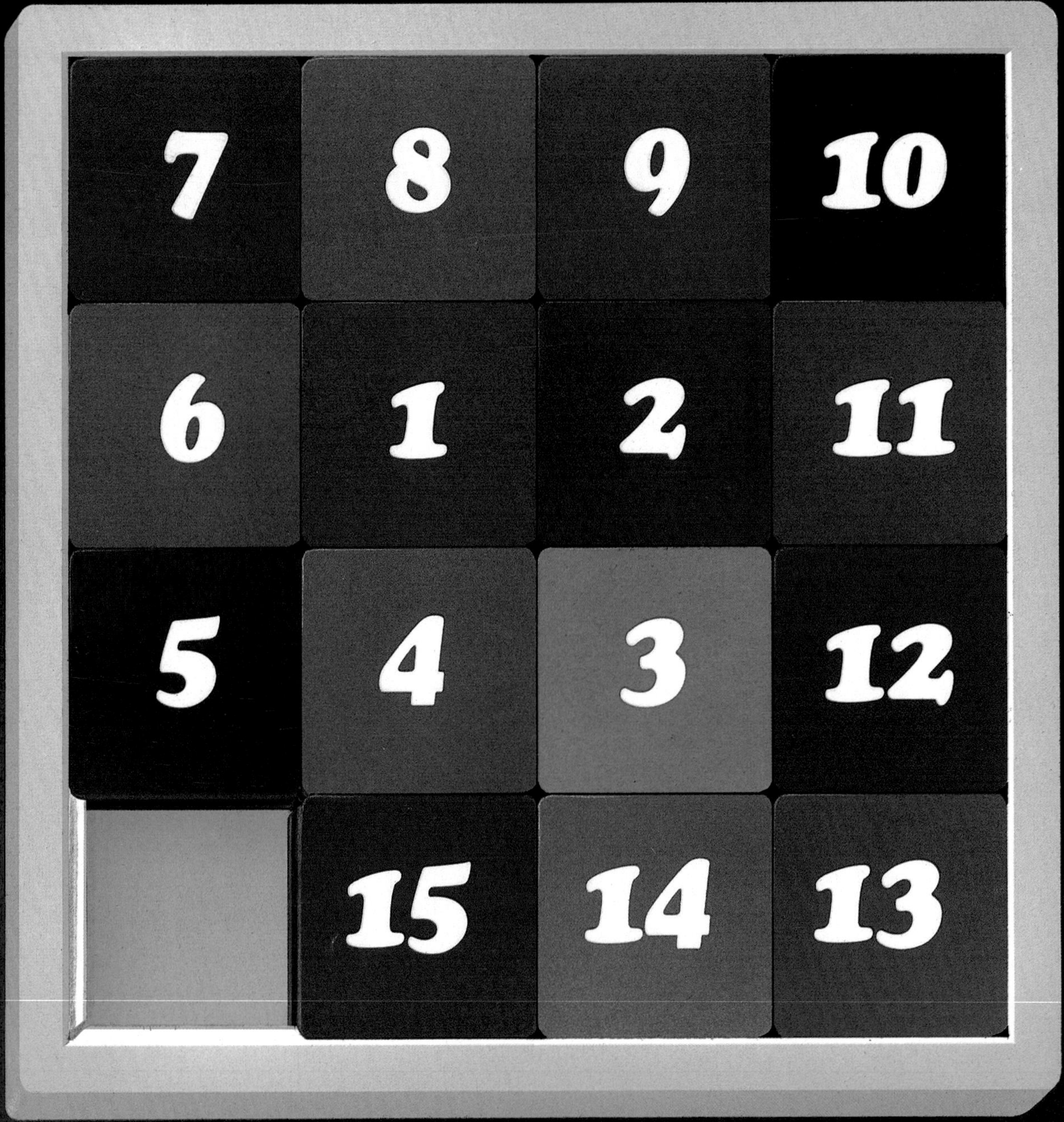
7
8
9
10
6
1
2
11
5
4
3
12
15
14
13

THE 14–15 PUZZLE

Short history

Not many years ago, one only had to board a bus to see some youngster engrossed in a Rubik's cube (a "magic" cube named after its inventor), or indeed even adults, similarly engrossed, twisting and turning the little coloured cubes of which the larger cube consisted. Legends grew up around this exceptional toy, and national and international championships were held. However, the craze was relatively short-lived and seemed to disappear like a mere fashion. Such is the way of things! Only a few decades previously, in the fifties, a close forebear of Rubik's cube—the "14–15 puzzle"—enjoyed a similar brief burst of popularity. As the Hungarian inventor of the cube himself admits, this game can be considered a two-dimensional ancestor of the later three-dimensional game. It was invented by the American Sam Loyd around 1870, and fast became a craze in the United States. A number of people consider Samuel Loyd the greatest inventor of games and pastimes ever to have lived. Much of what he invented can be found in the *Cyclopedia of Puzzles*, edited and published by his son, Samuel Loyd, Jr., in 1914.

How to play

The game is played with a square panel containing fifteen small movable square sections numbered 1–15 (whence the name), which occupy the whole area of the panel except for the equivalent of one extra (a sixteenth) small square (see *figure a*).
Given this space, the small squares can be shifted around, one space at a time, as on a chessboard. Normally one starts with them at random (see *figure b*) and tries to arrange them in some predetermined pattern by means of methodical intermediate moves.
The pattern might very well be that in *figure a*, reading horizontally.
The little squares can only be moved up or down or horizontally. It may at first sight appear an easy game: however, one can find onself with, for instance, a beautiful arrangement as in *figure a*—but with the 14 and 15 the wrong way around.

Some examples

Both children and adults find this game compelling, especially when the arrangement to be achieved is more complex than that illustrated in *figure a*. For instance, one could decide on a vertical ordering of the squares (*figure c*), with the numbers reading from top to bottom. Perhaps more difficult again would be a diagonal order (*figure d*, next page), starting from one in the bottom left-hand corner.
If any reader feels so inclined, it might also be worth trying a spiral arrangement, as shown in the colour plate opposite, with the numbering starting from one of the central squares and proceeding outward to 15 in a spiral direction.

fig. b

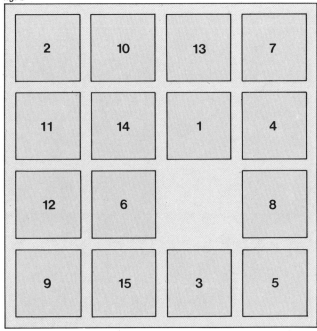

fig. a

1	2	3	4
5	6	7	8
9	10	11	12
13	14	15	

fig. c

1	5	9	13
2	6	10	14
3	7	11	15
4	8	12	

Some variants
If instead of 15 we take 31 squares, we get the rectangular game shown in *figure e*: this certainly offers greater possibilities, but at the same time it is more complicated. Fifteen squares afford a total of some 1,300 billion possible arrangements; and obviously with 31 this number will be even greater.

By replacing numbers with letters, we have an alphabetical version of this same game (*figure f*), which in turn offers a variety of possibilities.

One could, say, make the name of a friend out of the letters, from a higgledy-piggledy starting point. Or one could make words or short phrases and then make anagrams. After the initial craze for the game of "14–15," it fell out of vogue and is now only played by a few enthusiasts. (Bobby Fischer, the former world chess champion, could solve the puzzle blindfolded.)

fig. d

fig. e

fig. f

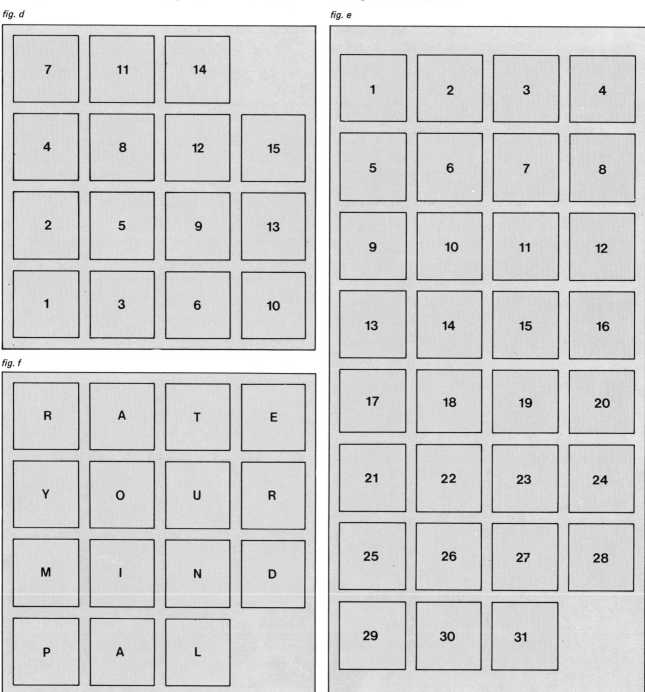

How do you make out in mathematics? (Five progressive easy problems)

1) Of thirty-six eggs in a basket, four in every dozen are bad. How many good eggs are there?

2) Peter spent half of what his mother had given him on chips, then with half of what he had spent on chips he bought some sweets. He was then left with thirty cents change. How much did he spend on chips?

3) The number y is as much higher than twenty-one as it is lower than thirty-seven. So what is y?

4) If a, b, and c are numbers, totalling d, is it true that d less a equals b plus c?

5) If a, b, and d are numbers, and d is the difference between a and b, what would be the necessary condition for d plus a to equal b?

Answers and comments on the clock games

1) c goes with f: since a shows 3:00, b shows 6:00, and c shows 9:00, the logical sequel is 12:00.

2) e. (Here it is not a question of looking at hours and minutes, but at the geometrical relation of the two hands; the second pair in each set of hands has been turned forty-five degrees clockwise.)

3) Now what we are faced with is a quite different kind of problem: to guess the time in e we must first identify the principle behind the times shown in a, b, c, and d: a shows 9:15, b 7:20, c 5:30, and d 3:45. Note that the hour lessens by two each time, while the minutes increase in multiples of five (5, 10, 15, 20 . . .). Thus we need simply take 2 from 3 and add 20 to 45 (giving us one hour and five minutes, or five past the hour): the time in e should therefore be 1:05.

4) This exercise is like the previous one but has the added complication of the seconds:

a 8:10:00
b 9:00:05
c 10:50:10
d 11:40:15

It is easy to use that the hours increase by one each time, while the minutes decrease by ten, and the seconds increase by five. Thus we just have to do a simple calculation:

23 + 1 = 24 (hours)
40 − 10 = 30 (minutes)
15 + 5 = 20 (seconds).

Therefore e will read 12:30:20.

Answers to the mathematical games

1) Twenty-four eggs. Since thirty-six eggs make three dozen, if four eggs in every dozen are bad, the other eight will be good. Hence there are $3 \times 8 = 24$ good eggs.

2) Sixty cents. Anyone at all familiar with basic algebra will easily solve this problem. What we are required to do is work out how much money Peter spent on chips. To denote this sum we shall use the symbol x. Now we know that what he spent on sweets was half of the total he spent on chips, $x/2$. This left him with thirty cents: in other words, if we subtract $x/2$ from x, we are left with 30 cents. We are now in a position to express this in algebraic form:

$$x - x/2 = 30$$
$$\frac{2x - x}{2} = 30$$
$$x/2 = 30$$
$$x = 30 \times 2$$
$$x = 60.$$

3) Twenty-nine. A correct answer could perhaps be given by intuition, but a simple algebraic calculation will be almost as quick:

$$\frac{37 - 21}{2} = x$$
$$16/2 = x$$
$$8 = x$$

Thus the number is $21 + 8 = 29$.

4) Yes. For the answer here, we need to do a calculation with letters: $a + b + c = d$. Now we also know that in an equation, if the same amount is added or subtracted on both sides, the value will not change.
   Thus:

$$a + b + c - a = d - a$$

which gives us:

$$b + c = d - a$$

5) d plus a would equal b on condition that b is greater than a. To see why this is so, we have only to do a simple calculation:

$$d + a = b \Leftrightarrow d = b - a.$$

Some comment ought to be made on these last two exercises. If we had used numbers instead of letters, they would probably have been quicker and easier to answer. Expressed as they were, they required more mental effort: for it is harder to calculate with letters, which can have any value, than with numbers. Stepping from numbers to letters (arithmetic to algebra) involves accepting a higher degree of generalization and abstraction. In that step we see an example of how mathematics develops.

The prince's legacy

Many years ago there was an Indian prince who had ruled wisely and peacefully, administering his territories and seeing that his eight children (six boys, two girls) were given the best possible upbringing.

Finally, sensing that his life was nearing its end, he decided to retire to one of his estates—a sort of paradise on earth, with sea all around it (see *figure 27*).

He decided at the same time to keep the palace and garden, which were at the heart of the estate, for

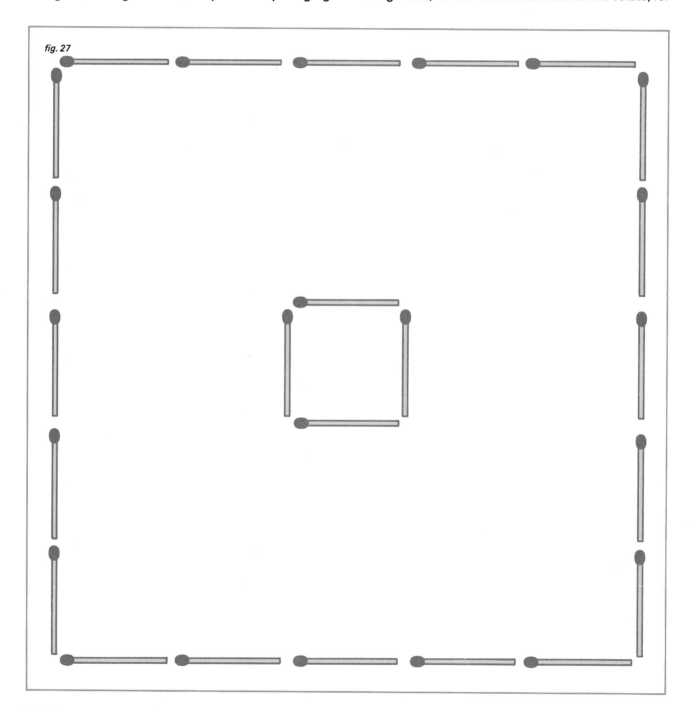

fig. 27

himself, and to divide the surrounding country and forest equally between his six sons.

How might he have done this while still keeping the central square intact?

One possible solution is given in *figure 28*.

Hardly had the poor prince sorted all this out when his wife, the princess, demanded fair treatment for her two daughters, claiming equal rights of inheritance for them. The prince loved his daughters so he set about dividing up the estate into eight equal portions. Perhaps the reader can help.

Figure 29 (next page) offers a solution.

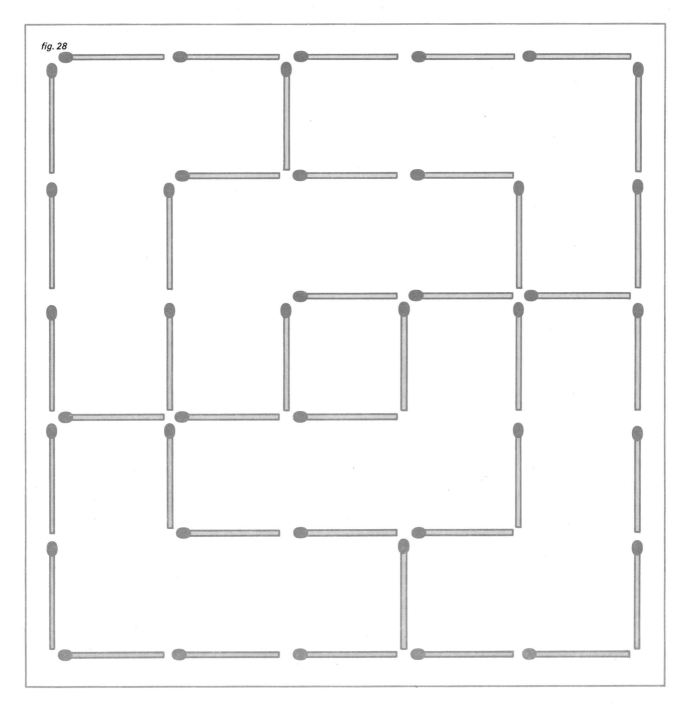

fig. 28

fig. 29

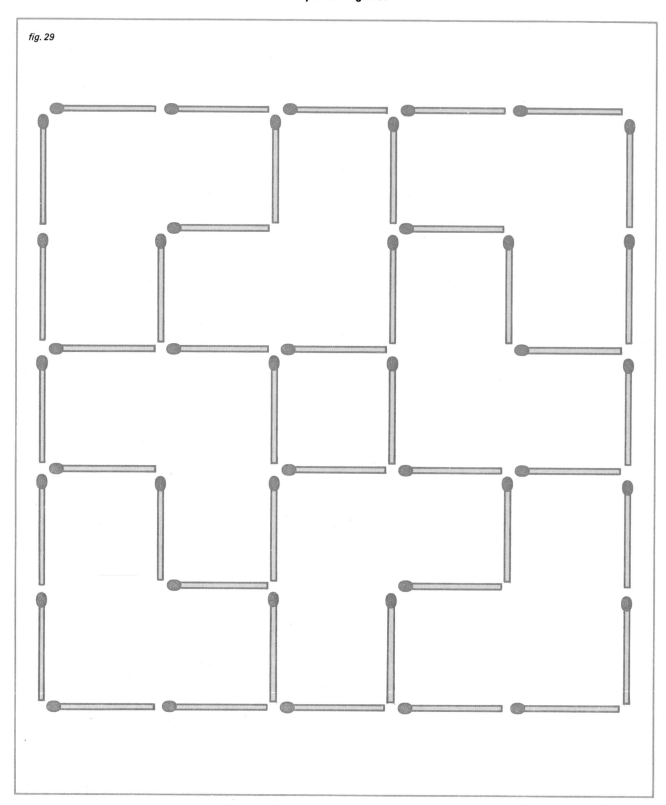

The trapezoid

Figure 30 is easily recognizable as an isosceles triangle, the base formed of three matches, and the other two equal sides of two each. By moving the matches around, is it possible to create a trapezoid —a four-sided figure with only two parallel sides?

Figure 31 suggests how.

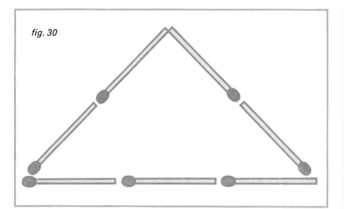

fig. 30

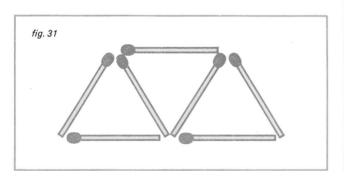

fig. 31

1985: rendezvous with Halley's comet

In 1682 the English astronomer Edmund Halley (1656–1742), a personal friend of Newton's, discovered the periodic nature of the comet that now bears his name. By a series of very precise calculations, he established that its orbit took exactly seventy-six years. Thus the last time it was seen passing was in 1986, and the next appearance will be in 2062. Halley's comet is thus visible only every seventy-six years, and many of us will not be alive to see its next appearance. For the astronomers of the present generation, therefore, 1986 saw a unique occurrence which was not to be missed. Hence the great interest in the comet recently and the attempts to achieve a "rendezvous" with the comet in space as it passed some tens of millions of miles from the earth. The comet even aroused a great deal of popular interest among those not normally much concerned with astronomy. By mid 1985, the comet was visible through most sorts of telescope used by amateurs for about a year. Visible with the naked eye in Britain around the end of 1985, it was to be seen clearly in southern Europe (forty degrees latitude) in the early months of 1986.

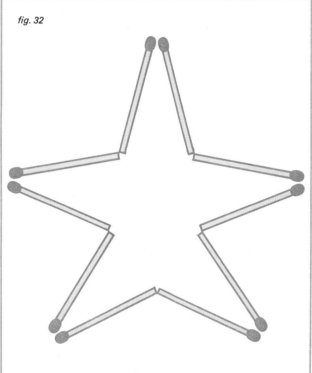

fig. 32

Giotto's Comet

Comets were often portrayed in medieval painting as stars with five points, similar to that represented with ten ordinary matches in *figure 32*.

There is one celebrated exception, however: that included by the Florentine painter Giotto in the fresco *Adoration of the Magi* in the Scrovegni Chapel in Padua. Here the head of the comet is no longer the traditional star shape, but a spherical body emitting rays of light.

Giotto, a master painter of the fourteenth century, was indeed a great innovator. But a comet star hardly seems worthy of such a definite iconographical break with tradition. How are we to explain it?

The most likely explanation is that in 1301, the very year when Giotto was decorating the

Scrovegni Chapel, Halley's comet appeared in the heavens, clearly visible to the naked eye. Undoubtedly the painter was among those who saw it, and he was struck by the fact that it was not so much starlike as spherical, diffusing light.

The crater

It is true to say that in all ages there has been fear of the catastrophic effects of the possible collision of a comet with the earth. A German astrologer predicted a disastrous collision between our planet and a comet on June 13, 1857, and in France this led to displays of collective panic. Perhaps even the appearance of Halley's comet in 1986 is seen by some people as a "rendezvous" with the end of our world.

With eight matches it is possible to create several geometrical figures (see *figures 33, 34, 35, 36*).

Using just eight matches, can you make a geometrical figure, consisting of four triangles and two squares, to represent the crater that would appear were Halley's comet to crash into the earth?

A suggestion is given in the bottom right-hand figure on this page (*figure 37*).

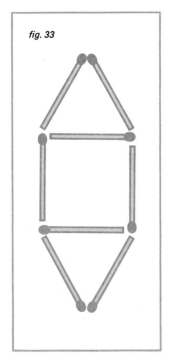

fig. 33

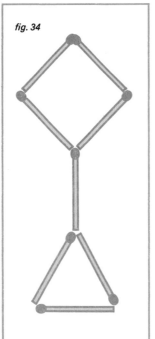

fig. 34

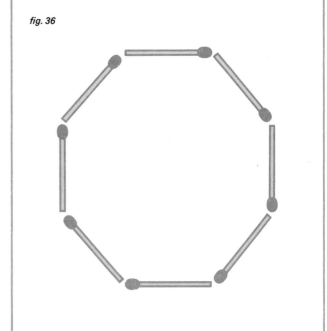

fig. 36

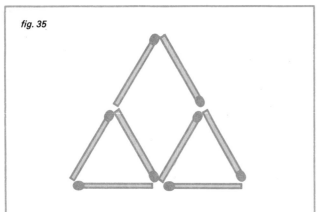

fig. 35

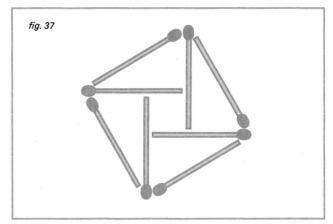

fig. 37

Select bibliography

General titles on games

For all kinds of information, curiosities, and games (not only mathematical and logical) and their variants, it is worth consulting Martin Gardner, an American writer on pastimes and mathematical questions, who up until 1983 contributed a section on mathematical games in the "Scientific American." The following books are of particular interest:

Gardner, M. *Mathematical Circus*, New York, 1979 and London, 1981

    Mathematical Puzzles and Diversions, New York, 1963 and London, 1961

    Mathematical Magic Show, New York and London, 1977

    The Magic Numbers of Doctor Matrix, Buffalo, N.Y., 1980

    N.B. Not all the games in these books are easy to grasp: some presuppose a mastery of mathematical and geometrical matters that perhaps some readers may lack.)

Other works

Arnold, A. *The World Book of Children's Games*, New York, 1972

Baslini, F. *Il "solitaire,"* Florence, 1970

Dossena, G. *Giochi da tavolo*, Milan, 1984

Girault, R. J. *Traité du jeu du Go*, Paris, 1972

Grunfeld, F. V. (ed.). *Games of the World*, New York, 1975

Games of logic

Logic has been treated very much in layman's terms in this book, without the use of technical "jargon" of symbols, and the answers are on the whole presented through processes of intuition and reasoning. Underlying this approach was a desire to introduce readers unfamiliar with this way of thinking to the basic language and methodology of science. Although our games, stories, and puzzles were arranged in increasing order of difficulty, as well as according to their own logical development, they do not claim to be a self-contained introduction to the problems of logic. Our aim was primarily to arouse interest and stimulate curiosity, and encourage further reading. The main sources for the games of logic are:

Copi, I. *Introduction to Logic*, 6th edn. New York, 1982

Johnson, D. A., Glenn, W. H., & Norton, M. S. *Logic and Reasoning*, Bologna, 1978

Smullyan, R. *The lady or the Tiger?*, New York, 1983

    What is the Name of this Book? The Riddles of Dracula and other Logical Puzzles, Englewood Cliffs, N.J., 1978 and London, 1981

Further reading

Dalla Chiara Scabia, M. L., *Logica*, Milan, 1981

Mendelson, E. *Introduction to Mathematical Logic*, New York 1976

Tarski, A. *Introduction to Logic*, New York, 1954

Wesley, S. C. *Elementary Logic*, Bologna, 1974

Mathematical stories and games

Although brief, the chapter dealing with mathematical stories and games constitutes a sort of history of numbers (with particular attention to the binary system) and a concise and readable account of the origins of arithmetic. Sources of the games are:

Aleme, Jean-Pierre. *Jeux de l'esprit et divertissements*, Paris, 1981

Berloquin, P. *Geometric Games*, London, 1980

Boyer, C. B. *History of Mathematics*, New York and London, 1968

Ifrah, G. *Histoire universelle des chiffres*, Paris, 1981

Johnson, D. A., & Glenn, W. H. *Exploring Mathematics on Your Own*, New York, 1972

Further reading
Courant, R., & Robbins, H. *What is Mathematics?*, London, 1941
Freudenthal, H. *Mathematics Observed*, New York and London, 1967
Waismann, F. *Introduction to Mathematical Thinking: The Formation of Concepts in Modern Mathematics*, New York, 1951 and London 1952

Intelligence puzzles and tests
The tests, verbal, visual, mathematical and otherwise, were taken primarily from:
Berloquin, P. *Testez votre intelligence*, Paris, 1974
Bernard, W., & Leopold, G. *Test Yourself*, Philadelphia and New York, 1962 and London, 1964
Eysenck, H. J. *Know Your Own I.Q.*, Harmondsworth, 1962

Intelligence, creativity and personality
For a discussion of problems relating to intelligence, creativity and personality, it is worth referring to the following books on psychology:
Anastasi, A. *Psychological Testing*, London, 1961
Eysenck, H. J., & Kamin, L. *Race, Intelligence and Education*, Hounslow, 1971

Harré, R., & Secord, P. F. *The Explanation of Social Behaviour*, Oxford, 1976
Hilgard, E. R., Atkinson, R. C., & Atkinson, R. L. *Introduction to Psychology*, New York and London, 1964

Games with matches
Neumüller, Anders. *Tündstickor – Konst och ek*, Stockholm, 1983

Jealousy test
The test on jealousy (pp. 114–116) is by Pino Gilioli, whose book *Personality Games* appeared in the same series (New York and London, 1986)

Other books in the series
Agostini, F. *Math and Logic Games*, New York, 1983
Mathematical and Logical Games, London, 1983
De Carlo, N. A. *Psychological Games*, New York and London, 1983
Gilioli, P. *Personality Games*, New York and London, 1986

Index of games